'Though the fundraising environment [...] the fundamental principles, tools and techniques of so[...] essential for fundraising success. Wh[...] y to day, including at a senior level, it'[...] ie tools that can help you see things fr[...] ok cover to cover or dip into the differe[...] newcomers to the sector and experie[...]
Beth Crackles, Director of Fundraising and Communications, [...] a Support

'This book is a really helpful companion for any fundraiser who wants to think more strategically about their work, or who has been tasked with leading a strategy process. The models and practices shared in the book can be redeployed as fundraising programmes develop and change, and as fundraisers' remits and responsibilities evolve and grow. I wish it had been available years ago when I was starting out!'
Louisa Johnson, Head of Fundraising, Full Fact

'Strategy is certainly the buzzword of all buzzwords these days with hundreds of books, courses and resources out there on the subject. Often, these are tailored for the business rather than the not-for-profit community – few are easy to understand and fewer relatable to our sector. So, if you are interested in fundraising strategy for your charity, I highly recommend this absolutely brilliant book. It is a clear and concise walk-through of developing your fundraising strategy, full of applicable examples that will help you tremendously. You'll need this one on your shelf as well as for your whole leadership team and board!'
Cherian Koshy CFRE, Director of Development, Des Moines Performing Arts

'At last! The book I wish I'd had 20 years ago. I feel I had to stumble towards this, drawing on a range of sources, but here it is: a definitive guide, grounded in real-world examples. I know this will help any fundraiser build and implement their strategy effectively, for I have seen the principles work. It should be standard issue across the sector.'
Matt Parkes, Director of Development, Diocese of Westminster, and Trustee of the Chartered Institute of Fundraising

'This is a fantastic book for anyone tasked with the (often daunting) assignment of writing a fundraising strategy. Whether you aren't sure where to start, are stuck in a rut with your current approach, or are eager to get others around you engaged with the process, there is something for you. The book's plethora of handy, clearly explained and accessible tools mean anyone can get stuck in.'
Leah Selinger, Director, Selinger Consultants

'This is a really welcome guide to the elements of creating and implementing a fundraising strategy, filled with useful and practical tools to create a fundraising plan grounded in insight. The content on fundraising ethics, inclusion and diversity, and emergent and agile strategy makes this book incredibly relevant in today's changing fundraising landscape.'
Katie Simmons, Director of Fundraising Strategy, British Red Cross

'It's one thing knowing you need a fundraising strategy, but it's a completely different thing being able to write one that is sensible and achievable. This book strikes a brilliant balance between walking you through the process of writing a meaningful strategy and explaining the rationale behind each step.

I particularly love the fact that Claire and Richard assess each tool in an impartial manner, addressing the weaknesses of each tool as well as the strengths. When you combine that with the case studies and the rich evidence base, you will have everything you need to get buy-in from even the most sceptical managers or trustees.

Whether you are writing your first fundraising strategy or your hundredth, you will find something in this book that will make your strategy stronger.'
David Burgess, Director, Apollo Fundraising

'Strategy is real work and it can be overwhelming. It requires fundraisers to roll up their sleeves, ask difficult questions and, ultimately, knuckle down and put pen to paper on a plan. This guide is one of the most honest I've read about how to navigate that process and build a dynamic fundraising strategy for your organisation. Richard and Claire have taken inordinate care to walk fundraisers through manageable steps as they distil both the science and art of strategy with reassuring aplomb. This is a resource that I shall myself have on my desk, and one that I will encourage all my charitable clients to also dig into. It is a book that every fundraiser should be referencing time and time again.'
Niduk D'Souza, Vice-President of Strategy and Marketing, Up Fundraising

Third edition

Fundraising Strategy

The Fundraising Series

Claire Routley and Richard Sved

directory of social change

In association with:

University of Kent | Centre for Philanthropy

Chartered Institute of Fundraising

Published by the Directory of Social Change (Registered Charity no. 800517 in England and Wales)

Office: Suite 103, 1 Old Hall Street, Liverpool L3 9HG

Tel: 020 4526 5995

Visit www.dsc.org.uk to find out more about our books, subscription funding website and training events. You can also sign up for e-newsletters so that you're always the first to hear about what's new.

The publisher welcomes suggestions and comments that will help to inform and improve future versions of this and all of our titles. Please give us your feedback by emailing publications@dsc.org.uk.

It should be understood that this publication is intended for guidance only and is not a substitute for professional advice. No responsibility for loss occasioned as a result of any person acting or refraining from acting can be accepted by the authors or publisher.

First edition published 1997 by the Charities Aid Foundation
Second edition published 2002 by the Directory of Social Change
Third and digital editions 2021

Copyright © Directory of Social Change 2002, 2021

All rights reserved. No part of the printed version of this book may be stored in a retrieval system or reproduced in any form whatsoever without prior permission in writing from the publisher. This book is sold subject to the condition that it shall not, by way of trade or otherwise, be lent, re-sold, hired out or otherwise circulated without the publisher's prior permission in any form of binding or cover other than that in which it is published, and without a similar condition including this condition being imposed on the subsequent purchaser.

The digital version of this publication may only be stored in a retrieval system for personal use. No part may be edited, amended, extracted or reproduced in any form whatsoever. It may not be distributed or made available to others without prior permission in writing from the publisher.

The publisher and authors have made every effort to contact copyright holders. If anyone believes that their copyright material has not been correctly acknowledged, please contact the publisher, who will be pleased to rectify the omission.

The moral rights of the authors has been asserted in accordance with the Copyrights, Designs and Patents Act 1988.

ISBN 978 1 78482 054 1 (print edition)
ISBN 978 1 78482 055 8 (digital edition)

British Library Cataloguing in Publication Data
A catalogue record for this book is available from the British Library

Cover and text design by Kate Griffith
Typeset by Marlinzo Services, Frome
Printed and bound in Great Britain by CPI Group, Croydon

To Neill and Kate, with love

Contents

About the Fundraising Series ix
About the Directory of Social Change x
About the authors xi
Acknowledgements xii
Foreword by Dhivya O'Connor xv

Introduction 1

CHAPTER ONE	The fundraising audit 7
CHAPTER TWO	The internal audit and SWOT analysis 22
CHAPTER THREE	Improving your strategy with research 42
CHAPTER FOUR	Setting objectives and identifying your audience 57
CHAPTER FIVE	Developing your message 76
CHAPTER SIX	Choosing your tactics 90
CHAPTER SEVEN	Scheduling and budgeting for your fundraising 110
CHAPTER EIGHT	Monitoring and controlling your fundraising performance 122
CHAPTER NINE	Getting internal buy-in and managing change 137
CHAPTER TEN	Fundraising ethics 149
CHAPTER ELEVEN	Contemporary issues in fundraising 167
CHAPTER TWELVE	Avoiding strategic wear-out 187

Index 203

About the Fundraising Series

For hundreds, if not thousands, of years generous people have given of their resources to improve the lives of others. Underpinning that benevolence are the people who ask for support on behalf of causes and for those in need – the fundraisers. As a group, they are often little known and little celebrated, but they are a driving force in enabling others to express their philanthropy and experience the joy of giving.

Over the last century or so, fundraisers' work has become more and more professionalised. The role of the fundraiser is achieving professional recognition through the establishment of the Chartered Institute of Fundraising (CIoF), the development of fundraising education and a growing interest in codifying professional ethics. Rightly, fundraisers are increasingly acknowledged as having a particular set of skills, and their knowledge base is growing in size and scope.

This series aims to help fundraisers build their skills and grow professionally. Each volume addresses a key part in the spectrum of fundraising techniques. As fundraising evolves and develops, new titles in the series are added and old ones revised. Each title explores a particular fundraising activity: looks at the current best practice; helps establish future strategy; and, where relevant, considers the historical, ethical and theoretical context for that activity. The series offers something for anyone who is aspiring to be a professional fundraiser, whatever the size or type of their organisation or the stage of their career.

The Centre for Philanthropy at the University of Kent is proud to partner with the Directory of Social Change and the CIoF in the development of the series, as part of our shared mission to open up insights from the academic world to practising fundraisers. We'd also like to pay tribute to fundraising academic Adrian Sargeant for his early championing and stewardship of the series.

This series wouldn't be possible without the hard work of many people from authors to contributors to the publishing team who shape the text; we thank everyone who has contributed to its development.

Dr Claire Routley
Dr Beth Breeze
Centre for Philanthropy
University of Kent

About the Directory of Social Change

At the Directory of Social Change (DSC), we believe that the world is made better by people coming together to serve their communities and each other. For us, an independent voluntary sector is at the heart of that social change and we exist to support charities, voluntary organisations and community groups in the work they do. Our role is to:

- **provide practical information** on a range of topics from fundraising to project management in both our printed publications and our e-books;

- **offer training** through public courses, events and in-house services;

- **research funders** and maintain a subscription database, *Funds Online*, with details on funding from grant-making charities, companies and government sources;

- **offer bespoke research** to voluntary sector organisations in order to evaluate projects, identify new opportunities and help make sense of existing data;

- **stimulate debate and campaign** on key issues that affect the voluntary sector, particularly to champion the concerns of smaller charities.

We are a registered charity ourselves but we self-fund most of our work. We charge for services, but cross-subsidise those which charities particularly need and cannot easily afford.

Visit our website **www.dsc.org.uk** to see how we can help you to help others and have a look at **www.fundsonline.org.uk** to see how DSC could improve your fundraising. Alternatively, call our friendly team at **020 4526 5995** to chat about your needs or drop us a line at **cs@dsc.org.uk**.

About the authors

Claire Routley

Claire Routley has worked in fundraising for almost 20 years for a number of different charities, ranging from a local hospice to Age UK. Claire is now a consultant specialising in legacy and in-memory fundraising and is an in-demand speaker at conferences across the UK. She is a fellow of the Chartered Institute of Fundraising where she also teaches across its range of fundraising qualifications. Claire holds the world's first PhD in Legacy Marketing and is also a chartered marketer.

Richard Sved

Richard is Director of 3rd Sector Mission Control. He is an experienced senior manager having, by the time of publication, led the fundraising team at nine national charities including Girlguiding, Epilepsy Society and the National Literacy Trust. Richard specialises in income generation, strategic planning and charity governance, and is a proud and enthusiastic consultant, trainer, fundraiser, blogger, trustee, volunteer and mentor. Outside work, Richard enjoys playing in a brass band and helping to organise his local parkrun.

Acknowledgements

Special thanks go to Cherian Koshy, Louisa Johnson and Beth Crackles, who reviewed the manuscript at its early stages to provide valuable feedback and helpful suggestions for further improvements. In particular, we thank Cherian for his insights on equality, equity, diversity and inclusion considerations in recency, frequency and value analysis in chapter 4.

We're also thankful to Ian MacQuillin, Cherian Koshy and Roewen Wishart for their comments on an initial draft of questions in the section 'Categorising ethical dilemmas' in chapter 10, and to Dr Haseeb Shabbir for reviewing the section 'Service user portrayal' in chapter 11, which is based on his work.

Richard would like to thank Claire for asking him to help write this book and Directory of Social Change's John Martin and Gabi Zagnojute, who have been a pleasure to work with.

The authors and publisher are grateful to the organisations and people that contributed text and illustrations and granted permission to re-use copyright materials, including:

- Wayne Murray for permission to use his quote in the introduction.

- Catriona Brickel for permission to adapt and use the case study on Church Mission Society audit in chapter 1.

- Caroline Danks for permission to use an excerpt from LarkOwl's report *The Calm before the Storm: UK fundraising ROI 2020* shown in figure 2.1.

- Oxford Publishing Limited for permission to adapt and reproduce the fundraising portfolio matrix shown in figure 2.4. Copyright Oxford Publishing Limited.

- Cherian Koshy for providing the 'When data collection goes wrong' section in chapter 3.

- Lesley Pinder for the case study on taking a blended research approach to understanding supporters in chapter 3.

- Jonathan Cook for the case study on using quantitative research to develop a training proposition at the Chartered Institute of Fundraising in chapter 3.

ACKNOWLEDGEMENTS

- Louisa James for permission to adapt and use the case study on using qualitative insight to develop a legacy proposition at St Peter's Hospice in chapter 3.

- Harvard Business Publishing for permission to adapt and reproduce the Ansoff's matrix model in chapter 4. Adapted and reprinted with permission from H. Igor Ansoff, 'Strategies for Diversification', *Harvard Business Review*, vol. 35, no. 5 (Sept/Oct), 1957. Copyright 1957 by Harvard Business Publishing; all rights reserved.

- Mari Sved for permission to use her photograph in figure 5.1.

- Bryony Doughty of MQ Mental Health Research and photographer Matt Holyoak for their permission to use portraits of Gillian Anderson, Melanie Chisholm and Nicola Adams from the charity's We Swear campaign shown in figure 5.3.

- Mike Johnston for permission to adapt and use the case study on Diabetes Canada in chapter 6.

- Maddy Scott for permission to adapt and use the case study on Arkansas Children's Foundation, based on Lindsay Doerr's text, in chapter 8.

- Stephen Cotterill and Gemma Sherrington for permission to feature a case study on Save the Children in chapter 12.

- Jen Love and John Lepp of fundraising agency Agents of Good for permission to include a case study on the Oregon Zoo Foundation in chapter 5.

- Advance HE for permission to reproduce the change matrix shown in figure 9.2. © 2003 Advance HE. All rights reserved.

- Jamie Byrne-McCollum for permission to feature a case study on University of Arkansas at Little Rock in chapter 9.

- Ian MacQuillin for permission to reproduce the Rogare's ethical decision-making model in chapter 10.

- Cancer Research UK for permission to feature a quote from the charity's EEDI strategy in the case study in chapter 11.

- Community-Centric Fundraising for permission to quote the ten core principles of the movement in chapter 11.

- Howard Lake for permission to use a case study on WaterAid's Untapped campaign in chapter 11.

- Giles Pegram for permission to use his quote in a case study on listening to donors in chapter 12.

- Vicky Reeves for providing the case study on design sprint in chapter 12.

- Carolina Herrera and Joanna Culling for permission to feature materials from The Showcase of Fundraising Innovation and Inspiration (SOFII) – figure 6.3 and cases studies in chapters 3 (on SolarAid), 4 (on St Michael's Hospital Foundation) and 8 (on Unicef). The SOFII website is a gift to you and to charitable fundraisers everywhere. An easily accessible free archive of the best fundraising creativity and innovation from around the world, it is available to you 24 hours a day, seven days a week. SOFII safeguards our fundraising history and adds new examples of fundraising greatness every week (see sofii.org).

Foreword

Charities have never had so many different sources of income, communication channels and content to choose from when trying to reach new donors and nurture relationships with long-term supporters. While off-line channels remain vital to the fundraising mix, digital transformation has permanently changed the way we interact with all supporters. All these new and exciting ways to inspire giving, raise the profile of your cause and further your organisation's mission mean that a robust fundraising strategy is even more critical.

The Chartered Institute of Fundraising (CIoF) is proud to partner with the Directory of Social Change and the University of Kent on the growing Fundraising Series, which covers so many key areas of fundraising. This title in particular provides an excellent step-by-step guide to creating and implementing a fundraising strategy for any fundraiser – whether you are a director looking to develop a joined-up organisation-wide strategy, or a head of a department trying to make the most of your team's capacity and resources. In addition to research-based guidance, this book features case studies from charities at the forefront of fundraising innovation, which demonstrate how the lessons of each chapter have been successfully implemented in practice. I am pleased that the CIoF's own South East and London volunteer group was able to share how it is using data and insight to enhance its training offering.

The COVID-19 pandemic forced the sector to re-evaluate how to develop a fundraising strategy and execute it at pace. In unprecedented and hugely challenging circumstances, fundraisers everywhere stepped up to bridge the income gap, proving that agility, innovation and great supporter experience will help a charity weather any storm. I hope that, through the experiences and guidance shared in this book, these lessons will not be forgotten.

Equally, as the sector adopts more inclusive practices and frameworks, I trust that the advice on equality, equity, diversity and inclusion detailed in this book (including research carried out by the Change Collective at the CIoF) will help your organisation make better decisions. As a sector, we are already making huge progress in this area, but we must keep working towards becoming an equal, diverse and inclusive profession. It is always important to listen to a range of viewpoints and perspectives. No successful strategy can be created in a vacuum.

FUNDRAISING STRATEGY

A good fundraising strategy generates income. A great fundraising strategy does this too; however, it also, as importantly, brings people along on the journey and leaves a lasting legacy. I hope that, with the help of this book, you will be able to shape your strategy from good to great.

**Dhivya O'Connor, Interim CEO,
Chartered Institute of Fundraising**

Introduction

What do we mean by 'strategy'?

This book explores the various elements of developing and implementing your fundraising strategy. However, before we begin to describe the process, it's helpful to define what exactly we mean when we use the word 'strategy'.

Henry Mintzberg, a Canadian academic who has written extensively on the subject, argues that there is no single definition of strategy, as the term is used in many different ways. His 'five Ps' of strategy encompass:

- **plan:** an intended course of action which is made in advance and developed purposefully;

- **ploy:** a specific manoeuvre designed to get the better of competitors;

- **pattern:** displaying consistent behaviour, whether or not by conscious intention – can be indicative of a strategy which is emerging;

- **position:** finding a distinctive place in the wider environment;

- **perspective:** patterns of thinking or culture, which can be difficult to change.[1]

Mintzberg's five Ps are naturally overlapping and interrelated, and may develop and occur in differing orders. For example, an organisation may fall into a **pattern** of behaviour, recognise that this is a successful way of working and then build it into a more consciously developed **plan**.

In this book, we focus primarily on strategy as a consciously developed **plan** and we outline a planning framework that will help you to develop your own organisation's strategy. This approach offers what we believe to be the best chance of success for your organisation. However, it's certainly worth being aware of Mintzberg's other definitions of strategy, as shown in the five Ps, as your colleagues and others might understand the term differently.

How will this book help you to develop a fundraising strategy?

Over the course of this book, we set out a process for conducting an audit of your organisation's environment, setting objectives, and then planning out a strategy and tactics to deliver that strategy. We explain how to analyse the external environment (chapter 1) in which your organisation is operating, from considering trends in the wider environment to assessing competitor activity and then reflecting on your organisation's specific market. Throughout the book, where relevant, we also take a more in-depth look at some of the key issues affecting fundraising at the time of writing.

We then show you how to consider the internal factors within your organisation, including how you can both summarise the big picture and focus more closely, and how you can identify your key opportunities by doing a SWOT (strengths, weaknesses, opportunities and threats) analysis (chapter 2). In chapter 3, we provide guidance on how you can use research to fill any knowledge gaps outstanding following the external and internal audits covered in chapters 1 and 2. Chapter 4 considers how you can translate the findings of your SWOT analysis into fundraising objectives, and chapter 5 looks at how those objectives might be delivered through your strategy – that is, how you can make decisions about your organisation's key audiences and messages. We then discuss how to draw up your organisation's tactics by examining the detail of delivering fundraising objectives on the ground and by looking at different fundraising streams (chapter 6). Chapter 7 covers how your strategy might be scheduled and budgeted, and chapter 8 suggests how to monitor and control your fundraising performance.

In the book's final chapters, we consider organisational and stakeholder buy-in, and how to manage change so as to give your strategy the best chance of success (chapter 9). We also discuss how you can ensure that your fundraising tactics are delivered in an ethical way (chapter 10) and consider some of the key issues facing contemporary fundraising (chapter 11). At the end of the book, we explore how you can avoid strategic wear-out, ensuring that your strategy remains effective over time (chapter 12).

Figure 1 illustrates how we suggest you should view the process of creating your fundraising strategy. While this book is arranged in what we feel is the most logical order, we do not advise that you consider each element strictly sequentially. Whereas, naturally, some elements of creating your fundraising strategy will come earlier in the process (such as undertaking a fundraising audit) and some will ordinarily take place towards the end of a cycle (such as monitoring and control), there are things which you will need to take into account throughout the whole process (such as ethical considerations and involving stakeholders). Most importantly, your fundraising shouldn't ever stop just because you are taking time to think strategically about it.

We believe that developing and implementing a fundraising strategy is an involved and involving process that goes far beyond simply producing a document that you can present to others. As charity strategist Wayne Murray puts it, 'Your strategy isn't a document. It's a set of mutually agreed decisions, created by all and owned by all. The document is just the receipt.'[2]

FIGURE 1 THE FUNDRAISING STRATEGY CYCLE

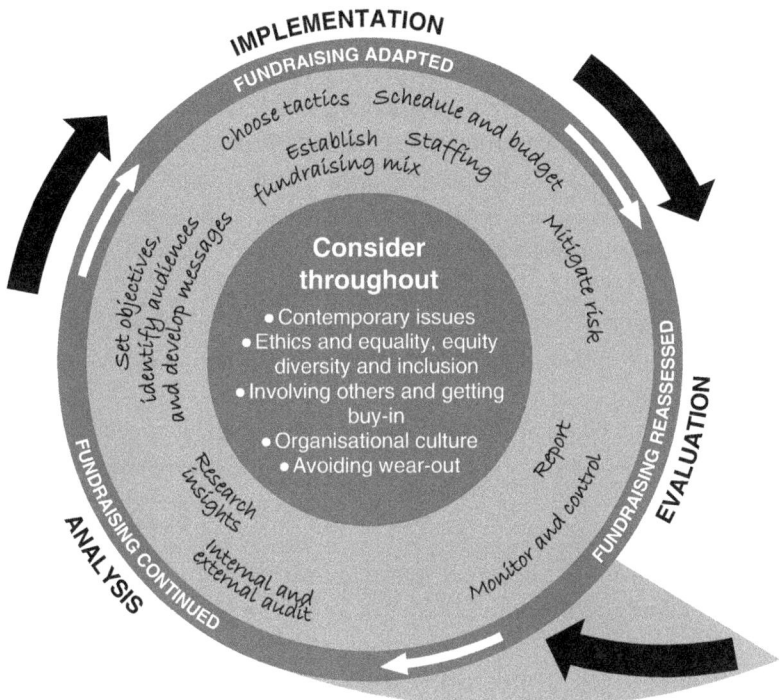

Why is having a fundraising strategy or plan important?

Why would you go through all of the detailed and time-consuming processes that we have described above? In short, taking the time to plan ensures that, rather than diving straight into your fundraising with a few ideas around current trends or hunches about what might work, you will have carefully thought through the actions you're going to take. These actions will be based on the highest-quality knowledge that is available about your external and internal environments, making it more likely that your fundraising will be successful. Given that your supporters' donations will be spent on this fundraising activity, engaging in this careful planning process is an ethical imperative.

There is some evidence to support the value of planning in charitable organisations specifically. In the 1990s, academic Julie Siciliano found that the studies to date had mostly established positive relationships between planning and performance in non-profits (although there were fewer studies of the relationship between planning and performance in non-profits than in the for-profit world). Her study of 240 branches of the YMCA found that those which followed the approach of developing formal strategies had higher levels of financial and social performance.[3]

More recently, in 2020, academics Adrian Sargeant and Kathryn Carpenter explored the connection between fundraising planning and performance.[4] In their study, 95% of respondents said that they believed fundraising planning was an immensely valuable process, while almost 90% said that having a formal fundraising plan increased their effectiveness. The authors also examined the idea of 'good practice', which in this book we would describe as having a plan in place, including strategies and tactics; integrating the plan into the organisational budget and allocating financial and/or staff resources to it; involving senior management; holding fundraisers accountable; and ensuring team members are committed. Sargeant and Carpenter found that the more a plan adhered to these principles of good practice, the more confidence the organisation had in achieving its targets.

Their analysis of actual results showed that organisations with a plan had higher levels of donor retention and were more likely to have increased income in the two years prior to taking the survey (while being less likely to have decreased income).[5]

There are a number of other benefits that can be derived from developing a fundraising strategy:

- It will enable you to set goals or objectives, which can make it clear to your colleagues (whether they are paid staff or volunteers) what they need to do and how that fits in with your wider team and organisation.

- The objectives you set when you develop your fundraising strategy can also become a guide against which you can measure performance.

- Your strategy can facilitate communication between team members and, indeed, wider staff and volunteer teams.

- Your strategy can ensure that your organisation is taking advantage of opportunities arising from the wider environment.

- Your strategy can reduce risk by helping you to minimise the effects of weaknesses and threats.

However, it would be remiss not to point out that there are potential downsides to this type of planning process, although you will be able to mitigate them (see table 1).

TABLE 1 WAYS TO MITIGATE THE POTENTIAL DOWNSIDES OF THE FUNDRAISING PLANNING PROCESS

Downsides	Ways to mitigate them
In a rapidly changing world – as evidenced by the COVID-19 pandemic – your organisation might need to change its approach, perhaps more rapidly than is common in standard three- or five-year planning cycles.	This can be mitigated through seeing the strategy as a living document and conducting regular assessments of how well it is being delivered and how the environment is changing around it.
A strategy could become inflexible or even stifle innovation.	This potential downside can again be avoided by ensuring that the plan stays 'live' and flexing it as appropriate.
The process of planning is relatively complex and potentially costly, at least in terms of staff time. As the rest of this book will illustrate, developing an effective strategy can be a time-consuming process.	This can't really be avoided but, ultimately, a carefully thought-through strategy can help your organisation to invest its limited resources in the most effective and efficient way.
Your strategy itself could be brilliant on paper but then fail if it is not implemented effectively in real life.	Therefore, as well as covering the principles of planning, this book discusses the more detailed and specific levels of planning, such as scheduling and budgeting, as well as exploring how to achieve buy-in from your colleagues.

On a final note, before beginning the process of auditing your environment and developing a strategy, we strongly recommend that you think carefully about who should be involved. This might partly be dictated by circumstance – if you're the sole fundraiser, then it's likely that much of the process will fall to you. However, even then it would be wise to consult other internal stakeholders, such as members of staff and volunteers, as you develop your strategy, as it's likely that success or failure will ultimately depend to some degree on them.

In a larger organisation, there may be more options as to who is directly involved in the process and how the strategy is pulled together, for example using interviews, conducting workshops or assigning different elements to different individuals or groups. Deliberately involving stakeholders at different stages of your strategy development in a process of co-creation can help to develop a sense of ownership of the strategy that is ultimately produced.[6] Therefore, although for convenience we use the term 'you' throughout this book, this will sometimes relate to a larger group of stakeholders rather than you, our specific reader.

We hope that this book will enable you to get 'out there' and strategise. It will be hugely important to the success of your organisation and, when you pull it off, it can be immensely satisfying. Through successful fundraising, you will help your organisation to do great things.

Assess. Plan. Fundraise. Change the world.

Good luck!

Notes

1. Henry Mintzberg, 'The Strategy Concept I: Five Ps for strategy', *California Management Review*, vol. 30, no. 1, 1987, pp. 11–24.
2. Wayne Murray, [Twitter post], https://twitter.com/WayneTheMurray/status/1391817574078365698, 10 May 2021.
3. Julie Siciliano, 'The Relationship between Formal Planning and Performance in Nonprofit Organizations', *Nonprofit Management and Leadership,* vol. 7, no. 4, 1996, pp. 387–403.
4. Adrian Sargeant and Kathryn Carpenter, *Development Plans and Fundraising Performance* [PDF], Institute for Sustainable Philanthropy, 2020, https://static1.squarespace.com/static/5e99b731e7ec45190a6bc6a6/t/5fa9137e4f8f02449ae4fbf3/1604916105527/Development_Fundraising-Report_2020.pdf, accessed 19 May 2021.
5. *Ibid.*
6. Kristi Hedges, 'How to get real buy-in for your idea' [web page], Forbes, 2015, www.forbes.com/sites/work-in-progress/2015/03/16/how-to-get-real-buy-in-for-your-idea, accessed 19 May 2021

CHAPTER ONE
The fundraising audit

Introduction

In this chapter, we start by thinking about the fundraising audit: what it is and why we do it. We then look at the first component of the audit: the external analysis. The external audit involves three key elements: a macro-environmental analysis (by which we mean seeking to understand the wider environment in which your organisation operates); an analysis of your organisation's competitors and/or peers; and a market analysis, which aims to understand your organisation's audience and trends in its focal area(s) of fundraising.

What is a fundraising audit?

A fundraising audit can help you to understand both the external and the internal environments in which your organisation does its fundraising. Working through an audit can give you more information and help you choose the most effective way forward.

Academic inquiry around charity fundraising audits is rooted in earlier research on marketing audits. Some of the earliest research on marketing audits came from Abe Shuchman, a professor of marketing at Columbia University, in the 1950s. In his introduction to an article titled 'The Marketing Audit', he noted that many organisations were already appraising elements of their practice regularly (for example, by assessing the results they had achieved). However, he argued that a marketing audit was different from such ordinary appraisals because it was integrated, co-ordinated, comprehensive and executed systematically.[1] Importantly, Shuchman also made the point that audits enable us to take a step back from the day to day and review our assumptions, conceptions, misconceptions and expectations about our practice. Later writers have emphasised the importance of carrying out an audit periodically rather than on an 'as and when' basis, so that we can assess how various factors change over time.[2]

Like a marketing audit, a fundraising audit can take a deep dive into either a specific area of your organisation's fundraising (for example, a particular income stream) or your fundraising as a whole, considering a range of different aspects using a proven set of tools and models. Adrian Sargeant and Jen Shang, academics specialising in fundraising, state that a fundraising audit is about gathering as much information as possible (about both your existing fundraising practice and the wider environment) in a systematic way. Importantly, they also point out that when auditing, you should consider how both the fundraising function and the wider environment might change and develop over the lifetime of the plan.[3]

Just like a marketing audit, a fundraising audit is an opportunity for you to take time out from your day-to-day work to think about what you do now and what might need to change to enable your organisation to optimise opportunities and minimise threats in the future.

Why do we audit?

In a busy, pressurised fundraising team where there is never enough time or money to devote to a fundraising audit, it can be tempting to skip over this stage when you're developing a fundraising plan. Indeed, in a survey on fundraising planning, Adrian Sargeant and Kathryn Carpenter found that while 72% of organisations said they had a plan, over 40% hadn't analysed the external environment.[4] However, the audit plays a crucial role in the success of the rest of the plan. It ensures that you're taking advantage of opportunities and have the internal capabilities to do so effectively.

You can use an audit to understand what external and internal factors might affect your fundraising practice. External factors, clearly, are derived from the world around us, so they might include issues like the impact of a change in legislation or changing economic circumstances. In contrast, internal factors are derived from within your organisation and might include issues like staffing, budgets or culture. An audit can enable your organisation to gain a picture of its historical performance and where its strengths and weaknesses lie (or indeed previously lay), but also sets up your priorities for the next planning period, making sure those priorities are based on your best estimates about the future. Alternatively, an audit can be both diagnostic and prognostic: you can use it not only to establish any problems in your fundraising performance but also to identify opportunities for future growth and development, and, as you proceed through the planning process, to enable you to set appropriate objectives for your fundraising.[5]

Finally, an audit can play a valuable role as an influencing tool. It can help other stakeholders – such as fundraising team members, senior management team members, trustees or funders – to understand the current situation of your fundraising and encourage them to take an objective perspective, grounded in data.[6]

An audit normally consists of three main sections: an external audit; an internal audit; and a SWOT (strengths, weaknesses, opportunities and threats) analysis, which synthesises the findings of the external and internal audits. In the remainder of this chapter, we will discuss how to focus your audit appropriately and then concentrate on the external audit. The auditing process conventionally starts from the outside and works in towards the organisation itself, which is why we recommend starting with the external audit. In chapter 2, we will look at the internal audit and SWOT analysis.

Step one: Identify your organisation's mission, vision and objectives

The first step in your audit is to reflect on your organisation's mission, vision and objectives. A vision portrays the world the organisation would like to see, while a mission statement describes how the organisation will bring that world to life.[7] Organisational objectives should provide the detail of how the mission and vision will be achieved. For most organisations, an effective fundraising strategy will underpin the delivery of these objectives and thus will be integral to achieving the mission and vision.[8]

The relationship between your organisation's fundraising strategy and its overarching strategy is illustrated in figure 1.1. As the figure indicates, your fundraising strategy will be shaped, and indeed driven by, what your wider organisation is trying to achieve. However, there has to be some two-way conversation: your organisation must be confident, drawing on input from its fundraisers and finance team, that the resources can be provided to deliver the organisational strategy in the context of both the wider environment and the organisation's internal capabilities. The audit is a vital step in assessing this.

FIGURE 1.1 THE RELATIONSHIP BETWEEN ORGANISATIONAL STRATEGY AND FUNDRAISING STRATEGY

Step two: Decide on your focus

Your audit can be either horizontal or vertical: it can either look at the entire fundraising function or focus on a specific income stream, such as individual giving or fundraising from grant-makers.[9] Which option you choose is likely to depend on your position and responsibilities in the organisation and the particular issues you are looking to address within the audit. If you are developing a broader fundraising strategy – say, as a sole fundraiser, a department head or a CEO – you may want to take a horizontal approach. If you are focusing on a specific area of fundraising, you may prefer to think vertically.

Whichever option you choose, it can help to focus on a specific question. A vast amount of data is available to anyone aiming to complete a fundraising audit, both from within your organisation and from external data and research (see chapter 3 for more on research). Therefore, once you've decided on the broad scope, it can be helpful to decide on an audit question to narrow your focus further and ensure that what you find is as relevant as possible to your fundraising practice. Again, the scope of the question is likely to differ depending on your role – a director of fundraising is likely to take a broader and more open view, whereas if you're responsible for a specific area of fundraising, your question might be narrower. Examples could include:

- How can we attract more millennial donors?
- How can we increase our income by 50%?
- How can we organise a successful new event?
- How can we reduce our dependence on specific income streams?

Your choice of question is likely to be guided by your overarching organisational or fundraising objectives. So, for example, if your organisation was seeking to serve twice as many people, it's likely that your fundraising income would have to double to deliver that aim.

Completing the external audit

Once you've completed steps one and two, you can begin your external audit, which will be guided by the outcomes of those steps. We suggest a three-phase external audit: a macro-environmental analysis, a competitor analysis and a market analysis (see figure 1.2). The macro-environmental analysis examines the wider context in which your fundraising takes place. The competitor analysis can examine both the past and predicted future actions of your direct competitors as well as those organisations that are exemplars of best practice. Lastly, the market analysis focuses on both the specific audience for your selected forms of fundraising and more general trends in your focal area(s).

FIGURE 1.2 THE THREE PHASES OF AN EXTERNAL AUDIT: MACRO-ENVIRONMENTAL ANALYSIS, COMPETITOR ANALYSIS AND MARKET ANALYSIS

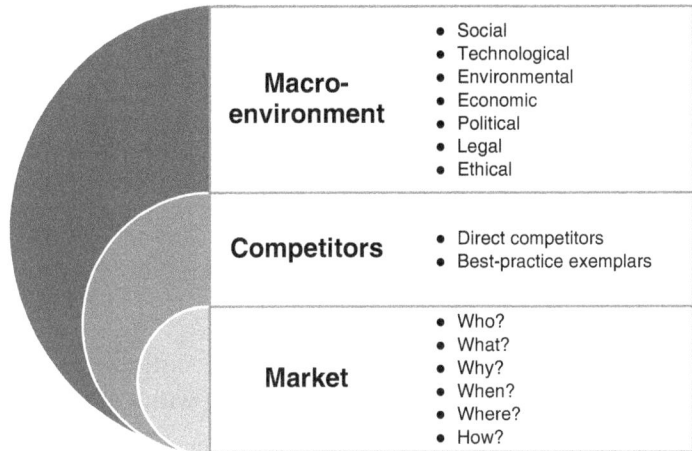

Step three: Macro-environmental analysis

Conventionally, an external audit begins with a macro-environmental analysis, in which you examine the forces that will affect the immediate and long-term future worlds within which your organisation will need to operate.[10] It's important to understand the macro-environmental situation because factors from the wider environment may well affect your fundraising but you will generally not be able to affect them. Therefore, you must be prepared to react to them appropriately. A good case in point is changes driven by the wider economy, which in turn may affect how likely individuals, corporates, trusts and foundations are to give, or the size and timing of those gifts. Individually at least, you're unlikely to be able to make a difference to the economic situation facing the country in which you operate, but you can make sure that your organisation is appropriately equipped to work within it.

A helpful acronym for the various aspects of the macro-environment is STEEPLE:

• **social**: for example, demographic information (such as the fact that the population is ageing) and attitudinal data (such as people's attitudes to your cause);

• **technological**: for example, hardware issues (such as adoption of particular devices – e.g. tablets) and software issues (such as the use of particular social media channels by your target audiences);

- **economic:** for example, levels of disposable income (which may affect the value of gifts given) and house price growth (which may affect legacy income);

- **environmental:** for example, attitudes towards the environment (such as concern about plastic used at fundraising events) and aspects of the local environment (such as ease of travel);

- **political:** for example, likelihood of policy change (which might directly affect your service users or your fundraising) and political attitudes towards charities providing services;

- **legal:** for example, legislation (such as the General Data Protection Regulation);[11]

- **ethical:** for example, attitudes towards the use of different fundraising tools (such as face-to-face fundraising) or working with vulnerable groups, and changes in codes of practice.

Note that you may see other acronyms used, such as PEST, SLEPT or PESTLE. These refer to the same broad concept of macro-environmental analysis. However, STEEPLE covers the fullest range of potential factors.

How then, practically, should you go about pulling together the data for your macro-environmental analysis? Firstly, identify data sources. Given that this analysis focuses on the wider environment, the most likely sources of information will be data and reports published by other organisations, such as the news media, government or industry.

Once you have started to source data, you will need to process it. Table 1.1 provides an example of a five-stage thinking process you might go through, in this case when looking at one economic factor in an audit focused on reducing attrition (donors leaving) in individual giving.

TABLE 1.1 EXAMPLE OF HOW TO PROCESS DATA IN A MACRO-ENVIRONMENTAL AUDIT, LOOKING AT REDUCING ATTRITION IN INDIVIDUAL GIVING

Stage	Questions to ask yourself	Thinking process
Create a frame	What [*economic*] factors do I think might affect my charity?	My sense is that things are looking up economically: there is likely to be a **recovery from the recession**.

Stage	Questions to ask yourself	Thinking process
Verify	Will the factor [*recovery from the recession*] affect my donors?	Possibly. But as they're typically individuals on an average wage, maybe there are more appropriate factors – maybe the factor I should be considering is **trends in income** instead?
Quantify and reference	Can I use research to source data and facts relevant to this factor? Can I find out if it is a one-off issue or a longer-term trend?	My factor becomes: **annual earnings are now more than 3% lower than in 2008 (*The Guardian*, 2018)**, which means that rather than there being a positive opportunity linked to the recovery, there is a possible threat to my fundraising if people have less disposable income.
Reflect	What is the likely impact of [*annual income being lower*] on our [*individual giving*]?	It may be **harder to recruit new donors** if people feel economically squeezed. Additionally, attrition levels may increase (i.e. donors will leave) if people have to make spending cuts.
Prioritise	How important is this factor to our individual giving, taking into account the likely impact?	Given one of our key aims is to reduce attrition, I'll rate this factor as **very important**.

Step four: Competitor analysis

The number of charities in the UK is growing. Since 2000, the number of charities registered with the Charity Commission for England and Wales has grown by almost 5%, from 159,845 to 168,186.[12] There are also around 25,000 charities registered with the Office of the Scottish Charity Regulator, 6,000–10,000 charities registered in Northern Ireland, an estimated 100,000 charities throughout the UK that are too small to register, plus around another 80,000 groups such as Scouts, Guides and churches.[13]

Although the number of charities is growing, the proportion of people giving is not. In their study of giving between 1978 and 2008, economists

Edd Cowley and Sarah Smith found that fewer households gave to charity in 2008 than 30 years before: in 2008, 27% of people reported having given to charity in the preceding two weeks, whereas in 1978 that figure was 32%. Giving had remained at the same share of total spending – 0.4% over that period.[14] More recent data seems to confirm this trend, with the Charities Aid Foundation finding that the proportion of people giving money to charity saw a steady decline between 2016 and 2018.[15] Alongside this backdrop, a majority of charities (65%) are experiencing increasing demand for their services, putting pressure on their fundraising resources.[16] This situation (falling income and increasing demand for services) has often been referred to as a 'perfect storm', particularly with the sector facing the effects of the global pandemic caused by COVID-19.[17]

These trends have created an increasingly competitive environment for charities. However, despite this, within some organisations there may be a reluctance to engage in competitive behaviour, with charities viewing other voluntary organisations as 'fellow travellers' rather than competitors.[18]

Your or your organisation's beliefs about competition in the sector may therefore affect your approach to competitor analysis. Nonetheless, even if you don't view other charities as competitors, it can still be helpful to undertake such an analysis in order to identify and learn from best practice in the sector. Indeed, around three-quarters of charities carry out competitor analyses.[19]

Identifying competitors

The first stage in a competitor analysis is to decide which competitors to focus on. Your choice of competitors is likely to depend on how you view this stage of the audit. If you see it as a way of analysing threats, you might choose to investigate those organisations that you view as direct competitors. This could include, for example, organisations that serve the same causal or geographic area. If, however, you view this stage as a way of identifying best practice, then you are likely to choose organisations from which you can learn the most, such as those that have grown their fundraising dramatically or that have been recognised for good practice. Indeed, researchers Roger Bennett and Sharmila Savani found that the fundraising campaigns of other charities are a primary source of new ideas for non-profits, both large and small. They point out that this is unsurprising, given that it's often very easy to see what other charities are doing via the campaigns they run in the public sphere – thus providing a cheap and easily accessible source of inspiration.[20]

Of course, it may be that you wish to carry out the analysis twice, looking at both direct competitors and those you can learn from. Whichever way you are looking at your competition, however, do remember the focus that you identified in step two (see page 9): ideally, you should choose to analyse those competitors which can best inform your specified focus. For example, if your aim is to double your income, then you may wish to look at other organisations which have achieved that aim, to understand and learn from how they did it.

In most analyses, it is helpful to look at around three to five competitors. This enables you to go into some depth with your analysis while also providing some sense of the competitive set in which you operate and enabling you to understand the commonalities between the various organisations. The number you choose to focus on will depend on your own requirements.

Analysing competitors

Before you can analyse your competitors' data, you need to find it. There are a number of sources of information you might choose to use:

- **published information:** for example, stories or case studies in the sector press, often about fundraising successes or sector award winners;

- **personal conversations:** often non-profits will be willing to share best practice via formal or informal networks in the sector;

- **annual reports:** available either from the charity directly or via the regulator's database;

- **sector reports:** for example, NCVO's *UK Civil Society Almanac*;[21]

- **conference presentations and write-ups:** often non-profits will share considerable detail on their approach at sector conferences or in articles and blogs;

- **tactics:** analysing tactical information (for example, a brochure, a mailing pack or a website) that a charity produces can enable you to infer quite a bit of information about the underlying strategy (for example, the size of a press advert and its placement might reveal something about the charity's expenditure, enable estimation of the likely response and tell you something about the type of supporter they are trying to recruit).

From the information that you gather, it's helpful to deduce:

- **The trend in results in your chosen area of fundraising:** if you want to learn from organisations that are fundraising effectively, then you need to understand their results to ensure that you learn from those whose income (or other key performance indicators) is growing. Therefore, it's wise to look at results over three to five years or longer, where that information is available.

- **The strategy and tactics underlying those results:** in order to understand how these results were achieved, it's important to deduce the overarching strategies and specific tactics that each organisation used to achieve them.

- **Key success factors:** you can take your analysis a step further and consider your competitors' key success factors. What particular aspect of their approach has led to their success? What distinguishes their approach from that of other charities? You can also consider what characteristics successful competitors share: if, for example, you find that a number of successful competitors all seem to share an internal commitment to investment in fundraising, then you can be more confident in identifying that as a key success factor. Analysing these factors can aid you in learning from their success and potentially replicating it on a scale that's appropriate for your organisation.

- **Future aspirations:** if you view this exercise as a way of analysing threats, then you are likely to be particularly concerned about your competitors' future aspirations. How are they planning to grow or develop in the future, and how might that activity affect your organisation?

As in the macro-environmental analysis (see table 1.1), it's always helpful to include some reflection about what these findings mean for you. What are your initial reflections on the impact of your analysis on your future strategy? What lessons might you apply in your organisation?

At this point, you might also find it helpful to read the section on benchmarking in chapter 2 (see page 23).

Avoiding copy and paste

It is very tempting to look at examples of other charities' successes and think that they can be replicated by your organisation, but this derivative strategy may not be successful unless you tailor it to your organisation and supporters. What is more, there is a real danger that if we copy each other's ideas too closely, we will risk homogenising the sector, narrowing our fundraising base, and becoming less innovative and less resilient as a result. Fundraiser Joe Jenkins has argued that, if we share too much, we may end up 'all doing exactly the same thing'. He says that we should challenge rather than be 'indoctrinated into' the status quo.[22]

This criticism is rooted in the writing of Paul DiMaggio and Walter Powell, who address the dangers of institutional isomorphism – essentially, the idea that organisations risk looking too much alike.[23] They argue that there are three main drivers of institutional isomorphism:

- **coercive isomorphism**, where organisations may essentially be driven or even forced down similar paths by legal or governmental mandates;

- **mimetic isomorphism**, which could be described as imitation due to uncertainty – for example, when investing in a new area of fundraising, organisations might be tempted to create similar ideas to those already in the market;

- **normative isomorphism,** driven by (for example) similar educational backgrounds or repeat hiring, underlining the importance of thinking about diversity within recruitment (see page 167 in chapter 11).

So, what might all this mean in practice? Haven't we just suggested learning from competitors? We would propose that, rather than lifting ideas wholesale from other organisations, you think more about the key principles underlying those ideas. For example, if you see a particularly effective fundraising campaign, consider *why* that campaign is successful. It might, for example, tap into an unmet need of your competitor charity's supporters – so, rather than recycling the campaign itself, you could gather insights on your supporters to see what specific unmet needs they might have.

Step five: Market analysis

Identifying your market

In order to conduct an effective analysis, you first have to understand who or what constitutes your market. If you already engage in the focal fundraising activity you chose in step two (see page 9), then you can analyse your internal data in order to understand who your audience is – in geographic, demographic and, if you hold relevant data, attitudinal terms. You might need to break down the analysis into a number of segments.

For new areas of fundraising, you might try to understand the demographics and attitudes of the external market. For example, if your organisation were contemplating putting on its first running event, you might try to understand which demographic groups would be most interested in running as a sport, and their attitudes towards different types of challenges and distances.

Understanding the individuals or institutions in your market

In order to understand your market, you can use a mix of internal research (for example, the results of supporter surveys if available) and research conducted by external bodies (see page 15 for examples). Through this mixed research, it can be helpful to understand:

- **Who** your audience is, in demographic and attitudinal terms.

- **Why** they support – or might support – your organisation, so that you can craft appropriate messages to them.

- **What** options might be attractive to them: might they give regularly, take part in events or share your social media posts?

- **Where** they spend time either geographically or digitally.

- **When** they might consider supporting you (for example, companies might decide on a charity partner at a specific time of year).

- **How** they might support you: do they prefer to support online, face to face or through the post?

Often, it's most useful when planning for the future to access trend data rather than snapshot data. For example, it will probably be more useful to understand that a market is growing by 15% a year than to know that at a particular point in time it constitutes a million people.

As with all the other elements of your external analysis, the data that you find should enable you to reflect on what the findings mean for you: what opportunities can you identify for your fundraising practice? Might your fundraising be hindered or threatened by the information you have identified? If you have access to both internal and external data, you can take your analysis a level deeper, comparing and contrasting the two sources in order to understand particular opportunities available to you – or areas where you might be able to improve your own practice. For example, using external data sources could tell you whether your focal demographic group is growing or shrinking in size, while internal data could indicate whether the number of people supporting you from this group is growing or shrinking accordingly. If the demographic group is growing yet the number of your supporters isn't, what might you do to make your offer more attractive to these people?

Understanding trends in the wider marketplace

As well as considering the particular individuals or institutions that make up your market, you can look at trends in the marketplace for your specific focal area(s) of fundraising. For example, if you are an events fundraiser, you might (at least prior to the COVID-19 pandemic) have noted an increasing trend for people to take part in MOB (mud, obstacles and beer) events, such as Tough Mudder-style endurance obstacle courses.[24] Noting this trend might have given you useful data in its own right, but it might also have suggested new information on your audience, allowing you to improve your understanding of the individuals or institutions that make up your market. For example, having noted the trend towards MOB events, you might have hypothesised that people were increasingly motivated by extreme physical challenges, that they enjoyed the experience of being part of a team, and that they valued the wider social experience surrounding a challenge (although you might have wanted to source additional data to verify these hunches). You could then have begun to design a team-based challenge event specifically tailored to your target demographic.

Case study: Church Mission Society audit

An audit carried out by Catriona Brickel, Individual Fundraising Team Leader for the Church Mission Society (CMS), shows the value of investing time in a detailed audit process.

With headlines showing that fewer people define themselves as Christian in the UK, without a thorough audit, fundraisers in Christian organisations might be forgiven for thinking that they are operating in a declining market and therefore that they are unlikely to be able to grow their income. However, by delving more deeply into the data, Catriona was able to uncover a number of potential opportunities for her organisation.

An analysis of the macro-environment showed that while it is true that fewer people define themselves as Christian today, that decline is partly explained by a decline in traditional Anglicanism. Research showed that two-thirds of UK denominations are actually experiencing growth, suggesting that it is possible for Christian charities to achieve growth. This initial analysis was supported by analysis of other Christian charities, which demonstrated that several were both growing their income and acquiring new supporters, partly through reaching out to these growing denominations.

Drilling down to understand in more depth how other Christian charities were achieving these results, Catriona found that, at an overarching level, they shared an organisation-wide focus on fundraising and had invested in growing their supporter bases. They had also obviously considered the value that they offered their supporters by creating products that could enrich their lives.

Catriona's analysis of the overall market painted a picture of a group of Christians who had a very high propensity to support charities and who gave generously to Christian causes. They also seemed to plan their giving, with direct debits often being preferred.

Ultimately, the audit highlighted a particular opportunity for CMS in value-exchange (or creating products that are valued by supporters, which may encourage them to give). CMS developed a Lent devotional that contributed to doubling Lent appeal income and gained the charity 350 good-quality postal contacts. The charity also developed a new product – asking people to make a monthly gift – using the lessons from the audit.

By taking the time to develop a deep understanding of her charity's external environment, Catriona was able not only to demonstrate that growth was possible within a Christian charity but also to identify specific opportunities that CMS could take forwards and that would fulfil an important need for its supporters.

Conclusion

Having researched and analysed the macro-environment in which you operate, the actions of other fundraising organisations and your specific market, you should be well equipped with potential opportunities and threats to your fundraising practice. The next chapter concludes by describing the SWOT analysis tool. However, before beginning to plan for the future in any detail, you need to consider your internal capabilities to ensure that you can take advantage of potential opportunities effectively and efficiently. The next chapter therefore begins by considering the next stage of the analysis: the internal audit.

Notes

1. Abe Shuchman, 'The Marketing Audit: Its nature, purposes and problems', in *AMA Management Report No. 32: Analysing and improving marketing performance*, Chicago, American Marketing Association, 1959, pp. 1–44.
2. Mehdi Taghian and Robin Shaw, 'The Marketing Audit and Organizational Performance: An empirical profiling', *Journal of Marketing Theory and Practice*, vol. 16, no. 4, 2008, pp. 341–49.
3. Adrian Sargeant and Jen Shang, *Fundraising Principles and Practice*, San Francisco, Jossey-Bass, 2010, p. 144.
4. Adrian Sargeant and Kathryn Carpenter, *Development Plans and Fundraising Performance* [PDF], Institute for Sustainable Philanthropy, 2020, https://static1.squarespace.com/static/5e99b731e7ec45190a6bc6a6/t/5fa9137e4f8f02449ae4fbf3/1604916105527/Development_Fundraising-Report_2020.pdf, accessed 19 May 2021.
5. Abe Shuchman, 'The Marketing Audit: Its nature, purposes and problems', in *AMA Management Report No. 32: Analysing and improving marketing performance*, Chicago, American Marketing Association, 1959, pp. 1–44 at p. 11.
6. Mehdi Taghian and Robin Shaw, 'The Marketing Audit and Organizational Performance: An empirical profiling', *Journal of Marketing Theory and Practice*, vol. 16, no. 4, 2008, pp. 341–49.
7. Adrian Sargeant and Elaine Jay, *Fundraising Management: Analysis, planning and practice*, London, Routledge, 2014.
8. *Ibid.*
9. James Rothe, Michael Harvey and Candice Jackson, 'The Marketing Audit: Five decades later', *Journal of Marketing Theory and Practice*, vol. 5, no. 3, pp. 1–16.
10. Alan Andreasen and Philip Kotler, *Strategic Marketing for Nonprofit Organizations*, New Jersey, Pearson, 2008, p. 80.
11. For guidance on data protection as it applies in the charity sector, see Paul Ticher, *Data Protection for Voluntary Organisations*, London, DSC, 2021.
12. 'Recent charity register statistics' [web page], Charity Commission for England and Wales, 2018, www.gov.uk/government/publications/charity-register-statistics/recent-charity-register-statistics-charity-commission, accessed 19 May 2021.

13 David Ainsworth, 'There are more than twice as many charities in the UK as you've been told' [web article], Civil Society Media, www.civilsociety.co.uk/voices/there-are-more-than-twice-as-many-charities-in-the-uk-as-you-ve-been-told.html, 22 September 2015; 'Charity search' [web page], Charity Commission for Northern Ireland, www.charitycommissionni.org.uk/charity-search, accessed 19 May 2021; 'Home' [web page], Office of the Scottish Charity Regulator, www.oscr.org.uk, accessed 19 May 2021.
14 Edd Cowley and Sarah Smith, *The State of Donation: Long-term trends in UK charitable giving* [PDF], Centre for Market and Public Organisation and Centre for Charitable Giving and Philanthropy, 2011, www.bristol.ac.uk/media-library/sites/cmpo/migrated/documents/smithcowley.pdf, accessed 19 May 2021.
15 *CAF UK Giving 2019: An overview of charitable giving in the UK* [PDF], Charities Aid Foundation, www.cafonline.org/docs/default-source/about-us-publications/caf-uk-giving-2019-report-an-overview-of-charitable-giving-in-the-uk.pdf, accessed 19 May 2021.
16 '"Managing in a new normal" series' [web page], Chartered Institute of Fundraising, 2016, https://ciof.org.uk/events-and-training/resources/managing-in-a-new-normal-series, accessed 19 May 2021.
17 'Charity looks ahead to 2021 after weathering 2020's "perfect storm"' [web article], Charity Today, www.charitytoday.co.uk/charity-looks-ahead-to-2021-after-weathering-2020s-perfect-storm, 25 January 2021.
18 Roger Bennett, 'Competitor Analysis Practices of British Charities', *Marketing Intelligence and Planning*, vol. 21, no. 6, 2003, pp. 335–45.
19 *Ibid*.
20 Roger Bennett and Sharmila Savani, 'Sources of New Ideas for Charity Fundraising: An empirical study', *Creativity and Innovation Management*, vol. 20, no. 2, 2011, pp. 121–38.
21 See https://data.ncvo.org.uk/about.
22 Joe Jenkins, 'Opinion: Share and share alike – until we're all doing exactly the same thing' [blog post], Critical Fundraising, http://blogs.plymouth.ac.uk/criticalfundraising/2016/05/25/opinion-share-and-share-alike-until-were-all-doing-exactly-the-same-thing, 25 May 2016.
23 Paul DiMaggio and Walter Powell, 'The Iron Cage Revisited: Institutional isomorphism and collective rationality in organizational fields', *American Sociological Review*, vol. 48, no. 2, 1983, pp. 147–60.
24 *Sports Fundraising Market Snapshot 2018* [PDF], Massive, 2018, http://wearemassive.co.uk/wp-content/uploads/2018/08/Sports-Snapshot-1.pdf, accessed 19 May 2020.

CHAPTER TWO
The internal audit and SWOT analysis

Introduction
In the previous chapter, we looked at the external environment in which your organisation operates. In this chapter, we consider the environment inside your organisation.

Alongside understanding what's happening outside your organisation, it's vital to understand the internal situation. Ultimately, this will enable you to appraise your organisation's strengths and weaknesses so that you can choose how to react most appropriately to the external situation. For example, if your organisation recognises the growth of digital fundraising as an important opportunity arising from the external environment, it still might not be possible to progress in this area if one of your weaknesses is that you lack staff or volunteers with digital skills.

We start this chapter by considering previous fundraising results and then look at understanding how and why these results were achieved. The chapter ends by describing SWOT (strengths, weaknesses, opportunities and threats) analysis, which brings together the findings from the external and internal analyses, and acts as the conclusion to the audit.

Analysing fundraising results
The first stage of an internal audit most commonly focuses on analysing your previous fundraising results. The results that you choose to analyse will depend on the focus you have chosen for your audit (see page 9 in chapter 1). The scope of your analysis will therefore be very different depending on whether you are analysing the entirety of your fundraising function or whether you are focusing on the performance of one income stream, such as fundraising from grant-making charities.

The first step in your analysis is to choose metrics that are appropriate for the focus you have selected. Very often, in a fundraising analysis, income and expenditure will be key metrics, but there might well be others that you will analyse as well as these (or indeed instead of them). For example, you might look at the number of event participants, people who have expressed interest in legacy giving, donor attrition (donors leaving) or levels of satisfaction among particular donor segments. You might also find it useful at this point to consider the discussion of key performance indicators as a particular type of metric, covered in chapter 8.

Ideally, you would then consider how these metrics have changed over time: analysing five or more years of data should enable you to begin to identify whether there are trends developing. Often, displaying your data graphically (for example, as charts) is the best way to make these trends apparent.

Sometimes, however, it's impossible to access the relevant data, or your audit may be considering an area of fundraising that's new to your organisation. In this case, you would need to consider any results available from a related area that might give you a sense of your organisation's competencies in this field. For example, if you were thinking about creating a new raffle and lottery programme, analysing direct marketing results could enable you to gain a sense of your organisation's competence in delivering a data-driven individual fundraising programme.

Benchmarking

As part of this analysis, you may also wish to benchmark your results, by which we mean compare them with a standard.[1] Benchmarking can be internal, as discussed above, where you track your metrics over time. It can also be external, where you compare your results with those of peers.

Figure 2.1 gives an example summary of results for a charity's peers. Once the charity knows its peers' results in terms of major gifts, expenditure and what they define as a major gift, it can conduct a comparison with its own results.

FIGURE 2.1 EXAMPLE OF BENCHMARKING[2]

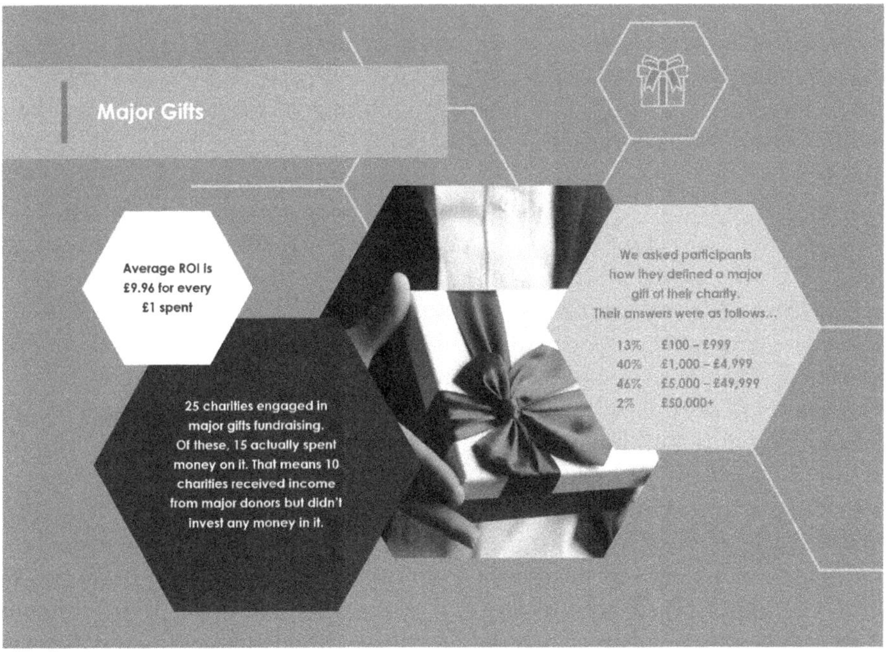

Major Gifts

Average ROI is £9.96 for every £1 spent

25 charities engaged in major gifts fundraising. Of these, 15 actually spent money on it. That means 10 charities received income from major donors but didn't invest any money in it.

We asked participants how they defined a major gift at their charity. Their answers were as follows...

13%   £100 – £999
40%   £1,000 – £4,999
46%   £5,000 – £49,999
2%   £50,000+

Benchmarking can bring additional context to your results, helping you to focus on what you do particularly well or where you perform particularly poorly. The range of areas you can benchmark is vast, from your strategic approach to the perception your donors have of your organisation. Most commonly, however, charities benchmark key metrics such as income, expenditure, return on investment (ROI), and donor retention and attrition.

Once you have decided precisely what you want to benchmark, you can focus on accessing the necessary data and then analysing it. You may be able to find published benchmarks, buy in to commercially available benchmarking projects or arrange your own project with other charities.

While benchmarking can add helpful context and be an effective tool for communicating with other people within your organisation (for example, regarding the need for investment), there are some caveats to be aware of. For example, it's important to compare like with like: if you're a small charity, you might not have the economies of scale of a larger organisation and therefore might find it a challenge to achieve a similar ROI, even if your organisation operates in the same field or cause as the charity you're comparing yourself with. Similarly, if you're a niche organisation serving a very specific cause, you might find it harder to engage in mass marketing than a peer with a broader appeal. There is also the danger that if you don't provide appropriate context, benchmarking figures may unwittingly provide trustees and other senior colleagues with a 'stick to beat you with' if your own performance – for whatever potentially entirely legitimate reason – does not match up.

It's also been argued that benchmarking is a conservative, large-organisation approach that can stifle innovation, with organisations seeking to replicate what's viewed as good practice rather than innovating themselves.[3] The likelihood of this happening, however, will depend more on how the results are used and the internal culture of the organisation. There is an important point here that strategies, and indeed more specifically fundraising strategies, can be dull, formulaic and uninspiring. While good use of data and benchmarking can help to persuade many to follow your new strategy, this shouldn't be at the expense of the creativity and innovation that will inspire others.

Once you have analysed the results themselves, you can begin to consider why you achieved this pattern of performance. Although the results in themselves are likely to be interesting, it's this part of the analysis – understanding the 'why' – that's likely to be most enlightening in terms of moving your fundraising strategy forwards. You can break down your internal situation into two core areas: the big picture (the wider internal situation of your organisation) and the more focused snapshot (the factors specifically affecting your focal area of fundraising). If you are a director of fundraising or solely responsible for fundraising, you might choose to consider big-picture issues, whereas if you are examining a particular type of fundraising or activity, you are more likely to concentrate on a focused snapshot of your work (though it would still be sensible to be aware of the bigger picture and how it affects your work).

The importance of return on investment in fundraising data

'How much should we be raising from our investment in fundraising?' is a question that fundraisers are asked very frequently, particularly by senior colleagues and trustees. Another way of phrasing this question is: what is likely to be the return from our fundraising if we continue to (or start to) invest in fundraisers, fundraising products and fundraising programmes? The answer can be very complicated, but this is an important question that every charity needs to address.

When the Chartered Institute of Fundraising (CIoF) stopped collating return on investment (ROI) data for its Fundratios project in 2013,[4] there ceased to be enough good UK-based data to help fundraisers and charity decision makers (senior managers) to work out which areas of fundraising they should be investing in and how those areas might perform. However, this has been rectified to an extent since 2019 by the fundraising consultancy LarkOwl, which stepped into the breach and collated ROI information in this area in both 2019 and 2020.[5] It is very helpful that we now have some more up-to-date data to help guide our decision-making, even though the sample size collated by LarkOwl is smaller than the data from the CIoF's Fundratios project.

ROI is a simple but important metric. If you raise £10 by spending £1 on a particular activity or income stream, your ROI for that event or type of fundraising is £10. And, simply put, your ROI needs to be £1 in order to break even.

It's easy to calculate ROI retrospectively, but you will need to be able to estimate ROI in advance of starting a new fundraising project or programme. Following are a few highlights from LarkOwl that may help you with that:[6]

- Fundraising from charitable trusts and foundations is a solid and increasingly important performer, with an ROI of just over £10 (increased by 23% from 2019) and an average amount raised per successful application just under £6,000. If well stewarded, trusts and foundations may give over a number of years, or pledge multi-year gifts, which will increase the ROI in this area.

- While raising money from trusts and foundations performs well in ROI terms, government money is hard to come by for charities, with less than a third of respondents raising income in this way. However, while this might mean that statutory income is hard to find, it could also be that not many charities are applying for such finding so it is not as competitive.

- The star of the show in ROI terms is legacy fundraising, with over £30 raised for every £1 spent. While it is often difficult to correlate the money invested in this area with the gifts in wills received in any given financial year, the high ROI is surely an argument to invest in legacy fundraising, if it is considered appropriate for your organisation, particularly if you have a cause that appeals to individual donors.

- Corporate fundraising performs well on average, but there is wide variety in success rates, with some charities losing money on it and others being very successful. Investing in corporate fundraising could be seen as risky area but one that can pay off handsomely if you get it right.

- Community and events fundraising each bring in around £5 for every £1 spent. They are therefore good performers in their own right, but they should also be seen as important gateways to other fundraising functions, such as individual giving and corporate fundraising.

If your ROI on an income stream increased by, say, 10% in 2020, it may look good in isolation, but of course it may not look quite as impressive when set against the national trend. Alternatively, an increase of only 6% may be stronger than the national trend, indicating that you are performing well in this area. Or maybe your return is better than it looked at first glance, due to the vagaries of average donation or grant size, for example.

Answering questions about ROI is complicated because there are a lot of factors that can push your ROI up or down. including size of organisation, area of operation, type of charity, duration of investment in fundraising so far, support of senior management and trustees, how much of a fundraising culture exists in the organisation, and potentially the diversity of the fundraising team.

At the time of writing, it is also unclear how much these figures will have been affected by the COVID-19 pandemic. However, a big lesson from 2020 is that organisations must not rely on single star performers in terms of ROI but need to maintain as diverse an income base as possible, in case a function is hit for reasons they cannot control. Not many organisations will have included a global pandemic in their risk registers.

Understanding the big picture

In terms of the big picture, it can be helpful to start your internal analysis by considering how well fundraising is embedded within your wider organisation. Consider how people, and in particular those in senior management positions, talk about fundraising within the organisation (see chapter 9 for more on getting internal buy-in). Is it seen as a necessary evil: something slightly unseemly that must be done in order for the organisation to do its 'real' work? Is it seen as an add-on to the organisation's core work, which belongs in an office down the corridor? Or is fundraising positioned as a key integrated part of how the organisation works to fulfil its mission? According to a report by fundraising academics Adrian Sargeant and Jen Shang, it is the last of these three which will enable true fundraising success.[7]

Sargeant and Shang carried out a series of interviews with fundraising directors and colleagues whom other sector leaders had identified as conducting great fundraising (i.e. doubling, tripling or even quadrupling income). One of the key findings of their analysis was that, although good fundraising could be a function of a successful charity, for great fundraising to happen, it needed to be at the charity's core.[8] Indeed, they found that successful fundraising directors had worked to embed the fundraising function deep within the organisation, such that other organisational processes, teams or systems were able to co-ordinate to enable fundraising success.

Sargeant and Shang went on to explore other big-picture questions around leadership, team and culture.

Leadership

Does your team have the right leader? Sargeant and Shang found that the fundraising directors they interviewed displayed characteristics linked with highly proficient leaders: specifically, they showed a combination of professional will and personal humility, as shown in table 2.1.

TABLE 2.1 THE CHARACTERISTICS OF HIGHLY PROFICIENT LEADERS[9]

Professional will	Personal humility
Prompts the transition from good to great. Achieves excellence.	Practises modesty and does not boast. Tries to avoid public praise.
Shows resolve to do whatever must be done to achieve the best results in the long term. Does not give up when faced with difficulty.	Demonstrates quiet and calm determination; motivates mainly through relying on inspired standards not inspiring charisma.

Professional will	Personal humility
Establishes a goal of creating an enduring great organisation and does not accept any lesser standard.	Directs ambition into the success of the organisation as a whole, not the self.
'Looks in the mirror' when assigning responsibility for poor results – shares liability rather blaming any one individual, external circumstances or bad luck.	'Looks out the window' when giving credit for the success of the organisation – acknowledges the performance of other people, external circumstances and good luck rather than self-congratulating.

Other characteristics of great fundraising leaders identified by Sargeant and Shang included:

- **Setting the right goals:** they ensured that they set objectives around the long-term drivers of donor value (i.e. those standards and behaviours that would add value for donors over the longer term).

- **Developing shared mental models:** they created mental representations of the key elements within their team's environment that were shared across members (for example, a shared representation of what it means to be donor-centric).

- **Excellent communication:** they used communication as a way of exerting power and influence in and on behalf of their team. They also listened carefully to those around them.

- **Systems thinking:** they were able to see the bigger picture (for example, how systems in the wider organisation were affecting fundraising over the longer term).

Team

Alongside having a great leader in place, Sargeant and Shang identify the importance of having the right team. They discuss the importance of having individuals in a team who have good technical skills but who also have the right characteristics: they are ambitious and determined to succeed, are good team players and are conscientious.

Culture

The other piece of the puzzle that Sargeant and Shang fit into place is organisational culture. Great fundraising organisations demonstrate an organisational learning culture, which means that they are effective at acquiring information, interpreting it and, ultimately, transforming it into knowledge.

Understanding the focused picture

Once you've considered the big-picture questions, you might like to take a focused snapshot of your fundraising activities – particularly if you're auditing a specific type of fundraising or activity. In order to do this, you can conduct an event factor review.[10] You could begin by looking at your results, identifying specific issues or activities (the 'events') to analyse. For example, were there particular years when your results improved or declined dramatically? Did particular fundraising activities perform particularly well or particularly poorly? Or have your results been on a steady upwards or downwards trend? (If this last outcome is the case, an analysis of your overarching approach might be appropriate.)

Once you've identified specific events to analyse or decided on the overarching approach, consider the roles the following factors may have played in your success or failure, and whether things have changed, or are planned to change, since the period you are analysing:

- **Senior-level support:** has your fundraising had support from senior members of your fundraising team, senior management and trustees?

- **Budget:** have you had sufficient funds to spend?

- **Database:** can your fundraising database facilitate your fundraising approach? Have you struggled to get data in or out of the system? Can your database cope with data from different sources, such as social media, email and direct mail campaigns?

- **Processes:** are there effective processes in place to deliver your fundraising? For example, is there a process to collect data correctly, to ensure that Gift Aid is maximised and/or that relevant stakeholders, such as trusts and foundations, receive reports when they are due?

- **Other equipment:** have you had the necessary equipment to facilitate your fundraising? This could involve anything from display boards to a company car to a mailing machine.

- **Outsourcing:** have you worked with external partners to deliver your fundraising? Has this worked effectively? What has gone well or poorly?

- **Case for support:** does your organisation have a compelling case for support that is shared with and understood by relevant stakeholder? (See chapter 5.)

- **Strategy:** is there currently a fundraising strategy in place? Are team members clear about their objectives and where they fit in the broader plan?

Some of these factors might bear more significance than others in your particular situation, and you may also want to consider the interrelationships between the above factors, in order to understand the root of any issues. For example, if fundraising doesn't have support from senior management, that might help to explain why there isn't sufficient budget available.

If you're in a situation where there is no relevant historical data to analyse – for example, if you are carrying out an audit with the view to developing a new area of fundraising – you could consider the factors above through a forward-looking lens: what is the current situation and how is it likely to affect your fundraising success?

Analysing your products' life cycle

Depending on the focus of your audit, it's likely that a key part of your internal analysis will be to consider the various 'products' within your fundraising portfolio. However you choose to analyse your portfolio, it's important to begin by defining what you mean by the term 'product'. This is likely to depend on your organisation and also your position within it. If you're the director of fundraising, you might choose to define your products as the different fundraising disciplines (for example, trust fundraising, events fundraising or corporate fundraising). If you are responsible for a particular discipline, you might instead choose to define your products as different ways in which people can give (for example, an individual-giving fundraiser might define their products as cash appeals, regular giving, raffles, lotteries and so on). You could also define products as 'bundles of need' (for example, a medical charity might pull together all of its research into a specific condition, or a social welfare charity might bring together its work with a particular group of people that it serves). This might also work particularly well for someone who is responsible for funding specific projects (for example, through trust funding or major donor fundraising).[11]

Once you've defined your products, you can begin to analyse them. A commonly used approach is to consider each product in terms of where it sits in the product life cycle. The product life cycle suggests that products typically go through four stages: introduction, growth, maturity and decline (see figure 2.2). Revenue from products will grow until the products reach maturity and then decrease as they enter the decline phase.

CHAPTER TWO **THE INTERNAL AUDIT AND SWOT ANALYSIS**

FIGURE 2.2 PRODUCT LIFE CYCLE

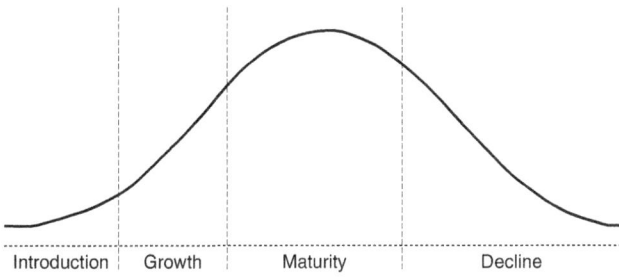

Considering where your products might be in their life cycle can be a useful exercise. At its most basic level, the tool encourages you to keep products that are making money and withdraw from those that are unprofitable. Understanding each product's life-cycle stage will also affect your likely future actions, such as how much you spend on promoting a product or how you actually promote that product.[12] In the fundraising context, when a product is in its growth stage, promotion is likely to be focused on informing people that it exists. However, once it has reached maturity – and other charities are likely to have developed similar products – the focus could instead be on differentiating that product from competitors. Once it is in decline, promotion might cease altogether.[13]

However, there are also a number of pitfalls of relying on the product life cycle as a model. Not all products will follow a life cycle that looks exactly like the one above: studies have identified at least 12 different curves.[14] Indeed, some seem not to follow this model at all – in fundraising, we could argue that while some mass participation events might seem to fit this model relatively well, a product like trust fundraising arguably sits in a more or less constant state of maturity. Other products might behave more like fads, seeing an explosion of interest followed by a fast decline: 2014's Ice Bucket Challenge would be a prime example of this.

Similarly, academics Paul Baines, Chris Fill and Kelly Page point out the difficulty of being sure of when a product has moved from one stage to another, suggesting that particular caution is needed when using the model in fast-moving, unstable environments.[15] This advice is especially appropriate given the pace of unforeseen change in fundraising brought about by the global pandemic beginning in 2019.

Finally, and perhaps most importantly, the model only considers products in isolation. It's important that, as a fundraiser, you consider the full range of products your organisation offers – your fundraising portfolio.[16]

However, even taking these weaknesses into account, if you are looking at a small number of products and they appear to fit well into the model, then it might be helpful to consider its insights in your future planning.

Analysing your fundraising portfolio
The Boston Matrix

One tool you can employ to overcome any shortcomings of the product life cycle is the Boston Matrix, which can be used to consider your fundraising products as a whole.[17] The original version of the matrix relies on the principle of market share, which can be difficult to apply in the charity sector.[18] However, the tool has been adapted by fundraising consultancy The Management Centre to focus on two key dimensions:

- **growth potential**: this can be either positive or negative and is assessed by considering either your competitors' activity or your perception of growth in the market;

- **return**: financial return (such as ROI, or gross or net income), which can also be positive or negative.[19]

Once you have decided whether a product's growth and return are positive or negative, it can be mapped onto a four-cell matrix like the one in figure 2.3. You can then repeat this for each of your products. In this case, the sizes of the ovals represent the return of each product relative to the overall fundraising target.

FIGURE 2.3 EXAMPLE OF THE BOSTON MATRIX[20]

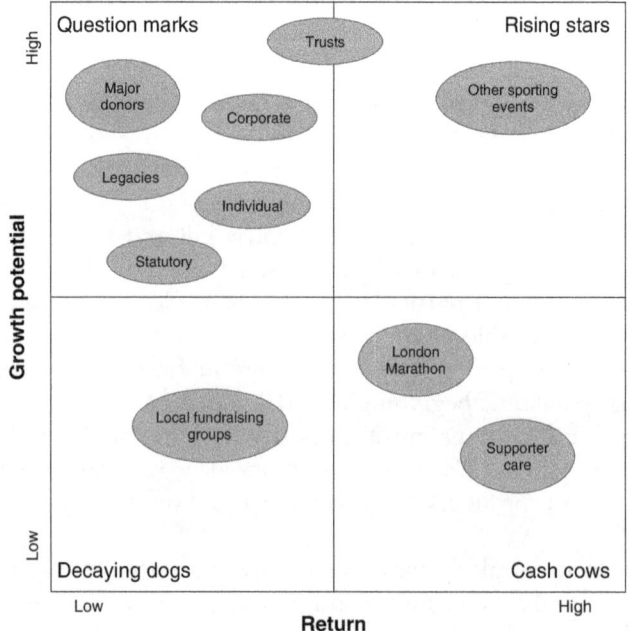

Each cell is named and suggests a different course of action:

- **Question marks** are products where other charities are performing well but you are not – you will need to make efforts to understand why this is the case.

- **Rising stars** are becoming mature, but they are likely to need continued time and money to come to full fruition.

- **Cash cows** are fully mature and produce good returns – although this may not continue in perpetuity.

- **Decaying dogs** produce low returns, and the market doesn't show growth – time and money should probably be invested elsewhere.

Mapping fundraising products onto this model enables you to consider your portfolio as a whole (rather than looking at products in isolation). You can consider whether your decaying dogs should be withdrawn from the market (with the time and energy redeployed more usefully); question whether you are looking after your cash cows appropriately, as important sources of income; consider whether you should focus on question marks or cut your losses; and reflect on whether you have enough rising stars and whether they are capable of eventually becoming cash cows. You can also consider whether your portfolio is correctly balanced between the various quadrants: for example, things might feel like they are going well if all your products are cash cows, but where will the cash cows of the future come from?[21]

Essentially, this model enables you to think about the lifetime journey of any given fundraising product. While you're piloting it or conceiving it, it will be a question mark. But what happens next? Will it become a decaying dog (stop doing it) or a rising star (keep growing it), and will it in the end become a cash cow (continue but know when to stop)?

The Boston Matrix is a particularly useful tool in events-based fundraising. You will clearly be able to plot the 'journey' across the matrix of sector initiatives like the Ice Bucket Challenge, which happened at high speed, and Race for Life, which has matured over a number of years. However, the tool will also help you to consider the investment time frame and risk mitigation needed for your own initiatives.

The alternative fundraising portfolio matrix

Although the Boston Matrix can help you to consider your products in combination, it has also been critiqued. A particular critique is that growth is not the only factor that makes a market attractive.[22] In the charity sector, for example, we might want to consider subtleties such as how reaching a particular market through fundraising could help to raise awareness of our core message. Various alternative portfolio analysis models have been created for use in the commercial sector, but academic Adrian Sargeant suggested a matrix adapted for fundraising specifically. It assesses fundraising products in terms of their internal appropriateness and external attractiveness.[23]

In order to create such a matrix, you first need to define what factors contribute to the internal appropriateness of a product in your organisation. These factors could include:

- perceived or potential impact on service users;
- ethical or values match;
- previous growth;
- availability of people or skills;
- profitability.

Similarly, you would then decide which factors contribute to the external attractiveness of a particular product. These could include:[24]

- level of competition;
- size of the market;
- growth of the market;
- speed or likelihood of change in the market.

The precise factors you choose to include in your assessments of internal and external attractiveness are entirely up to you. Once you have decided which factors you will include, you can weight them by allocating each a percentage score, so that each list adds up to 100%. This is important as some factors might be more significant to you than others. For example, in fundraising, the profitability of a product is commonly deemed to be very important, whereas you might see the availability of skills as only moderately important (if, for example, you could buy these in elsewhere). You should obviously give higher scores to the factors you deem more important.

The next step is to give each product a relative score from 1 to 10 against each internal factor. Then you multiply each score by the weighting and add all the weighted scores together to give an overall score for each product for internal attractiveness. The exercise is then repeated for external attractiveness. A worked example is given in table 2.2 (you would end up with two tables like this: one for internal attractiveness and one for external attractiveness).

CHAPTER TWO **THE INTERNAL AUDIT AND SWOT ANALYSIS**

TABLE 2.2 EXAMPLE OF THE FUNDRAISING PORTFOLIO MATRIX FOR EXTERNAL ATTRACTIVENESS

External attractiveness		10k run		Walk		Ball		Fete	
Factor	Weight	Score	Weighted score	Score	Weighted score	Score	Weighted score	Score	Weighted score
Number of potential participants	25%	6	1.50	3	0.75	3	0.75	10	2.50
Income potential	35%	4	1.40	3	1.05	4	1.40	5	1.75
Potential for repeat participants	20%	7	1.40	4	0.80	2	0.40	10	2.00
Connection to cause	20%	6	1.20	4	0.80	2	0.40	10	2.00
Overall score			5.50		3.40		2.95		8.25

Once each product has a score for internal appropriateness and external attractiveness, it can be mapped on a matrix like the one in figure 2.4. Note also that the maximum weighted score should always be 10 in this example. This means that if you added or removed factors, you would need to adjust the weighting percentages so that they always added up to 100%.

As in the Boston Matrix, you could add an additional layer of data by representing products as circles, the sizes of which show the comparative levels of income generated by each product.

FIGURE 2.4 FUNDRAISING PORTFOLIO MATRIX[25]

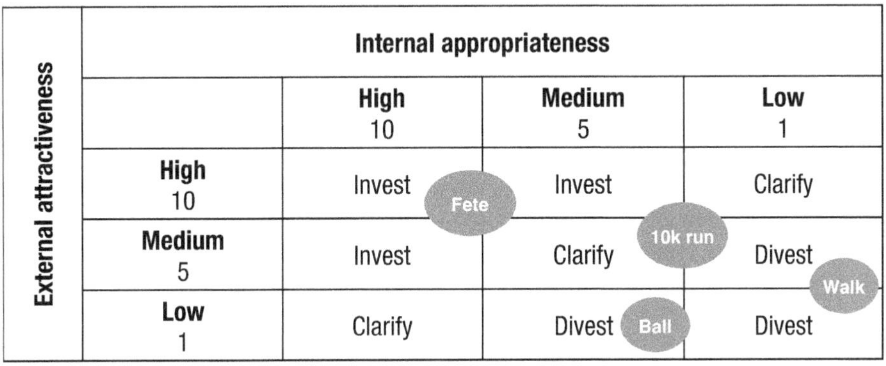

External attractiveness	Internal appropriateness		
	High 10	**Medium** 5	**Low** 1
High 10	Invest (Fete)	Invest	Clarify
Medium 5	Invest	Clarify (10k run)	Divest (Walk)
Low 1	Clarify	Divest (Ball)	Divest

35

The model suggests that any product which lands in the top third (like the fete) should receive additional investment and those which land in the middle third (like the 10k run) should be evaluated further (for example, you could consider whether undertaking additional training might improve internal appropriateness, and thus make the product more attractive for investment). Finally, those products which land in the bottom third (like the ball and walk) should, in due course and if they can't be 'turned around', be dropped as an unnecessary drain on resources.

While the prescription offered by the matrix might seem fairly simple, organisations should always think through the results of such an analysis carefully:

- Are the ratings biased? Might you have subconsciously given a higher rating to a product that you're fond of? Involving several people in the process can help to reduce this risk.

- Is the product new to the market? If so, it may take time before your internal ability to manage the product improves. Such products should probably be given time and evaluated again before action is taken.

- Are there other reasons to keep products which evaluate relatively poorly? For example, are they beloved by volunteers? Might there be other ways to improve their overall attractiveness (for example, a redesign to make them more attractive to the market)?

- How much income comes in from a particular product? For example, does a product appear in the 'divest' area but is also your largest source of income? Although admittedly unlikely, this is theoretically possible!

- If the analysis suggests you should be investing in a number of products, are there human and financial resources available to do this?

SWOT analysis

Once you have completed your external and internal audits, you will need to find a way to process what you have uncovered: an organising framework to summarise the information. A SWOT analysis can be an effective way to do this. Indeed, a SWOT analysis has been described as the best and the most familiar example of such an organising framework.[26] A SWOT analysis enables you to consider the information from your audit in context and helps you to make appropriate decisions as to how to move forwards with your fundraising strategy. It's a relatively simple yet potentially powerful tool.

In a SWOT analysis, strengths and weaknesses are identified through your internal audit, and opportunities and threats are identified through your external audit. Strengths and opportunities are positive and likely to have a helpful impact on your fundraising programme, while weaknesses and threats are negative and are likely to have a harmful impact.

In order to identify these strengths, weaknesses, opportunities and threats, the first step is to go back through your preceding analyses (the external audit in chapter 1 and the internal audit in this chapter). You will need to identify whether each factor identified by your internal audit is a strength or a weakness, and whether each factor identified by your external audit is an opportunity or threat. (This is also a good test of your previous audit work – if a factor is not a strength, weakness, opportunity or threat, you could ask yourself whether it should appear in the audit at all.) For a SWOT analysis to be a truly valuable tool, this is a crucially important stage. The outcome of any SWOT analysis is only likely to be as good as the information which goes into it, so it relies on your ability to draw on the results of thoroughly completed external and internal audit.

It can sometimes be challenging to understand whether a factor is a positive (i.e. a strength or an opportunity) or a negative (i.e. a weakness or a threat), and indeed it might not yet be apparent at this early stage. Some factors therefore might be included as both, with a note as to potential positive and negative implications. For example, in the area of corporate fundraising, an audit might show that brands are increasingly taking a stand on social issues.[27] This might be an opportunity for corporate fundraising if brands want to partner with charities around these issues – or it might be a threat if brands want to associate themselves with these issues directly, taking action themselves. It might also be useful to draw on the expertise of colleagues and other stakeholders here, as incorporating multiple opinions on the impact of the various factors may reduce subjectivity in your analysis.

Each factor that you choose should be:[28]

- **Concise:** the list may only have four or five items.

- **Actionable:** the items included should be actionable rather than vague weaknesses, such as 'database'.

- **Significant:** the items on the list should have (or be capable of having) a substantial impact on your organisation.

- **Authentic:** the items should be based on data rather than wishful thinking (for example, if a strength is something like 'we have a strong brand', what evidence do you actually have for this?).

Table 2.3 shows a brief, simple worked example of a SWOT analysis showing factors for an imaginary charity.

TABLE 2.3 EXAMPLE SWOT ANALYSIS

Strengths	Weaknesses
• Strong core group of committed regular individual givers and grant-makers • Strong core of digital campaigners (via Facebook and Twitter) who are allied to our cause • Good roster of community fundraising events • Two new trustees who have some good connections and are keen to make introductions	• Our 'offer' to regular supporters is not currently clearly defined • Some 'churn' in regular givers in recent years • Our operations team and fundraising team do not currently speak with one voice
Opportunities	**Threats**
• Potential to take advantage of predicted growth in legacy giving by communicating legacies more prominently to our committed supporters • Increasing interest in our cause means the potential for a continued strong pipeline of potential financial supporters • Trusts and foundations are increasingly open to supporting our cause	• Expected cuts in statutory income • In-person challenge events may not recover sufficiently even after the COVID-19 pandemic recedes

At this stage, you will have a simple list of factors (like the one shown in table 2.3) rather than a definitive guide to action. To realise the full power of your SWOT analysis, you need to process the list of factors you have uncovered. By doing this, you can examine how strengths can be leveraged to realise opportunities – or, more negatively, how weaknesses might magnify threats or slow down progress.[29] This will enable you to fully appreciate the connections between your fundraising programme and its environment.

The first layer of processing may be to prioritise the factors. Which are the most important strengths, weaknesses, opportunities and threats? You could do this relatively simply by using your intuition to organise them into priority order, or you could potentially assess and score each factor against a set of weighted criteria, in a similar way to what is suggested in the section above on the fundraising portfolio matrix (see page 34).

The next layer of data-processing could be to find matches between the various categories, as illustrated in table 2.4. This exercise helps to establish the forward-looking elements of your strategy by pointing towards how you can leverage your internal abilities to take advantage of opportunities that are arising (and avoid potential pitfalls on the way). Table 2.4 shows a worked example of a SWOT matching exercise for a fictional hospice charity (you may well be able to identify alternative matches). Completing this exercise should put you in an excellent position to move forwards with setting objectives and developing your strategy – a strategy that is grounded in robust knowledge about the external and internal situation of your organisation.

TABLE 2.4 EXAMPLE OF A SWOT MATCHING EXERCISE[30]

	Strengths • Excellent unprompted brand awareness • New state-of-the-art database • Above-average supporter loyalty • Trustees committed to investment in fundraising	Weaknesses • Slow to move on new opportunities • Difficult to recruit fundraisers • No fundraising strategy in place
Opportunities • Number of people giving online increasing • Growing interest in running events • Growing interest in extreme challenges (such as Tough Mudder-style events)	S/O approaches (use strengths to take advantages of opportunities) • Use brand awareness to reach out to potential participants and their sponsors via digital channels • Use database to develop supporter journeys to retain new event participants	O/W approaches (overcome weaknesses by taking advantage of opportunities) • Purchase places in existing running and challenge events to minimise strain on fundraising team while recruiting new fundraisers
Threats • Ageing population • Competition from St Amanda's Children's Hospice • Decline in average event revenue nationally • Increasingly unpredictable weather patterns	T/S approaches (use strengths to avoid threats) • Consider investing in less strenuous event options for older, loyal supporters • Incentivise different fundraising targets for existing, loyal donors	T/W approaches (minimise weaknesses and avoid threats) • Implement new strategy • Consider virtual events that are less weather dependent

Conclusion

We opened this chapter by talking about the importance of understanding not just fundraising results but also, crucially, why those results are achieved. We moved on to discuss the broader internal situation, how fundraising is positioned within an organisation and the specific factors likely to affect the success of a fundraising activity. We then looked at fundraising products, considering them both individually and in terms of how they fit together into a healthy product portfolio. Finally, we discussed how you can bring together the results of both parts of your audit (external and internal) using a SWOT analysis and start to map out the best way forwards. We look at how you use those findings to go about developing objectives and setting strategy in chapter 4. Firstly, chapter 3 examines how you can use research to strengthen and improve your strategy and to fill in any gaps not available from existing data.

Notes

1. Zach Shefska, 'The Future of Fundraising Benchmarks' [web page], Fundraising Report Card, 2017, https://fundraisingreportcard.com/fundraising-benchmarks, accessed 19 May 2021.
2. *The Calm before the Storm: UK fundraising ROI 2020* [PDF], LarkOwl, 2020, https://larkowl.uk/fundraising-benchmarking-2019, accessed 19 May 2021.
3. Scott Lenet, 'The importance of benchmarking' [web page], Forbes, 2018, www.forbes.com/sites/scottlenet/2018/12/12/the-importance-of-benchmarking, accessed 19 May 2021.
4. See 'Fundratios 2013: Overview of results' [web page], Centre for Interfirm Comparison/Chartered Institute of Fundraising, 2013, www.cifc.co.uk/Fundratios13.html, accessed 19 May 2021.
5. 'Benchmarking' [web page], LarkOwl, 2020, https://larkowl.uk/fundraising-benchmarking-2019, accessed 19 May 2021.
6. *The Calm before the Storm: UK fundraising ROI 2020* [PDF], LarkOwl, 2020, https://larkowl.uk/fundraising-benchmarking-2019, accessed 19 May 2021.
7. Adrian Sargeant and Jen Shang, *Great Fundraising* [PDF], Clayton Burnett, 2013, https://www.philanthropy-institute.org.uk/reports-sign-up, accessed 19 May 2021.
8. *Ibid.*
9. Adapted from *ibid.*, which is based on Joyce S. Osland, Marlene E. Turner and David A. Kolb (eds), *The Organizational Behaviour Reader*, 9th edition, Upper Saddle River, Pearson, 2011, p. 461.
10. Alex Coman and Boaz Roneb, 'Focused SWOT: Diagnosing critical strengths and weaknesses', *International Journal of Production Research*, vol. 47, no. 20, 2009, pp. 5677–89.
11. Adrian Sargeant and Elaine Jay, *Fundraising Management: Analysis, planning and practice*, Abingdon, Routledge, 2014, p. 29.
12. Orville Walker, Harper Boyd, John Mullins and Jean-Claude Larreche, *Marketing Strategy: A decision-focused approach*, New York, McGraw Hill, 2003.
13. Adrian Sargeant and Elaine Jay, *Fundraising Management: Analysis, planning and practice*, London, Routledge, 2014, p. 29.
14. Orville Walker, Harper Boyd, John Mullins and Jean-Claude Larreche, *Marketing Strategy: A decision-focused approach*, New York, McGraw Hill, 2003.
15. Paul Baines, Chris Fill and Kelly Page, *Marketing*, Oxford, Oxford University Press, 2011.
16. Adrian Sargeant and Elaine Jay, *Fundraising Management: Analysis, planning and practice*, London, Routledge, 2014, p. 29.

17 See Bruce Henderson, 'The product portfolio' [web article], Boston Consulting Group, www.bcg.com/publications/1970/strategy-the-product-portfolio, 1 January 1970.
18 Adrian Sargeant and Elaine Jay, *Fundraising Management: Analysis, planning and practice*, London, Routledge, 2014, p. 30.
19 'The Boston Matrix in fundraising' [web page], The Management Centre, 2016, www.managementcentre.co.uk/the-boston-matrix-in-fundraising, accessed 2 March 2020.
20 Adapted from 'The Boston Matrix in fundraising' [web page], The Management Centre, 2016, www.managementcentre.co.uk/the-boston-matrix-in-fundraising, accessed 2 March 2020.
21 *Ibid.*
22 Orville Walker, Harper Boyd, John Mullins and Jean-Claude Larreche, *Marketing Strategy: A decision-focused approach*, New York, McGraw Hill, 2003.
23 Adrian Sargeant, *Marketing Management for Nonprofit Organizations*, 2nd edition, Oxford, Oxford University Press, 2004, p. 64.
24 *Ibid.*
25 Based on Adrian Sargeant, *Marketing Management for Nonprofit Organizations*, 2nd edition, Oxford, Oxford University Press, 2004, p. 64. Adapted figure reproduced with permission from Oxford Publishing Limited through PLSclear. Copyright Oxford Publishing Limited.
26 John Kay, Peter Mckiernan and David Faulkner, 'The History of Strategy and Some Thoughts about the Future', in *The Oxford Handbook of Strategy: A strategy overview and competitive strategy*, edited by Andrew Campbell and David O. Faulkner, Oxford, Oxford University Press, 2003, pp. 18–36.
27 Nikki Gilliland, '10 brand campaigns that took a stand on social issues' [web article], Econsultancy, https://econsultancy.com/brand-campaigns-that-took-a-stand-on-social-issues, 18 February 2021.
28 Alex Coman and Boaz Ronen, 'Focused SWOT: Diagnosing critical strengths and weaknesses', *International Journal of Production Research*, vol. 47, no. 20, 2009, pp. 5677–89.
29 Marilyn Helms and Judy Nixon, 'Exploring SWOT analysis – where are we now? A review of academic research from the last decade', *Journal of Strategy and Management*, vol. 3, no. 3, 2010, pp. 215–51.
30 Heinz Weihrich, 'The TOWS matrix – A tool for situational analysis', *Long Range Planning*, vol. 15, no. 2, 1982, pp. 54–66.

CHAPTER THREE
Improving your strategy with research

Introduction
If you have completed your audit and there are still significant gaps in your knowledge, you may decide there's a need to carry out some additional primary research. This could be to understand a variety of issues, such as the demographic make-up of your supporter base, the general public's opinion of your organisation or the motives of your supporters. This chapter covers the benefits of investing in research and the different options for carrying it out.

Listening and informal research
Before we start talking about the merits of investing in formal research projects, we wanted to add a word or two about the importance of listening to and reflecting on what supporters might tell you informally. We mention in more detail later in this book the importance of learning from front-line staff who speak to donors on a regular basis, and how valuable their input can be in shaping your strategy at the earliest stage of its development and throughout the process (see page 193). And, even if you don't feel it's appropriate to carry out a formal research project, it may be appropriate to test your thinking at an early stage with some of your valued supporters who may be affected by your strategy, particularly if they are high-value financial supporters (often referred to as major donors) or people whom you are keen to bring into the fold more centrally. They will be able to give you an indication of whether you are on the right track – and hopefully they will also, if you pitch your enquiry correctly, be flattered that you are keen to hear their thoughts. This may then lead to a deeper relationship with them. In our experience, the old adage 'ask for money, get advice; ask for advice, get money' has often proven true.

> **Case study: Listening to donors at SolarAid**
> SolarAid's experience (as told by Richard Turner) illustrates the importance of listening to donors.
>
> > We introduced a simple free text box after people gave on line, that asks **why** they had donated. What was great is we would get some lovely messages from donors. So, each week I would pick the best and send them around the entire organisation, including our offices in

> Africa and our trustees. It was a really easy way to get across the passion of supporters and that in turn started to help generate a great respect for them within SolarAid.
>
> Occasionally we would get some insights too. This was how we learned people were giving to us to offset their carbon footprint. As a result we changed our SEO [search engine optimisation] terms so that [for] anyone searching for 'carbon offset charity', SolarAid would pop up.[1]

Why research?

To return to research in the more formal sense, when we use the term 'research' in this chapter, we mean the collection, analysis and communication of information which will ultimately assist your decision-making about fundraising.[2]

Using research to inform your fundraising strategy comes at a cost in terms of time and, generally, money. Why then would you choose to invest in this way? Here are some potential answers to that question:

• Research can help you to understand your supporters (and particularly their motivations) better, which will enable you to create a strategy that is supporter focused and meets their needs.

• Research can help you to understand how and why your colleagues or predecessors made the decisions they did in the past, as well as helping you to explore how various events were interlinked.

• Research may help you to predict future behaviour by your supporters and also may help you to develop new, creative ideas for your audience.

• Research can help you to demonstrate the evidence behind your thinking and explain your rationale more clearly, and it may also give you metrics against which you can track the progress of your fundraising strategy.

• Research may also help you to identify potential new audiences and new markets for particular products or propositions.[3]

The research process

So, if understanding more about your supporters can benefit both those supporters and your organisation, how do you go about it? The process of designing and developing a research project is illustrated in figure 3.1, and the stages will be discussed below in more detail.

FIGURE 3.1 THE STAGES OF THE RESEARCH PROCESS[4]

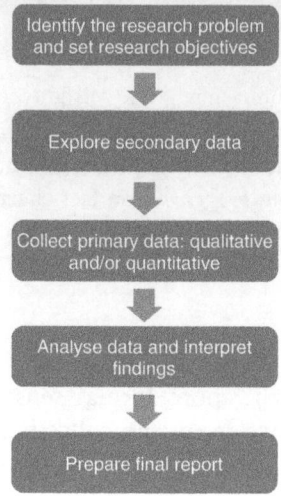

Identifying the research problem and setting research objectives

Identifying the research problem or opportunity is the most important step in any research project.[5] Without absolute clarity at this stage, it can be very easy to waste time and money during the research process – or even design a project that will not deliver the information you need. In order to get the most out of your research work, you can define two things: a marketing *decision* problem (or question) and a marketing *research* problem.

In the context of a fundraising strategy, your marketing decision problem might be something like, 'How can we best steward our existing supporters so that they will continue to support us?' Another way of conceptualising the marketing decision problem is by starting at the end, aiming to understand the decisions that will need to be taken as a result of the research (i.e. exactly what you will do with the data you acquire).[6] For example, you might hope to understand more about why some donors are stopping giving. If you can understand your supporters better, you can tailor your communications with them in order to build relationships more effectively. In this way, your chosen marketing decision problem should form the foundation of your entire study.

You can then move on to defining your marketing research problem. This involves determining what information you will need to address your marketing decision problem. In the case of the example above, your marketing research problem might be, 'To understand what donors want to get out of a relationship with our organisation.'

Once you have identified and expressed your marketing research problem, it can be translated into a set of research objectives that specify precisely what it is that you would like to find out. In our example, they might include:

- to describe the tangible benefits that donors may appreciate (for example, tax breaks);

- to determine the intangible benefits that donors may value (for example, 'warm glow' – a sense of joy or satisfaction).

Clear objectives can also help you to choose the most appropriate research method. Very broadly, objectives which are concerned with understanding 'how much' or 'how many' point towards a quantitative methodology (based on numbers and facts), while those concerned with understanding 'why' tend to point towards a qualitative methodology (based on opinions and perspectives).

Exploring secondary data

The best place to start in most research projects is with secondary research, by which we mean data and research that already exists, such as in externally published sources or internal reports and databases. However, for the purposes of this chapter, we'll assume that you have already explored that material as part of your internal audit (see chapter 2) and ascertained that the information you need hasn't already been published elsewhere. You'll therefore need to carry out some primary research – research that creates new data.

Collecting primary data

Quantitative research

Quantitative research involves collecting information about a sample of people in a population that can be quantified (put in the form of numbers) in order to understand that population's demographics, behaviour, motivations or attitudes.[7] Commonly, quantitative data is gathered through structured interviews or surveys. These can be delivered through several channels, such as online, by post, by telephone or face to face. The channel(s) you choose for your research project will depend on a number of considerations. For many charities, cost will be a key factor, and therefore the online channel can be a very cost-effective choice, while face to face would normally be the most expensive option. However, you should also consider issues such as reach (for example, how many of your audience have an email address?), representativeness (for example, do those people with email addresses reflect the audience you're interested in?) and accessibility (for example, are your older donors comfortable completing surveys online?).

In order to gather useful data, you will also need to pay particular attention to the design of your survey to ensure that you can generate the data you require. This includes the topics you cover, the types of questions you ask (see the survey question don'ts below), the wording you use, the order in which your questions appear, and the overall length and design.

> **Examples of poor questions to include in a survey**
>
> - **Why did you have such a terrible experience with our charity?** This is called a leading question, because pre-defining the experience as terrible will lead people to answer in a particular way.
>
> - **What about your experience with our charity encouraged you to complain and to do so by telephone?** This is asking two questions in one, and you won't be sure which one your donor is answering.
>
> - **Why wouldn't you not give to us in the future?** Convoluted constructions such as double negatives are difficult for people to comprehend.
>
> - **Why did you lapse as a charity supporter?** This uses fundraising jargon that a donor is unlikely to understand.
>
> - **Are we better than other charities you support?** This question is too broad and ultimately wouldn't give you much useful data. Ideally, you would want to break down the different ways you might differ from other charities (for example, your speed of response or the impact of your work).

The other key element of research methodology to be aware of is sampling, or making sure that you are selecting a representative group of people to contact. It is unlikely that you will have the budget or time to reach all of your potential audience. However, you can use sampling methods to select a smaller group. The power of statistical analysis means that you can then extrapolate from this smaller group to say with a specified degree of accuracy that, for example, around 25% of your organisation's supporters value the tax benefits that they receive when making a gift. (There are various calculators available online that can help you to determine what size of group you need to sample in order for your results to be statistically significant, such as www.surveysystem.com/sscalc.htm.)

The downside of quantitative research is that, while it can tell you *how many* people think a particular thing, it is not so effective at determining *why* that might be the case, and it can be easy for researchers to impose their views on their audience with leading questions or poorly designed closed questions. Closed questions (where respondents must pick from a predetermined list) are not bad in themselves, but they must be designed carefully to ensure people can answer fully and accurately. For example, in a survey, a researcher might list a range of possible motivations for supporting a charity and then count how many people tick each box; however, in compiling the list, the researcher may not have included a motivation that would have been key for a number of people.

Case study: Using quantitative research to develop a training proposition at the Chartered Institute of Fundraising

This case study, provided by Jonathan Cook, Director at Insight-ful, gives a helpful illustration of the value of investing in quantitative research when you need to understand the requirements of different groups of donors – or, in this case, fundraisers themselves.

The Chartered Institute of Fundraising (CIoF) London and South East regional group wished to develop its training offer for fundraisers in the region. Traditionally the training offered by the group, both at its free monthly seminars and in its paid sessions with external trainers, was curated by the committee members. As a result, it was only possible to know whether the training courses on offer were required by fundraisers from the number of ticket sales and post-training feedback. The committee members decided to conduct a large online survey with regional members to understand their training requirements.

The survey went to all members of the CIoF based in the south-east of England and London as well as being advertised on social media and emailed to the CIoF London and South East regional group's mailing list.

The survey was split into three main areas of data capture:

- training content questions;
- location and time questions;
- segmentation questions.

The training content questions sought to understand what the respondents wanted from the future training programmes. Question asked were:

- What are the key areas of fundraising you would like to gain more expertise in (e.g. major donors, events, trusts)?
- What skills or knowledge would you like to gain in order to help you raise more money (e.g. copywriting, digital skills, presentation skills)?

- What type of personal development do you like (e.g. formal courses, mentoring, webinars)?

The location and time questions primarily sought to understand the barriers people faced in accessing training, so these could be overcome. Questions were also asked about distance from work or home to the training location, the time of day the training was run and the cost of the course.

The segmentation questions allowed the CIoF to understand the different requirements of the different audience groups. Questions were asked about the type of charity they worked for (animals, health, etc.), their seniority within the charity and their experience in the sector. The survey also asked for their postcode so as to be able to plot the respondents on a map.

The objective of the research was to be able to offer different types of training based on the individual, their style of learning, the topic they were interested in and their location.

All of the questions were quantifiable, so the answers could be counted or displayed in graphical form. Only two had options for free text (in an 'Other' field).

The results were presented as a series of charts in a dashboard. At the top, there were buttons displaying the segmentation elements of the survey. This allowed the CIoF to select everyone at manager level with less than three years' experience (for example), and the charts changed to show the views of just those segments.

The CIoF was then able to devise a full training and development programme for people with different levels of experience and those who worked for large, medium and small charities. It was able to work out when, where and how those programmes should be delivered and to ensure that training was available for all levels of budget.

For example, people new to the sector wanted training on strategy, planning and negotiating, whereas people with more than ten years' experience were particularly interested in training in regulation and insight. People new to the sector also had far more of a digital learning style, whereas people with more than ten years' experience were looking for more masterclass-style events.

This survey and the insights gained were used to develop the CIoF London and South East regional group's entire training programme for the following few years.

Testing

As human beings, we don't always understand the reasons we behave as we do, and we can't always articulate them clearly. And, sometimes, our actual behaviour differs from how we believe we might have behaved in a given situation. Therefore, rather than applying methods that ask people whether they might do something (such as give to your organisation in the future) or whether they might be influenced by a certain approach, you can test some of your ideas in a real-life situation. For example, you can try out different versions of text in social media advertising or different versions of copy in direct marketing.

Testing properly can be a challenge, however. Firstly, it is important to ensure that you are testing in sufficient volumes for the results to be statistically significant (see the information above on sampling on page 46 for more detail). Secondly, you must design your tests carefully. If you want to know which of two mailing packs works better, then you can test two quite different packs against each other and measure the difference in, for example, response rates or gift amounts. However, if you want to understand *why* there is a difference in the response rates, then you have to change only one thing at a time – perhaps something as small as a word or two in a letter or telephone fundraising script. All other factors (such as timing when a message is sent) should be held constant. Without these controls, it can be easy to impute meaning to results which aren't justified given the design of the research or the statistical significance of the results.

Qualitative research

Qualitative research is research undertaken with a comparatively small number of individuals that produces deep – but generally non-quantifiable – insights into their behaviour, motivations and attitudes.[8] Qualitative data can be gathered through a number of methods, most commonly focus groups and interviews.

Focus groups are typically made up of six to ten people who meet for one to two hours to discuss a specific topic, most typically face to face, although it is also possible to facilitate focus groups online (increasingly using videoconferencing). According to authors Adrian Sargeant and Elaine Jay, typically a project might involve six to eight groups in order to hear a range of opinions from a variety of stakeholders.[9]

Interviews are often conducted one to one, although they can occasionally involve couples or trios. They can be carried out on the phone, online (using videoconferencing software) or face to face. In both interviews and focus groups, the researcher tends to have a guide to the topics to be covered, although they can build in flexibility to follow up on interesting themes that emerge through the conversations.

While both focus groups and interviews enable in-depth understanding, they each have their own strengths and weaknesses. In-depth interviews can be particularly useful for understanding the experience, journey or views of people on an individual basis. They can also work well where there might be a concern over sensitivity, where people might not want to share their views in a group environment and/or where the researcher may need to adapt their approach depending on the reaction of the individual. Therefore, for example, they might be an appropriate tool when discussing supporters' personal experiences of your organisation's work. Focus groups, on the other hand, can work well where there might be research benefits from the social interaction between more than two people that occurs – for example, they might be a good forum to discuss new fundraising materials, where the discussion can build on the inputs from the various members of the group.

Case study: Using qualitative insight to develop a legacy proposition at St Peter's Hospice

Qualitative research can be particularly helpful when exploring reactions to different fundraising ideas or, in this case, fundraising messages.

The team at St Peter's Hospice were keen to develop messaging for their legacy fundraising that was grounded in supporter insight. Before the project began, they had carried out a supporter survey which included questions about supporters' interest in legacy giving alongside other questions about their reasons for supporting the hospice and what St Peter's meant to them. This enabled the external researcher to pull out responses from people with an interest in legacy giving and to understand what might make them different from the hospice's wider group of supporters. In particular, the analysis suggested that people with an interest in legacy giving were more engaged with the hospice and significantly more likely than other supporters to be motivated by remembering a loved one.

Using the findings from the survey, the hospice worked with its creative agency to develop four different ideas for legacy messages. These ideas were then shared with stakeholders in three focus groups, alongside materials from other charities, to allow the participants to identify comparisons and contrasts. There was consistency across the groups around two messages that resonated with them and two that didn't, giving St Peter's the confidence to move forwards with either of the ideas that resonated. The participants also drew out important principles for future messaging, including a preference for a particular brand colour that was strongly associated with the hospice, the need to show how the work affected people directly and the need to ensure that the area's diverse community was represented in imagery.

The key benefit of qualitative research is the opportunity to gain in-depth understanding, particularly around supporters' 'whys' (such as why they are motivated by your cause). Its flexible, exploratory nature means that you may discover completely new or unexpected information that you might not find from a more structured survey. The downside of the flexibility of the method and the smaller number of people involved is that you can't tell with any degree of certainty how widely these opinions are shared among your audience.

Combining qualitative and quantitative methods

Qualitative and quantitative research can be used together in a single project, where the strengths of one method may be used to address the weaknesses of the other. Commonly, qualitative research is used to gauge opinions, perceptions or motivations, and quantitative research is then used to measure how many people share those ideas.

Case study: Taking a blended research approach to understanding supporters

Lesley Pinder, Supporter Experience Expert, explains how quantitative and qualitative insights can be used together in practice:

> Since 2014 I've been employing a user-centred approach to solve supporter experience problems or to develop new ways for people to support a charity they care about. This approach means that a project starts with an audience, a problem or opportunity, and questions about both and then decides how best to answer those questions. Usually this means using a whole range of different sources of insight, or research tools, and building them up layer by layer until a holistic picture starts to emerge.
>
> **I start with discovering what has happened and what is happening now.** If you want to understand what people did in the past, data and web analytics are absolutely the best place to start. Asking people to remember what they have done will always have its flaws, whereas data is usually a pretty good record. If you then also want to

understand *how* they do it now, then data and analytics can help to suggest possible scenarios. However, to really understand this, you will need to consider ethnographic research, where you observe people in real life or online (either in a public place or with their consent). You might use this if you are seeking to understand how people use your organisation's shops or how someone navigates your website to make a donation. Between data and observation, you can get a really good understanding of the past and the now.

If you want to understand how people feel, you need to talk to them. It can be easy to rely on surveys to gain insight into people's motivations and interests. I use them, as they help me to get a broad understanding of how an organisation is doing and what its supporters are interested in. But surveys don't tell me how people really feel and why. That is why I always find an opportunity to speak to supporters by phone, in person or sometimes online. Interviews and discussions allow you to dive deeper, to read body language and go on unexpected tangents that reveal deep truths.

Don't ask people what you need to learn from data, observation or tests. I have lost count of how many times someone has said that qualitative research is flawed as 'people say one thing and do the other'. You should never ask someone to project how they might behave. It is better to ask them to reflect on something they have already experienced. Qualitative research is for finding out how people feel, their values and their needs, not trying to accurately predict how they will behave, what they will pay or how many emails they will open.

Research and insight aren't foolproof – the real world is unexpected. Only once something is live and in the wild can you ever really fully understand whether the insight you gathered is leading you in the right direction. Up-front insight isn't foolproof and it doesn't give you all the answers. Research is always limited so try to find a balance between putting effort into research up front to help you make good decisions and getting something live quickly so you can test it.

Working with an agency or a consultant

In charities in general, and smaller charities in particular, budgets available for research can be extremely limited. Many of the research approaches discussed above can be undertaken by paid staff or qualified volunteers or through creative solutions, such as working with local college students. However, where the budget is available, your project might well benefit from professional research input. The benefits of working with agencies include:

- **Time and cost:** agencies' experience might mean that they can carry out the research more efficiently than less experienced internal staff, which can mean that, when you take into account the cost of staff time, an agency is the cheaper option.

- **Facilities:** agencies may have access to specific facilities (such as recording equipment), which can be expensive to purchase for limited use.

- **Know-how:** agencies have specific expertise (such as focus group facilitation and data analysis) which might be difficult to replicate internally.[10]

The first, and often the most important, step in working with an outside agency (or in briefing internal staff or volunteers) is to create a research brief, so that prospective agencies and your organisation share the same perspectives on the project and particularly what needs to be understood. Typically, this might include:

- background information on your organisation and the project;
- research and fundraising objectives;
- target audience to be researched;
- initial thoughts on methodology, if appropriate;
- budget and timescale;
- details of how the project will be managed;
- information on how you will choose an agency (key criteria, method of supporter engagement, etc.).

Once you have developed the brief, you can circulate it to several agencies, which are likely to respond with a detailed research proposal describing how they would address your research brief. There are several types of agencies that address fundraising research projects, from individual freelancers to international market research agencies. Your choice is likely to depend on a combination of your available budget, the quality of each agency's proposal, the agency's experience in undertaking fundraising research, personal recommendations, and fit between the agency and your organisation.

Judging the quality of research outputs

During the process of carrying out the research – and, of course, once you have completed your project or received a report from an agency – it's helpful to consider its quality. You will need to be sure that the research is of high quality before you go about applying the findings to your practice. It's sensible to consider research quality differently, depending on whether the research is quantitative or qualitative.

There are three key criteria for judging the quality of quantitative research:

- **Validity** is whether you're measuring what you originally set out to measure. For example, if you measured donor satisfaction in a survey, are you confident that all the relevant questions related to that key topic?

- **Reliability** relates to the level of measurement error. For example, if a survey question was worded in a confusing way, participants might have guessed at an answer.

- **Generalisability** relates to the extent to which results from a sample can be applied to a wider population. It relies on you sending your survey to a large enough sample size to be representative (see page 46) and analysing your results using appropriate statistical techniques which account for the combined influence of various factors.[11]

The quality criteria for qualitative research are less clear. While some researchers have attempted to adapt the principles of validity, reliability and generalisability to suit qualitative outputs, it's probably more sensible to judge qualitative research differently, using criteria that match its particular strengths. Jane Meyrick, a research consultant, has developed a model for assessing qualitative research which ultimately boils down to two key questions:

- **Is the research systematic?** For research to be considered systematic, the researcher should lay out their objectives, the methods for achieving them, their process for data collection and analysis, and how this data has shaped their conclusions.

- **Is the research transparent?** For research to be considered transparent, the sample (for example, the interviewees) should be described (for example, 'We spoke to eight members of staff at charity X'), as should potentially the researcher's personal view on the subject. Any changes in focus in response to participants' answers should be made clear, and any findings should be clearly grounded in data.[12]

> ### When data collection goes wrong[13]
> Having read this and previous chapters, you might think that the more data you have, the better. However, as Cherian Koshy argues, that isn't always the case – and poor data can result in poor insight.

Whether you are looking at data collected from the external environment, internally within your organisation or from research that you commission, it can be easy to fall into certain traps. These can result in you wasting resources collecting data that can't be used or, worse still, making poor decisions. For example:

- **Collecting data that you don't have the capacity to use or can't act upon:** always ask yourself whether you're actually going to be able to make a decision based on the data you're acquiring. Similarly, consider whether you can act upon what you discover – for example, there's little point understanding whether your donor base is wealthy if you don't have the capacity to fundraise from major donors.

- **Collecting too little data (or not having enough variety in your metrics):** while too much data that's not practically useful can be problematic, often a single metric isn't enough. If, for example, you were only counting money raised, you might never invest in recruiting new donors, as organisations often lose money in that process – you would have to have a view of the longer-term potential of that relationship, such as lifetime value (see page 126 in chapter 8).

- **Collecting the wrong data:** sometimes a metric can look good on paper but might not be particularly useful for decision-making. For example, asking your donors for a net promoter score (a single number score that expresses how likely they are to recommend your organisation) is unlikely to be helpful unless you understand why each supporter has given the score they have.

- **Collecting inappropriate data:** you may know the phrase 'garbage in, garbage out'. If you're collecting data in an inappropriate form, or that data isn't clean (for example, incorrect or incomplete), it's unlikely to be helpful in your decision-making – and might even point you in the wrong direction.

- **Collecting biased data:** it's easy to insert our own biases into the data we collect, whether that's by asking questions in a particular way or seeking out data that confirms our existing expectations. In some scenarios, these biases can have implications for equality, equity, diversity and inclusion (EEDI). For example, if you've only ever reached out to white, middle-class donors, then your data is likely to only reflect the opinions and preferences of that group. (See page 167 in chapter 11 for more on EEDI.)

Conclusion

Investing in research can offer you a range of benefits, from understanding your audiences better to supporting the development of new fundraising ideas to shedding light on supporter behaviour. It can benefit your organisation by ensuring that you have a robust, well-informed fundraising strategy. And, importantly, it can benefit your supporters by ensuring that you develop a fundraising approach that meets their needs.

For your research project to do this, it's vital that you're absolutely clear, and as precise as possible, about what it is that you need to know. Once you've achieved this clarity, you can apply a variety of techniques and approaches to the problem, from reading what others have written to conducting a full-scale project generating new data through a combination of focus groups and surveys. Armed with insight and information from your research, you will be fully ready to think about your fundraising objectives and your audiences, which are covered in the next chapter.

Notes

1. Commission on the Donor Experience, 'CDE project 16 section 2: Case examples, tips and links' [web article], The Showcase of Fundraising Innovation and Inspiration (SOFII), https://sofii.org/article/cde-project-16-section-2-case-examples-tips-and-links, 30 April 2017.
2. Alan Wilson, *Marketing Research: An integrated approach*, Harlow, Pearson Education, 2003, p. 4.
3. D. V. L. Smith, 'The Role and Changing Nature of Marketing Intelligence', in *Market Research Handbook*, edited by Mario van Hamersveld and Cees de Bont, 5th edition, Chichester, John Wiley & Sons, 2012, pp. 1–36.
4. Based on figure 3.1 in Adrian Sargeant and Elaine Jay's *Fundraising Management: Analysis, planning and practice*, London, Routledge, 2014, p. 40.
5. Naresh Malhotra, David Birks and Peter Wills, *Marketing Research: An applied approach*, Harlow, Pearson Education, 2007.
6. D. V. L. Smith, 'The Role and Changing Nature of Marketing Intelligence', in *Market Research Handbook*, edited by Mario van Hamersveld and Cees de Bont, 5th edition, Chichester, John Wiley & Sons, 2012, pp. 1–36.
7. Alan Wilson, *Marketing Research: An integrated approach*, Harlow, Pearson Education, 2003, p. 135.
8. *Ibid.*, p. 37.
9. Adrian Sargeant and Elaine Jay, *Fundraising Management: Analysis, planning and practice*, London, Routledge, 2014, p. 45.
10. *Ibid.*, p. 27.
11. Daniel Muijs, *Doing Quantitative Research in Education with SPSS*, London, Sage, 2011.
12. Jane Meyrick, 'What is Good Qualitative Research? A first step towards a comprehensive approach to judging rigour/quality', *Journal of Health Psychology*, vol. 11, no. 5, 2006, pp. 799–808.
13. Based on information provided by Cherian Koshy.

CHAPTER FOUR
Setting objectives and identifying your audience

Introduction

By this point in the strategy development process, you should have a good understanding of the wider situation and your organisation's position within it. A full SWOT (strengths, weaknesses, opportunities and threats) analysis should have helped you to begin to think about the future direction of your fundraising. In this chapter, we look at two crucial elements of clarifying your future direction: setting your objectives (which will clarify the focus of your strategy) and identifying the audience or audiences that you will reach through your fundraising.

Setting objectives

Before you can progress with developing any sort of strategy, it's important to set clear overall objectives. Indeed, there's a very long history of thought on the importance of having a clearly defined end goal: as early as the sixth century BC, the great military strategist and philosopher Sun Tzu pointed out the value of setting an ultimate goal by saying, 'In war, then, let your great object be victory, not lengthy campaigns.'[1]

The value of objectives in management specifically has been discussed throughout the twentieth century, with the principle of 'management by objectives' generally credited to business guru Peter Drucker.[2] He states that every area where performance and results directly affect the survival and prosperity of an organisation should be managed through objectives – and in most charities, surely, fundraising is vitally important to both survival and prosperity! Drucker also points out that to be effective, it's essential that objectives are carefully thought through. However, he argues that in the vast majority of cases, they are not.[3]

So, how do you go about ensuring that your objectives are indeed carefully thought through? In chapter 2, we discussed the importance of the SWOT analysis – not only as a summary of your audit findings but also as a guide to moving forwards. Therefore, in order to formulate effective objectives, you should return to your completed SWOT analysis and consider the various options you identified to use strengths to take advantage of opportunities, overcome weaknesses by taking advantage of opportunities, use strengths to avoid threats, and minimise weaknesses and avoid threats. Indeed, you might find it helpful to put those options into what you believe to be order of priority, so that you know where you can most effectively focus your future fundraising. You could prioritise the options based on your experience and instinct as an experienced fundraiser, or perhaps develop a set of criteria to score them against, such as fit with your existing fundraising programme or income growth potential.

Once you've considered the available options, you can translate them into objectives. In many strategies, the most important ways forward are found when you align your strengths and opportunities, while the other elements of the SWOT analysis might feed into your wider strategy. For example, if you identified that there might be an opportunity to take advantage of a growing millennial audience by using your existing skills in digital fundraising, you might set an objective that is structured around recruiting a number of new, younger donors through online channels.

Ideally, your objectives should meet SMART criteria.[4] That is, they should be:

- **Specific:** clear and well defined (rather than general and broad-brush, such as 'to raise more money').

- **Measurable:** so that you can measure progress towards them and know whether you achieved them.

- **Achievable:** if a goal is impossible to achieve given the internal or external situation, then that may well be demotivating to all concerned. Reflecting on your audit should be helpful in making sure that you set objectives that, according to the best available evidence, can be achieved.

- **Relevant:** fit well with your wider fundraising, organisation, brand and audience.

- **Time-bound:** that is, it's clear what the deadline is to achieve them, ideally with milestones along the way.

SMART or not?

To grow fundraised income by 20%

While this might be a specific, measurable objective, because it's not time-bound, it's not clear by when it will need to be achieved. If the time frame were 20 years, it might be relatively easy, especially when inflation is taken into account. However, achieving it in six months would be much more challenging! Making an objective time-bound tells you one of the constraints within which you're working.

To increase brand awareness by August 20XX

While growing awareness might well be helpful for an organisation, for many (particularly smaller organisations) it's difficult to measure. Ideally, an organisation would have a measure of what awareness currently is; then it could set a specific, measurable objective to grow it.

To recruit 47 new donors by January 20XX

On the face of it, this looks fairly SMART. However, making it more specific would help to determine future direction. For example, would the organisation want to recruit donors giving £5 a month or £500 a month? In each case, the approach it takes is likely to be quite different.

To implement a new database by December 20XX

Again, this might look like a fairly reasonable objective. However, it's probably more of a tactic to get the organisation to where it wants to be, rather than an outcome the organisation is looking to achieve in its own right.

In addition, fundraising objectives should set out:

- the amount of income to be raised;
- the types of donor that will supply these funds;
- the acceptable cost of raising the funds.[5]

Taking the example we introduced above, the broad goal – 'recruit a number of new, younger donors through online channels' – might become something like 'to recruit 250 one-off donors aged between 20 and 30 giving an average gift of £7 each via Facebook by the end of the financial year at a cost of £1,500'.

The number of objectives you set is likely to vary according to the complexity and duration of your plan, and the number of income streams you are dealing with. For example, a director of fundraising creating a strategy for multiple income streams may need to include more objectives than someone who is looking after a single type of fundraising. However, it's always worth thinking carefully about your capacity to deliver the objectives. While each might be achievable individually, will they also be achievable collectively? It's better to have fewer, focused objectives than to dilute your efforts across many that you won't have the capacity to deliver.

You might also find it helpful to consider how your objectives interrelate. Some people find it helpful to have an overarching objective (for example, to double event income within three years) and then to break down that overarching objective into a series of sub-objectives (for example, increase the number of event participants by 10% relative to the baseline in year one, a further 40% in year two and the final 50% in year three). You might also find it helpful to lay out milestones along the path – for example, you could add three new events to your portfolio, as illustrated in figure 4.1.

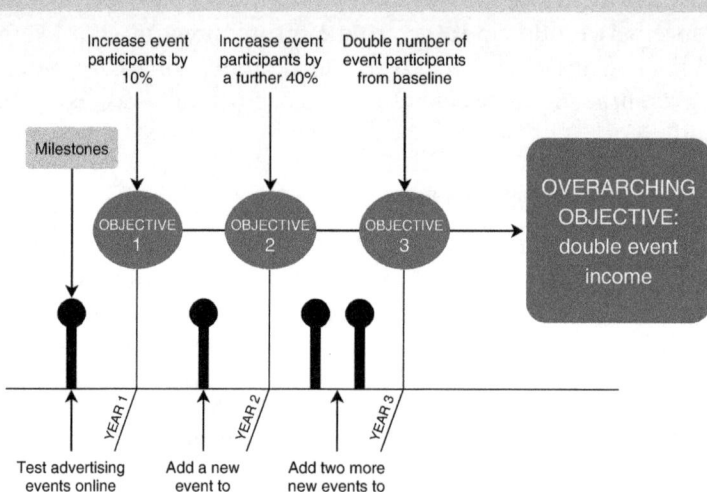

FIGURE 4.1 EXAMPLE OF A TIMELINE OF OBJECTIVES

Now that we have considered setting your objectives, in the remainder of this chapter we will move on to developing the truly strategic elements of your overall strategy. It can sometimes be difficult to differentiate between strategy and tactics. We define the strategy as the broad principles that underly your fundraising (who to talk to and what to say) and tactics as how your strategy is delivered on the ground (see chapter 6 for more detail on tactics).

In this chapter, we will focus on using several different strategy tools to identify the audience or audiences for your fundraising techniques, while the following chapter focuses on developing your messages for specific audiences. These two elements of strategy – also known as 'where to play' (your audience) and 'how to win' (your message) – are said to ultimately determine success in strategic planning.[6]

Identifying your audience

In practice, regardless of whether you have taken time out to reflect on your strategic approach or have developed a formal written strategy, you will be making ongoing key strategic decisions in two areas:

- which groups of donors to appeal to;

- how to make a case as to why someone should support your organisation (for example, as part of a speech to a local group).

Taking the time to think through these strategic decisions in a formalised way ensures your decisions are as considered, effective and co-ordinated as possible.

Ansoff's Growth Matrix

The first strategy tool we'll examine in this chapter is Ansoff's Growth Matrix, developed by mathematician turned business guru Igor Ansoff.[7] We'll assume that, as you're reading this book, you're likely to be seeking to grow your fundraising income. Ansoff's matrix is a useful tool in helping you to map out an overall direction for how you can increase your fundraising income, as it is focused on different ways an organisation can grow.

The matrix has two axes: products and markets. As explored in the discussion of portfolio analysis in chapter 2 (see page 32), you can define your 'product' at different levels depending on your role in your organisation. For example, as a fundraising director, you might consider your organisation's different income streams as products. Alternatively, as an events fundraiser, you might work through the different individual events your organisation offers. Each axis is divided into 'existing' and 'new' segments, creating four quadrants, as shown in figure 4.2.

FIGURE 4.2 ANSOFF'S GROWTH MATRIX[8]

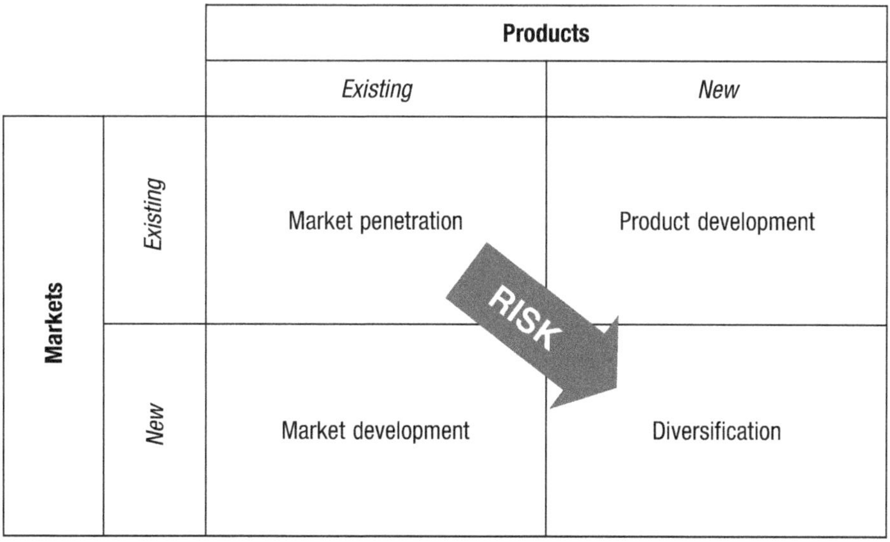

		Products	
		Existing	New
Markets	Existing	Market penetration	Product development
	New	Market development	Diversification

Each quadrant equates to a way of growing fundraising. The first quadrant is market penetration, which focuses on promoting existing products to existing markets. If you have an audience of people giving occasional gifts through direct mail, you might choose to put more budget into reaching that audience or refine the fundraising asks that you make to them (for example, by tailoring the amount of money you request to their previous giving history). This option involves the least risk, as you are likely to know the market well and understand the products you are working with. Growth is achieved by doing more of the same.

The second quadrant is product development, which involves developing new products for existing markets. For example, if you have an audience of individuals who occasionally give gifts, you could create a regular-giving product for them.

Conversely, the third quadrant (market development) focuses on promoting existing products to new markets. For example, if the donors giving occasional gifts above are predominantly women aged 45–65, you might test this product with women aged 35–44. The options in the second and third quadrants will be of medium risk: you'll be unfamiliar with either the product or the market.

The final quadrant, diversification, focuses on developing new products for new markets. This quadrant carries the highest risk as both the market and the product will be new to your organisation. To continue our example above, you might create a new regular-giving product targeted towards women aged 35–44. This example is illustrated in figure 4.3.

FIGURE 4.3 ANSOFF'S GROWTH MATRIX: COMPLETED EXAMPLE[9]

		Products	
		Existing	*New*
Markets	*Existing*	Asks for occasional gifts, primarily targeted to an audience of women aged 45–65 – could increase budgeted spend or make asks more effective	Development of a regular-giving product, primarily targeted to an audience of women aged 45–65
	New	Asks for occasional gifts to a new audience of women aged 35–44	Development of a regular-giving product to a new audience of women aged 35–44

There are several different ways the tool can be used in practice. For example, you can decide which broad quadrant to focus on while you are planning a particular type of fundraising, such as developing a range of new products. Using the matrix in this way may be particularly appropriate if you're a director of fundraising or solely responsible for fundraising and want to take a bigger-picture approach. However, if you're responsible for a specific income stream, it may be more useful to be a little more granular in your approach and to begin by listing all of your products and markets in the market penetration quadrant. Then, you can work systemically through each of the other quadrants, considering as many options as possible. Indeed, it's been argued that the value of the model comes from how it enables organisations to consider all the available alternatives and then choose between them.[10] Once the process of working through existing and potential products and markets is complete, the model also enables you to consider the different risks of the options, and potentially ensure a balance of risk moving forwards.

Several alternative models to Ansoff's matrix have been proposed. You might find an amended model, like that of Graeme Drummond, John Ensor and Ruth Ashford, helpful (see figure 4.4).[11] Rather than focusing solely on existing and new categories, the authors divide the matrix into current, related and unrelated products and markets. This might provide a useful additional lens through which to consider your approach if you are looking for a wider range of options to consider. So, returning to our example above, if you were fundraising from women aged 45–65, women aged 35–44 might be a related market – but men aged 18–25 might be an unrelated market, as their needs and the way you approach them might be quite different. Similarly, moving from one-off asks to regular giving might be related – but starting an events programme may be unrelated, as, again, it's a different form of fundraising necessitating different skills and approaches.

FIGURE 4.4 EXPANDED ANSOFF'S GROWTH MATRIX[12]

		Product	
Market	Current	New	
		Related	Unrelated
Current	Asks for occasional gifts, primarily targeted to an audience of women aged 45–65	Development of a regular-giving product, primarily targeted to an audience of women aged 45–65	Development of an events programme, primarily targeted to an audience of women aged 45–65

		Product		
Market		Current	New	
			Related	Unrelated
New	Related	Asks for occasional gifts to a new audience of women aged 35–44	Development of a regular-giving product, targeted to a new audience of women aged 35–44	Development of an events programme, targeted to a new audience of women aged 35–44
	Unrelated	Asks for occasional gifts to a new audience of men aged 18–25	Development of a regular-giving product, targeted to a new audience of men aged 18–25	Development of an events programme, targeted to a new audience of men aged 18–25

Segmentation and targeting

Segmentation in fundraising is the process of breaking down a wider market into smaller groups which can be targeted (or not) with particular fundraising products. The idea of segmentation as an important success factor in marketing was first introduced by Wendell Smith, who discussed the importance of adapting the product and marketing efforts to consumer requirements, and pointed out that increasing segmentation is driven by increasing competition for consumer expenditure.[13] This idea of segmentation was subsequently adapted from marketing into fundraising.

Segmentation is based on the basic principle that people and organisations in markets have diverse needs.[14] It is the process of dividing up your existing or potential donor base (whether individuals, companies, trusts or foundations) into different groups. Each group should ideally share the same or similar needs which can be satisfied by a specific fundraising offer.

There are a number of reasons to segment your markets, rather than treating all donors in the same way:

- **Specificity:** donors have different needs. By dividing them into different groups, you can meet those needs more effectively by crafting your messages and designing your fundraising to suit them. For example, someone with personal experience of a charity's work might be spoken to in a very different way from someone who is completely new to the cause. And similarly, you might reach an 18-year-old student through different channels from those you would use to reach an 85-year-old grandmother.

- **Efficiency:** through segmentation, you can concentrate your resources on those groups that are more likely to take a desired action or be interested in your offer – and, ultimately, those that are likely to be higher-value supporters of your organisation.

- **Relationship development:** effective segmentation can help to support the development of relationships, as segmentation and relationship marketing are inherently intertwined.[15]

As fundraising academic Adrian Sargeant neatly sums up, at the centre of segmentation is the ability to ask different donor groups for different amounts at different times.[16] Sargeant also points out that for some organisations that serve a very specific need or group (for example, benevolent funds aimed at members of a specific profession), segmentation is arguably essential for survival. In contrast, organisations with a wider pool of service users (for example, cancer charities) may be able to focus on a broader audience.

> **Case study: Using segmentation in planned (legacy) giving**
>
> The value of analysing a database of supporters to understand more about who they are – and then using those insights to target messaging more effectively – has been shown by St Michael's Hospital Foundation in inner-city Toronto.
>
> St Michael's Hospital Foundation supports a major Catholic teaching and research hospital affiliated with the University of Toronto. When the foundation adopted a new data-based segmentation approach to reach out to potential planned-giving supporters, it began by profiling its existing planned-giving donors. It found that it was only approaching donors who had given 35 gifts or more in the past, whereas, on average, these supporters had given 27 times. The foundation also scored donors based on their likelihood of making a mid-level ($5,000–$15,000) gift and found many of the people it was approaching at the time scored relatively low on that scale. A geo-demographic analysis confirmed that the people the foundation was talking to at the time were more likely to be from less affluent groups.
>
> Based on this analysis, St Michael's was able to launch a more targeted campaign to an audience that more closely resembled its existing planned-giving donors. It was then also able to tailor its messaging more appropriately to appeal to this specific group. Ultimately, response rates increased 118% over previous campaigns.[17]
>
> In planned or legacy giving, the high value of gifts means that even a small increase in response can lead to a relatively large increase in income. This further underlines the value of understanding, segmenting and targeting your audience appropriately.

So, how do you go about segmenting your audience?

Step one: Define the market

The first stage in the process is to be as clear as possible about who or what constitutes your overall market, in its widest sense. Geography is one possible example of segmentation criteria: for some organisations, the market may be international; for many, it might be the whole of the UK; and for others, the market might be limited to particular regions or even towns. The overall market might also be defined in terms of gender, a particular profession or a specific religion – depending, for example, on the non-profit organisation and the constituency it exists to serve. If you are focusing your strategy on a specific area of fundraising, your market might be narrowed further – for example, to individuals, companies, charitable trusts or foundations.

Step two: Identify the best segmentation criteria

For organisations that already have a number of supporters, whether individuals, organisations, trusts or foundations, one way of deciding where to focus future efforts might be to analyse or profile these existing supporters, particularly those who are loyal or higher-value donors. By understanding who these 'best' supporters are, in terms of their demographics or other factors, you can seek to recruit more supporters who will behave in a similar way. While this is a good starting point, be aware that if you focus solely on your existing supporters, you might miss out on broadening and diversifying you supporter base. Make sure to consider other types of supporter that might share only *some* characteristics with your current donors. For organisations that don't have existing supporters, market research – understanding who gives and why, or who gives to specific types of charities and why – might provide a helpful list of segmentation criteria.

With supporters who are already in your database, you will have access to a range of segmentation criteria based on past behaviours. More generally, there is a range of possible segmentation criteria. Those that might be applied to individuals include:

- **Demographic:** age, family status, income, education and so on. However, while these variables are often used, as they tend to be relatively easy to apply, people with similar demographics can behave very differently. Therefore, ideally, you should also apply a deeper level of insight by using one or more of the categories below in addition to this criterion.[18]

- **Geographic:** the country, region, town or area in which supporters are based.

- **Geo-demographic:** the principle that people with similar demographic profiles tend to live in similar areas (for example, older people in retirement villages or students residing in the areas around universities). Geo-demographic data is normally overlaid onto databases via commercial providers.[19]

- **Psychographic:** attitudes, lifestyles and values. This information is more rarely found in typical charity databases, although nowadays it can be used in digital targeting. In theory, given that charities are values-based, it would be useful to store and use this data in segmentation – although organisations would have to be very careful to adhere to data protection legislation.

There are often differences in response between new and existing donors, which may mean that one of the first segmentation criteria to consider is whether the audience you are segmenting is 'cold' (i.e. new to your organisation) or 'warm' (i.e. existing supporters).[20] Similarly, Sargeant lists a number of common ways in which an audience could be segmented, differentiating between approaches for warm and cold supporters (table 4.1 expands upon his list).

TABLE 4.1 SEGMENTATION CRITERIA[21]

Warm	Cold
Mode of donation	Demographics
Frequency	Lifestyle
Amount given	Similar audiences
Date of and time since last gift	Affinity to cause

With the widespread adoption of digital marketing, there are a range of criteria you can use when reaching out to either warm or cold audiences. Google, for example, advises that you can target paid advertising on its platforms by:

- **demographics:** such as age, location or gender;
- **affinity:** people with particular hobbies or interests;
- **in market:** people who have been searching for similar products or services;
- **customer intent:** people who are most likely to engage with your offer;

- **similar audiences:** people who 'look like' your existing audiences in demographic or attitudinal terms;

- **re-marketing:** users who have already engaged with your messages.

You can also target your advertising by content or the device being used.[22]

A number of charities have been able to use these tools effectively. WWF, for example, used Facebook targeting to reach an audience who were unfamiliar with the climate debate. The organisation was able to segment its audiences into groups (which it classified as 'hot', 'warm', 'cold' and 'frozen') and reached out to them using interest-based and look-alike (similarity) targeting. It was particularly able to reach into the frozen segment, driving both awareness and advocacy.[23]

As mentioned above, once a charity has accumulated a number of donors, it's also possible to segment by behaviour. One of the most common ways of applying behavioural segmentation is through recency, frequency and value (RFV) analysis, which takes into account when a donor last gave, how often they have given and the value of their gifts, and allocates a score accordingly. RFV analysis is based on the principle that the best predictor of how someone will behave in the future is how they behaved in the past.[24] See the box below for more information on RFV analysis.

Another way to apply behavioural segmentation is to use expected future lifetime value (LTV) – or the total net worth to an organisation of its relationship with a particular donor (income minus costs).[25] For more information on calculating donor LTV, see page 126 in chapter 8.)

Recency, frequency and value analysis

Recency, frequency and value (RFV) analysis – sometimes referred to as RFM (with the 'M' standing for monetary value) – is a commonly used segmentation tool in both the commercial and non-profit worlds. It looks at:

- **recency:** how recently a supporter gave a donation;
- **frequency:** how many donations a supporter has given;
- **value:** the average value of a supporter's donations.

In order to apply RFV analysis in practice, you would extract data on your supporters' RFV of giving and – most commonly – divide each into quintiles (or groups of five) ordered from the highest to the lowest. Each quintile is given a score from 5 to 1. So, for example, the division for recency might look as shown in table 4.2. You would then conduct a similar process for frequency and monetary value, with the top 20% of each group being given the top score of five, the second 20% a score of 4 and so on.

TABLE 4.2 EXAMPLE QUINTILES FOR A RECENCY, FREQUENCY AND VALUE ANALYSIS

5	0–6 months
4	7–12 months
3	13–18 months
2	19–24 months
1	25+ months

Once you have calculated your supporters' scores for RFV, you can add those scores together to give each supporter a total RFV score. Very simply, the higher a supporter's RFV score, the better a donor they're likely to be.

However, rather than simply looking for – and fundraising from – your best-scoring supporters, it's also possible to use the tool in a more sophisticated way, such as by upweighting one of the scores. For example, if you were seeking new major donors, then you might upweight monetary value. You might also use the tool to adapt your message to different groups. For example, those who have a high recency score but a low frequency score are likely to be new supporters, while those who have high frequency and value scores but low recency scores may be formerly strong supporters in danger of ceasing their giving to your organisation. Each group is likely to need different things from your organisation's communications.

RFV segmentation remains popular as it can boost fundraising results over no or limited segmentation and it is relatively easy to apply even without sophisticated data-analysis skills. However, the tool has been critiqued in recent years, particularly as more sophisticated segmentation tools have become available. Some criticisms include:

- The tool assumes that past behaviour predicts future behaviour, which is not always the case.

- It neglects the wider range of data potentially available to fundraisers.

- It doesn't enable you to understand why a supporter behaves in a particular way.[26]

- The idea that past behaviour predicts the future can be problematic from an equality, equity, diversity and inclusion (EEDI) perspective

> (see page 167 in chapter 11 for more on EEDI). If fundraising was historically targeted at the needs and preferences of predominantly White supporters, basing your future actions on this type of analysis can inadvertently discriminate by reaffirming those approaches.
>
> Organisations should at least consider, therefore, whether the tool is ideal to meet their current needs.

So far, we've discussed segmentation criteria that predominantly apply to individuals. However, organisations, such as corporates and trusts, might be segmented using similar criteria, including:

- **demographic:** organisation size, type of industry or cause supported;
- **geographic:** the country, region, town or area in which organisations are based or that their work covers;
- **donor behaviour:** how organisations make decisions about whom to support or sponsor;
- **culture:** how organisations do things.

For both individuals and organisations, one criterion is not necessarily better than another: instead, the best segmentation criterion is likely to depend on the context in which you're working. Geography is likely to be particularly important if you're organising an event, for example, while demographic criteria – particularly wealth – are more likely to be important when soliciting a major gift.

Segmentation criteria also don't have to be used in isolation. You might choose to use a number of criteria in concert. To continue the analogy around events and major donors above, you might use both geography and wealth when deciding whom to invite to a charity ball. Consideration of potential major donors is also likely to cover three factors: their capacity to give (i.e. an understanding of their wealth), their affiliation with your cause, and whether you have a way of reaching them (i.e. someone who can introduce you to them). Larger organisations may also have enough data to combine variables in sophisticated response models. Direct marketing specialist John Lister explains that these models generally use the best mix of data or predictor variables to analyse the likelihood of whether someone will respond to a particular communication, stratifying contacts accordingly – for example, by giving them a score from 1 to 100 and then focusing on those who score the highest.[27]

Case study: Using sophisticated response modelling in practice[28]

Soon after the turn of the millennium, older people's charity Help the Aged (now Age UK) needed to work out who, among its supporters, would be the best prospects to contact about legacy giving. It started the project by analysing its data. This analysis then enabled the charity to profile its existing legacy supporters by comparing data on that group to the wider donor base in order to understand the differences between them.

Once the profiles had been built, the charity could build a model to predict which people in the general donor base would be most likely to be interested in legacy giving – in practice, which supporters from the general donor base were most like its legacy supporters. In order to build the model, the charity drew on data about previous giving as well as data supplied by external agencies, including estimated age and geo-demographic data (which uses a postcode to impute characteristics about people living in an area).

The final model drew on the number of relationships (for example, as a donor, a volunteer or a customer) between the donor and the charity, individuals' donor status and number of enquiries made, and their estimated age and history of giving. When the model was tested in real-life campaigns, the charity found that response rates to legacy communications among people with high scores were significantly higher than among those with low scores.

Step three: Apply the criteria and divide the market

Once the segmentation criteria have been defined, the audience can be divided up appropriately.

Step four: Identify the priority segments

Once you have divided up the market, the various segments can be assessed in order to decide on whom your organisation will focus its time and efforts. You will need to consider how attractive a segment is in its own right, but also, importantly, how well your organisation can serve that segment. You should seek to focus on those segments which are attractive but which you also have a strong ability to serve.

Those market segments that are attractive (for example, they might be growing in number, be likely to give higher-value gifts or display high levels of loyalty) and whom you have a strong ability to serve (for example, you might be proficient at using their favoured communication channels or active in their geographical area) will become your primary focus. Those that are averagely attractive but whom you have a strong ability to serve (or vice versa) will become secondary targets. Those that fall somewhere in the middle on both their attractiveness and your ability to serve them might be possibilities to consider – for example, there might be internal changes that you could make that would improve your ability to serve them. Finally, those who are less attractive and whom you have less ability to serve should be avoided (or strongly avoided).[29]

In choosing a market segment or segments to focus on, you should consider carefully whether you will focus on one or a few segments, or choose several. There are advantages and disadvantages to both approaches: focusing on just one or two segments helps an organisation to really understand the needs and behaviours of its audience. However, there can also be a higher level of risk with this tighter focus – for example, if the segment is badly affected by economic changes or your organisation's offer begins to be seen as less relevant to them.

Step five: Evaluate your choices

Once you have chosen a segment – or segments – to focus on, you can do a final check of your choices before proceeding.[30] A segment should be:

- **Measurable:** information about the segment and its characteristics should be accessible, enabling it to be measured.

- **Accessible:** it should be possible to target the segment in a cost-effective way. For example, if you were an individual-giving fundraiser, could you reach this audience through relevant media? If you were a community fundraiser, could you relatively easily travel to the particular geographical area?

- **Substantial:** it should be large enough to fundraise cost-effectively from the segment. (However, this is likely to be less of an issue in certain forms of fundraising, such as major gifts or trusts, where average gifts tend to be significantly larger.)

- **Stable:** its behaviour should be relatively stable over time, in order for your organisation to plan ahead. For example, it would be difficult to focus a direct mail campaign around university students, who are likely to be changing address frequently.

- **Appropriate:** it should be appropriate for your organisation to raise funds from this segment. For example, non-profits might not want to solicit funds from organisations whose values conflict with their own.

- **Unique:** it should respond differently to fundraising offers from other segments, otherwise it makes little sense for it to be a separate segment. For example, two groups might be very different in demographic terms;

however, if they respond in the same way to an appeal, then they can be part of the same segment.

- **Sustainable:** your organisation should be able to sustain its relationship with the segment over time. For example, an organisation might attract an audience with a very low-value ask of £1 or £2, but, over the long term, it is unlikely to be able to serve that segment profitably unless they choose to give at a higher level.

Checking your final segmentation and targeting choices against the above criteria can ensure that those choices are robust and likely to work effectively as you begin to implement your strategy.

Conclusion

Hopefully, you now feel confident about setting objectives, or identifying the end goal of your strategy. Once those objectives are in place, you should be in a position to identify the most appropriate audiences to focus on. Our suggested next step is to consider the most appropriate messages to communicate to your chosen audiences. The next chapter therefore focuses on how messages can be developed.

Notes

1. Lionel Giles, *Sun Tzu on the Art of War: The oldest military treatise in the world*, London, Luzac & Co., 1910, p. 16.
2. Peter Drucker, *The Practice of Management*, New York, Harper and Row, 1954.
3. *Ibid.*, p. 110.
4. George Doran, 'There's a S.M.A.R.T. Way to Write Management's Goals and Objectives', *Management Review*, vol. 70. no. 11, 1981, pp. 35–6.
5. Adrian Sargeant and Elaine Jay, *Fundraising Management: Analysis, planning and practice*, London, Routledge, 2014, p. 96.
6. Roger Martin, 'The big lie of strategic planning' [web article], *Harvard Business Review*, https://hbr.org/2014/01/the-big-lie-of-strategic-planning, January–February 2014.
7. Igor Ansoff, 'Strategies for Diversification', *Harvard Business Review*, vol. 35, no. 5, 1957, pp. 113–24.
8. Adapted and reprinted with permission from Igor Ansoff, 'Strategies for Diversification', *Harvard Business Review*, vol. 35, no. 5, 1957, pp. 113–24. Copyright 1957 by Harvard Business Publishing; all rights reserved.
9. *Ibid.* Copyright 1957 by Harvard Business Publishing; all rights reserved.
10. Adrian Sargeant and Elaine Jay, *Fundraising Management: Analysis, planning and practice*, London, Routledge, 2014, p. 100.
11. Graeme Drummond, John Ensor and Ruth Ashford, *Strategic Marketing: Planning and control*, Abingdon, Butterworth Heinemann, 2008.
12. *Ibid.*
13. Wendell Smith, 'Product Differentiation and Marketing Segmentation as Alternative Marketing Strategies', *Journal of Marketing*, July 1956, pp. 3–8.

14. James McAlexander, Harold Koenig and Beth DuFault, 'Millennials and Boomers: Increasing alumni affinity and intent to give by target market segmentation', *International Journal of Nonprofit and Voluntary Sector Marketing*, vol. 21, no. 2, 2016, pp. 82–95.
15. Charles O'Reilly, Jennifer Chatman and David Caldwell, 'People and Organizational Culture: A profile comparison approach to assessing person–organization fit', *Academy of Management Journal*, vol. 34, no. 3, 1991, pp. 487–516; Christine Rupp, Sarah Kern and Bernd Helmig, 'Segmenting Nonprofit Stakeholders to Enable Successful Relationship Marketing: A review', *International Journal of Nonprofit and Voluntary Sector Marketing*, vol. 19, no. 2, 2014, pp. 76–91.
16. Adrian Sargeant, 'Market Segmentation: Are UK charities making the most of the potential?', *Journal of Philanthropy and Marketing*, vol. 1, no. 2, 1996, pp. 132–43.
17. Dwayne DiPasquale, 'St Michael's Hospital Foundation: Data-based planned giving campaign delivers heavenly results' [web article], The Showcase of Fundraising Innovation and Inspiration (SOFII), https://sofii.org/case-study/st-michaels-hospital-foundations-data-based-planned-giving-campaign-delivers-heavenly-results, 13 August 2013.
18. Christine Rupp, Sarah Kern and Bernd Helmig, 'Segmenting Nonprofit Stakeholders to Enable Successful Relationship Marketing: A review', *International Journal of Nonprofit and Voluntary Sector Marketing*, vol. 19, no. 2, 2014, pp. 76–91.
19. For example, Acorn (https://acorn.caci.co.uk) or Mosaic (www.theaudienceagency.org/insight/mosaic).
20. William Diamond and Sara Gooding-Williams, 'Using Advertising Constructs and Methods to Understand Direct Mail Fundraising Appeals', *Nonprofit Management and Leadership*, vol. 12, no. 3, 2002, pp. 225–42.
21. Expanded from Adrian Sargeant, 'Market Segmentation: Are UK charities making the most of the potential?', *Journal of Philanthropy and Marketing*, vol. 1, no. 2, 1996, pp. 132–43.
22. 'Targeting your ads' [web page], Google, https://support.google.com/google-ads/answer/1704368?hl=en-GB, accessed 19 May 2021.
23. 'World Wide Fund for Nature UK: Raising brand awareness with Facebook video ads' [web page], Facebook for Business, www.facebook.com/business/success/world-wide-fund-for-nature-uk, accessed 19 May 2021.
24. Arthur Hughes, 'Making a Database Pay Off Using Recency, Frequency, and Monetary Analysis', *Journal of Database Marketing*, vol. 3, no. 1, 1995, pp. 77–89.
25. Adrian Sargeant, 'Using Donor Lifetime Value to Inform Fundraising Strategy', *Nonprofit Management and Leadership*, vol. 12, no. 1, 2001, pp. 25–38.
26. See Noah Barnett, 'Beyond RFM: The key insights every nonprofit should know' [web article], *Philanthropy Journal*, https://pj.news.chass.ncsu.edu/2019/09/09/beyond-rfm-the-key-insights-every-nonprofit-should-know, 9 September 2019.
27. John Lister, 'Database Segmentation: An alternative to recency, frequency, value', *International Journal of Nonprofit and Voluntary Sector Marketing*, vol. 1, no. 4, 1996, pp. 337–42.
28. Based on Karen Cole, Rachel Dingle and Rajesh Bhayani, 'Pledger Modelling: Help the Aged case study', *International Journal of Nonprofit and Voluntary Sector Marketing*, vol. 10, no. 1, 2005, pp. 43–52.

29 John Robinson, Robert Hitchens and Dave Wade, 'The Directional Policy Matrix: Tool for strategic planning', *Long Range Planning*, vol. 11, no. 3, 1978, pp. 8–15.
30 Adrian Sargeant and Elaine Jay, *Fundraising Management: Analysis, planning and practice*, London, Routledge, 2014.

CHAPTER FIVE
Developing your message

Introduction
In chapter 4, we looked at identifying the audience for your fundraising: establishing who you're talking to (the 'where to play' mentioned in the previous chapter[1]). In this chapter, we consider how to go about crafting your messaging – or identifying what it is you're going to say – for this audience through the tools of positioning, branding and case for support ('how to win'[2]).

Who are your supporters?
Before you begin to develop your message, it can be helpful to have a clear idea in your mind of who you're developing this targeted communication for. That way, you can write with that specific audience in mind, whether it is made up of individual supporters or, for example, key decision makers in companies, foundations or trusts. You might find it helpful to use the information you gathered in the previous chapter to create pen portraits (often termed 'personas') of your supporters, giving each audience you identified a name, age, occupation and so on, so as to be able to develop messaging targeted at a specific (hypothetical) person. A fictional persona for a retired supporter giving digitally, as an example, is given in figure 5.1.

Positioning
The first element of messaging is deciding on your position in the market. According to marketing experts Philip Kotler and Kevin Keller, positioning is the act of designing a company's offering and image to inhabit a distinct place in the mind of the target audience.[3] In the charity sector specifically, however, it's been argued that positioning is an underused concept that is often done unconsciously rather than consciously. This could result in organisations being less than ideally positioned: for example, they may not be clearly differentiated from other organisations, or perceptions about them might not align with the reality of their work.[4]

In their seminal text on positioning, advertising executives Al Ries and Jack Trout argue that positioning is not about what you do to your organisation (or, in our sector, your organisation or your fundraising products); it's about each individual supporter – or, more specifically, how you position yourself in their mind.[5] When Ries and Trout were writing around the year

CHAPTER FIVE **DEVELOPING YOUR MESSAGE**

FIGURE 5.1 EXAMPLE PERSONA FOR A RETIRED SUPPORTER GIVING DIGITALLY

Kathy
Age: 68
Gender: Female
Work experience: Retired teacher
Volunteer experience: Women's Institute, Parish Council
Personal details:

- Widowed
- Childless
- Lives in Bournemouth
- Enjoys reading, craft and Pilates

Preferred digital channels:

- Email
- Facebook
- Charity's website

Preferred digital content: Video

2000, consumers might have seen several hundred ads per day; today, the average consumer probably sees more than 6,000 advertising messages daily.[6] Clearly, therefore, positioning your organisation in the mind of your target audience is a key way to make yourself stand out. You need to identify a niche and fill it.

Given the cluttered, complex world in which we operate, Ries and Trout argue that it's easier to work from the position that's already there, rather than try to develop a new position from scratch.[7] Indeed, in the non-profit world, where we are generally working with lower communications budgets than our corporate cousins and therefore can spend less on changing people's minds, this advice is particularly salient.

You also need to understand where other charities are positioned. As Ries and Trout argue, understanding the competition enables you to find a position that no one else occupies.[8] In contrast, engaging in head-to-head competition can be much more challenging (and in the charity sector arguably less palatable).[9]

Ries and Trout suggest beginning any positioning exercise by understanding the niche that you currently occupy in the minds of your donors. You can do this by mapping your and your competitors' relative positions against key dimensions on a perceptual map. This is depicted in figure 5.2, which shows a fictional perceptual map for some cultural organisations, positioning them on the dimensions of local/national and education/entertainment. Ideally, this mapping exercise would be informed by actual data on the target market's perceptions. However, with relatively few charitable organisations having access to – or budget to acquire – such data, it can be constructed using your perception of what donors think (keeping in mind the danger that this may lead to misconceptions, fallacies and biases).[10] At the very least, however, being clear about your position (or desired position) will help you to ensure your messages are consistent and co-ordinated.

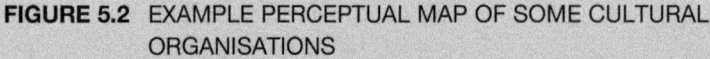

FIGURE 5.2 EXAMPLE PERCEPTUAL MAP OF SOME CULTURAL ORGANISATIONS

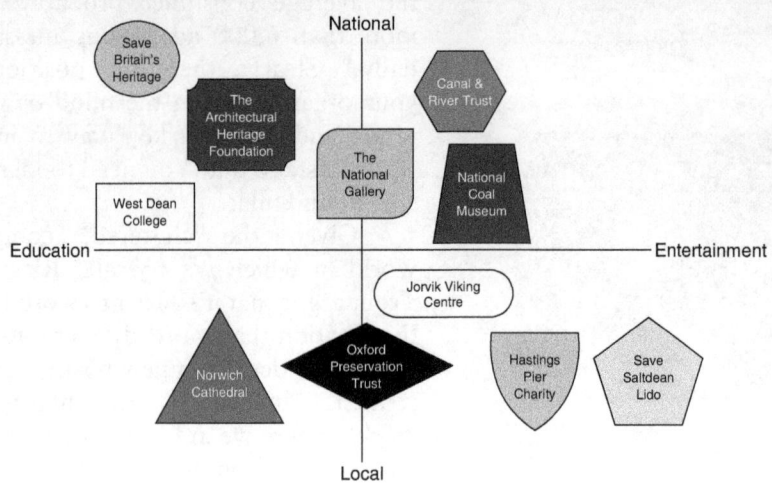

Mapping organisations in this way allows you to clearly see where other charities sit in the minds of the audience and whether there might be the potential for confusion between you and them. Additionally, understanding both your current position and how that sits versus other charities enables you to decide upon the area you ultimately wish to occupy, or indeed move towards it. Ries and Trout give several pieces of advice for those looking to develop a clear position:

- In order to occupy a clear, distinct space, you have to develop a simple, uncluttered message.

- Be aware that it costs time and money to establish and maintain a position, and that you should be in it for the long term. Similarly, changes of position should be relatively rare.

- The rest of your marketing approach, and particularly your communications, should match your position.[11]

In order to position yourself, you have to decide on the key dimensions you will use (like local/national and education/entertainment in figure 5.2). These should be key differentiators which are based on your organisation's major distinctive strengths. Examples include:

- perceived quality of service (for example, low to high);

- superior product benefits to users (for example, focusing on support in the here and now versus improving a situation in the future);

- provision of specialist services (for example, research could be positioned versus care);
- your organisation's mission (for example, to work nationally or locally; to support humans or animals);
- strong relationships and networks (for example, depth of relationships could be positioned versus breadth of relationships).[12]

To some extent, these areas may well be outside the control and remit of your fundraising function and will reflect the core purpose and work of your organisation, rather than fundraising per se. However, fundraisers and/or others working in communication functions can choose which aspects of their organisation are emphasised in communications.

As well as positioning the whole organisation, it is also possible to position individual products, although of course this would be influenced by the positioning of the wider organisation.[13] Depending on the focus of your strategy, therefore, it may make sense to consider positioning at a product level – for example, if you run fundraising events, where might they sit within the wider market of fundraising events in which an individual can participate? An example of a fundraising event product with its own positioning is Stand Up To Cancer, which was developed by Cancer Research UK and Channel 4 but retains its own distinctive brand and irreverent feel.

Branding

Closely linked to the idea of positioning is the idea of branding. Brand has been described as a shorthand in the mind of your audience for what your organisation might offer.[14] It can also be thought of as a psychological construct which everyone aware of your organisation holds in their mind.[15]

Often the first things that come to mind when we think about branding are an organisation's logo, the colours or fonts it uses, and its slogan. However, a brand should be embedded much more deeply than that. Writing about non-profits, authors Adrian Sargeant and John Ford describe brand as an amalgam of everything an organisation is, as well as what it says and does.[16]

There can be some scepticism about the concept of branding in the charity sector, which can discourage leaders from investing in the area.[17] However, Sargeant and Ford conducted a study of this area using a combination of focus groups and questionnaires, and they point out why it's important for fundraisers to think about branding:

- **Brands enhance learning** by functioning as a mental hook on which donors can 'hang' information about the organisation in their minds. For example, charities that have well-known brands may find fundraising easier, as prospective donors are likely to already have a good idea of who they are and what they do.

- **Brands reduce risk** by associating a cause with the delivery of high-quality goods and services. This reassures donors – who may not have experienced a charity's services for themselves – that their money will be spent effectively.

- **Brands provide insurance** by enabling organisations to withstand short-term negative publicity because they have a strong existing reputation.

- **Brands build loyalty** by enabling donors to express something of their own personality through the brand – for example, the brand might emphasise values that a donor and the charity will share. A homelessness charity might emphasise values such as a commitment to social justice, while a medical research charity might emphasise its focus on excellence.[18]

Individuals are also motivated to offer higher levels of loyalty and support to differentiated brands. However, alongside that finding, Sargeant and Ford also established that a lack of differentiation is a key weakness in the charity sector. Indeed, they discovered that most people find it difficult to discriminate between even the leading non-profit brands, seeing them as identical in many ways. This might be because of particular brand values. Examples such as 'caring', 'supportive' and 'sympathetic' are seen as non-profit values, shared across the sector.[19]

How, in that case, can we go about differentiating our brands? Sargeant and Ford suggest brands can be differentiated in four keys ways: emotional stimulation, service, tradition and voice.[20] For example:

- **Emotional stimulation:** does the brand display traits that have the potential to stimulate an emotional response in donors? These might be traits such as exciting, innovative or heroic. A prime example of heroism in action is the White Helmets in Syria: unarmed volunteers who risk their lives to help people injured in the Syrian conflict.

- **Service:** as well as through its brand, an organisation could differentiate itself by how it delivers its services. The organisation Charity: Water, which links its donors to specific water projects and enables them to watch the wells they have supported being drilled through video link, is an example of a non-profit that differentiates itself by being very clear about the services it offers, as well as its successes and failures.

- **Tradition:** some non-profits may be viewed as almost part of the fabric of society, and giving to them may be perceived as a duty, particularly during certain seasons. The most obvious example might be The Royal British Legion: the wearing of the poppy could arguably be characterised as 'almost obligatory' in some circles during the run-up to Remembrance Sunday.

- **Voice:** the brand might be differentiated by the tone of voice it uses. The mental health charity MQ Mental Health Research speaks in a distinctive tone of voice, directly addressing the issue of mental health in young people (see figure 5.3).

FIGURE 5.3 EXAMPLE OF TONE OF VOICE AS USED IN MQ MENTAL HEALTH RESEARCH'S ADVERTS[21]

Portraits by Matt Holyoak.

At a practical level, Sargeant and Ford give the following four key pieces of advice to fundraisers looking to differentiate their brands:

- **Map your organisation using the four dimensions of emotional stimulation, voice, service and tradition.** Consider whether there are opportunities to be distinctive in one or more – perhaps even all – of the four dimensions.

- **Emphasise what is distinctive about your organisation.** Understand, ideally through research with donors, what makes your organisation distinct from others and emphasise those aspects.

- **Pay close attention to the perceptions of your donors.** Ultimately, as suggested in the definitions at the start of this section, a brand is in the eye of its beholder. Organisations, therefore, need to understand donors' views and map them against how they desire to be perceived, taking action accordingly.

- **Understand which of your traits are shared with others.** Given that people see all non-profits as sharing similar traits, organisations that want to be perceived as benevolent or progressive only need to be recognised as non-profits. This can save resources that could more valuably be used elsewhere.[22]

> ### Case study: Rebranding
>
> The discussion above focuses on branding – but what about rebranding, which can involve anything from a change of name to a change of logo to a fully redeveloped identity? Blind Veterans UK rebranded from St Dunstan's in 2012 and the rebrand had an almost immediate positive impact on people expressing interest in its fundraising, with 22% of the public saying that they would consider supporting Blind Veterans as opposed to 16% for St Dunstan's – an increase of more than a third. This was mirrored by actual results from fundraising activity, with response rates from donor acquisition activities increasing by almost a third and the number of online event applications increasing by nearly two-thirds. The charity also developed a partnership with Specsavers for a key fundraising event.[23]
>
> However, before rushing into a rebrand, it should be noted that not all rebrands will have a positive impact on fundraising results. Fundraising consultant Jeff Brooks reports that, in his experience, most rebranding exercises have a negative impact on revenue – potentially, he argues, because changes can make materials less readable or their offer less clear, as well as affecting the connection that charities have with their donors.[24]
>
> While examples like Blind Veterans UK show that rebranding can be successful for fundraising, Brooks's figures show that, before any rebranding exercise, organisations need to think very carefully about the potential impact on fundraising income and ensure that donors are considered – and consulted – during the process.

Case for support

The final key dimension of your messaging is your case for support. You may hear the term 'case for support' used in different ways. For example, it may be used to refer to a brochure or an appeal document produced for a grant-making trust or other funders and supporters. However, here, we mean an internal document from which external donor communications are developed. According to the author of *Developing Your Case for Support*, Timothy Seiler, a case for support is the overarching argument as to why a charitable organisation deserves financial support.[25] Seiler describes it as the foundation of your fundraising: the source from which other fundraising messages flow.

Developing a case for support has several benefits. At a brand level, it can help you to develop an appropriate message (or messages) and use it (or them) consistently throughout your communications. At a practical level, it can help you to save time and have messages ready and waiting to go whenever you have the opportunity to share them. Most importantly, it's the cornerstone of any fundraising activity, which enables you to communicate why you do what you do, and what the results are, to inspire and motivate people to support you.[26]

Alongside the phrase 'case for support', you may encounter related terms such as 'case statement' (a shorter version of the case, made up of a specific illustration of some of the case elements) or 'case expression' (a specific document, such as a direct mail letter or a grant application, that contains a case statement).[27]

Case statement: Heart of the Oregon Zoo

It might be helpful at this point to see an extract from a real-life case statement. The case statement below was developed by Jen Love and John Lepp of fundraising agency Agents of Good for the Oregon Zoo Foundation. The Oregon Zoo Foundation wanted to create a case centred on its dreams of developing new habitats, investing in animal welfare and supporting education and conservation programmes. Jen and John grounded the case in interviews with people who loved the zoo, asking them 'Where is your heart in the zoo?'. The words of Julie Fitzgerald, the foundation's Executive Director, invite visitors to become part of the zoo's story:

> Our zoo is a place for people. People like you and me. The Oregon Zoo reflects a tradition of strong community involvement across generations. Today, our zoo is a place to learn first-hand about wildlife – and about the realities of our natural world, right here in our own back yard. Our world today has challenges: deforestation, climate change, competition for habitat. I believe it is a privilege and a responsibility for the people of Oregon today to stand up and stand together to support our zoo. Our zoo is a place to celebrate the joy and delight of nature. To every one of our neighbors – including you – I want to say this: let's imagine what is possible and let's work together to make our dreams come true.
>
> Today, my heart is at the entrance to our zoo, where I see people come in with excitement and curiosity as they start their day at the zoo. Today, I am welcoming you![28]

The full case statement – and its accompanying custom-made illustrations – can be seen at https://agentsofgood.org/portfolio-1/ozf.

So, how do you go about creating a case for support? At an early stage in the process, you will need to decide who will be involved in the process of developing the case. Including stakeholders such as board members, volunteers and donors could help to both gather varied perspectives and, ultimately, achieve buy-in from those people who will use the case for support.

According to Seiler, in order to develop a case for support, you'll need to gather together – or perhaps even develop – a range of information, including:

- **Mission:** illustrates awareness of the cause and/or problem addressed by your organisation.

- **Goals and objectives:** communicates the achievement that will solve the problem.

- **Programmes and services:** brings the organisation's work to life through stories about its work with and for its service users or people with lived experience.

- **Finances:** outlines the cost of providing the programmes and services.

- **Governance:** demonstrates the quality and character of the organisation.

- **Staffing:** underlines the strengths of the organisation's staffing.

- **Service delivery:** emphasises the effectiveness and strengths of the organisation's programme delivery.

- **Planning and evaluation:** demonstrates organisational strengths, impact and effectiveness.

- **History:** brings in story-telling and implies credibility through success over time.[29]

Looking at the list above will help you to create a document that's internally focused – but we would stress that it's important that your case for support is not seen as something to be put in front of donors but as a source that externally focused communications can draw from.

As part of this exercise, you should ensure that any 'donor-facing' materials are truly focused on donors. To do this, you can add to Seiler's list all available information on the needs and preferences of donors, which will enable you to tailor your case appropriately.[30]

Fundraising academics Adrian Sargeant and Jen Shang draw on the insights of fundraising consultant and trainer Alan Clayton, who argues that all charities should be able to express their case as a 'Big Idea'. The Big Idea harnesses the emotions that make people passionate about a cause and stimulates internal support for fundraising as much as it drives external donations. The Big Idea is a new ambition: more than just expressing what the organisation is trying to achieve it should:

- be boldly ambitious;
- state the problem and solution;
- show the donor why the world will be different after they give;
- be simple and quickly understood;
- be active (i.e. have a clear aim);
- be inspiring;
- be emotional;
- have fundraising at its core.[31]

An example of a strong Big Idea is Save the Children's No Child Born To Die campaign, launched in 2011.[32] Other examples are NSPCC's Full Stop appeal, with the strapline 'Together we can end cruelty to children. Full Stop', which began in the 1990s,[33] and Cancer Research UK and the National Cancer Institute's Cancer Grand Challenges (from 2020), which aim to tackle some of the biggest challenges in cancer research on a global scale.[34]

There are a number of techniques you could apply when thinking about how your case can be adapted to create external communications or case expressions. It has been suggested that fundraisers should ask three questions:

- **Why us?** Why is your organisation uniquely effective?
- **Why now?** Why is it urgent that you find donor support?
- **Why would a donor care?** What positive effects will be realised by a donor's support?[35]

Mark Phillips, director of the fundraising agency Bluefrog, argues that it's common for organisations to create an internally focused document that doesn't take into account the reasons donors give. He also poses three questions that charities should focus on answering in order to make their case donor-centric:[36]

- What can you offer your donors that other charities can't or won't?
- How can you make your appeal as emotionally rewarding as possible?
- How can you allow your donors to be part of the narrative?

Another useful technique for expressing your case in external communications is the Four Pillars.[37] The Four Pillars approach can help you to focus on the underpinning elements of any external communication. They are:

- **Vision:** what would the world be like if your organisation no longer needed to exist? Your organisation may be one part of a collaborative contribution towards this vision.

- **Enemy:** who or what is stopping the vision being achieved?

- **Hero:** who fights the enemy to achieve the vision? Who can the donor stand alongside in their support of the charity?

- **Recipient:** who will benefit from the work? What is the most compelling way to express this to the donor?

An example Four Pillars analysis for a fictional animal sanctuary is given in table 5.1.

TABLE 5.1 EXAMPLE FOUR PILLARS ANALYSIS

Vision	Enemy	Hero	Recipient
Every dog has a safe and loving home	The cruelty and neglect of callous owners	Caring volunteers who rehabilitate dogs and find them forever homes	Innocent, trusting dogs

You can then use your Four Pillars analysis to construct the core fundraising proposition that communicates why someone should make a donation right now. The proposition should include three central components: the need, the solution to that need and why a donor should give now. A proposition based on the example Four Pillars analysis above, and encompassing those core elements, might read something like:

> Like you, we believe that every dog deserves a safe home with a family that loves them. But every week, hundreds of innocent and trusting dogs are cruelly mistreated or abandoned by callous owners. Your gift will enable our caring volunteers to teach a dog how to trust people again and find them their forever home.

Case expressions: Different versions of your case for support

When using your case for support to draft case expressions, you may also need to consider your different audiences: for example, grantmakers may require very different messages compared to companies or individual supporters. If you were a medical charity researching cancer treatments, for instance, a charitable trust might be particularly interested to know about the innovative nature of your research and the excellent CVs of your researchers. In contrast, an individual supporter might be more motivated by stories of how your research has helped to develop treatments and the difference those treatments have made to people's lives.

Similarly, you may want to consider developing separate case expressions for each of your projects, especially if they are substantively different from each other. For example, someone might give to support a new building – perhaps because they are motivated by permanence. This might be quite different from the reason someone supports your everyday work (perhaps motivated by their personal experience) or take part in an event on your behalf (perhaps motivated by the event itself).

Conclusion

In this chapter we've considered messaging, focusing in on developing a distinct position in the eyes of your supporters and then moving on to consider your organisation's branding. We then discussed the vital tool of the case for support and how the full case can be refined down into a short, snappy fundraising proposition.

Having considered the vital strategic issues of who to talk to (chapter 4) and what to say (this chapter), we can now turn our attention to the details of how fundraising is delivered, or fundraising tactics. This topic is explored in the next chapter.

Notes

1. Roger Martin, 'The big lie of strategic planning', *Harvard Business Review*, https://hbr.org/2014/01/the-big-lie-of-strategic-planning, January–February 2014.
2. *Ibid.*
3. Philip Kotler and Kevin Keller, *Marketing Management*, London, Pearson, 2006.
4. Celine Chew and Stephen Osborne, 'Identifying the Factors that Influence Positioning Strategies in UK Charitable Organisations that Provide Public Services: Towards an integrating model', *Nonprofit and Voluntary Sector Quarterly*, vol. 38, no. 1, 2009, pp. 29–50.
5. Al Ries and Jack Trout, *Positioning: The battle for your mind*, New York, McGraw Hill, 2001.

6   Sam Carr, 'How many ads do we see a day in 2021?' [web article], PPC Protect, https://ppcprotect.com/how-many-ads-do-we-see-a-day, 15 February 2021.
7   Al Ries and Jack Trout, *Positioning: The battle for your mind*, New York, McGraw Hill, 2001.
8   Ibid.
9   'Inputs to perceptual maps' [web page], Market Segmentation Study Guide, 2012, www.segmentationstudyguide.com/understanding-perceptual-maps/inputs-to-perceptual-maps, accessed 19 May 2021.
10 Al Ries and Jack Trout, *Positioning: The battle for your mind*, New York, McGraw Hill, 2001.
11 Ibid.
12 Celine Chew and Stephen Osborne, 'Identifying the Factors that Influence Positioning Strategies in UK Charitable Organisations that Provide Public Services: Towards an integrating model', *Nonprofit and Voluntary Sector Quarterly*, vol. 38, no. 1, 2009, pp. 29–50.
13 Adrian Sargeant, *Marketing Management for Nonprofit Organisations*, 3rd edition, Oxford, Oxford University Press, 2009.
14 Alan Andreasen and Philip Kotler, *Strategic Marketing for Nonprofit Organisations*, New Jersey, Pearson, 2008.
15 Nathalie Kylander and Christopher Stone, 'The Role of Brand in the Nonprofit Sector', *Stanford Social Innovation Review*, spring 2012, pp. 36–41.
16 Adrian Sargeant and John Ford, 'The Power of Brands', *Stanford Social Innovation Review*, winter 2007, pp. 41–7.
17 Nathalie Kylander and Christopher Stone, 'The Role of Brand in the Nonprofit Sector', *Stanford Social Innovation Review*, spring 2012, pp. 36–41.
18 Adrian Sargeant and John Ford, 'The Power of Brands', *Stanford Social Innovation Review*, winter 2007, pp. 41–7.
19 Ibid.
20 Ibid.
21 Portraits of Gillian Anderson, Melanie Chisholm and Nicola Adams by Matt Holyoak were used in MQ's We Swear campaign, which ran between 2017 and 2019. Reproduced with permission from the charity.
22 Adrian Sargeant and John Ford, 'The Power of Brands', *Stanford Social Innovation Review*, winter 2007, pp. 41–7.
23 Vicky Browning, 'Branding inside out: A best practice guide' [web article], CharityComms, www.charitycomms.org.uk/branding-inside-out-a-best-practice-guide, 23 November 2021.
24 Jeff Brooks, 'How a brand change will impact revenue: Real-life figures' [blog post], Future Fundraising Now, www.futurefundraisingnow.com/future-fundraising/2011/03/how-a-brand-change-will-impact-revenue-real-life-figures.html, 9 March 2011.
25 Timothy Seiler, *Developing Your Case for Support*, San Francisco, Jossey-Bass, 2001.
26 Adrian Sargeant and Jen Shang, *Fundraising Principles and Practice*, Hoboken, Wiley, 2017.
27 Timothy Seiler, *Developing Your Case for Support*, San Francisco, Jossey-Bass, 2001.
28 Jen Love and John Lepp, *Heart of the Oregon Zoo* [PDF], Agents of Good, https://tinyurl.com/mjd2zm86, accessed 1 September 2021.
29 Timothy Seiler, *Developing Your Case for Support*, San Francisco, Jossey-Bass, 2001.

30 Adrian Sargeant and Jen Shang, *Fundraising Principles and Practice*, Hoboken, Wiley, 2017.
31 *Ibid.*
32 See 'No Child Born To Die' [web page], Save the Children, 2021, https://stories.savethechildren.org.uk/no-child-born-to-die, accessed 19 May 2021.
33 See Giles Pegram, 'NSPCC's Full Stop campaign: A fundraising triumph. Part two: The launch and beyond' [web article], The Showcase of Fundraising Innovation and Inspiration (SOFII), https://sofii.org/article/nspccs-full-stop-campaign-part-two, 29 November 2017.
34 See https://cancergrandchallenges.org.
35 Megan Venzin, 'Keys to Writing a Compelling Case for Support', *Major Gifts Report*, vol. 18, no. 4, 2016, p. 1.
36 Mark Phillips, 'The case against the case for support' [web page], Queer Ideas, 2011, https://queerideas.co.uk/2011/11/the-case-against-the-case-for-support.html, accessed 19 May 2021.
37 Stephen Pidgeon, *How to Love Your Donors (to Death)*, London, DSC, 2015.

CHAPTER SIX
Choosing your tactics

Introduction

In this chapter, we think through the tactics you might use to deliver your strategy. In the first part of the chapter, we consider the fundraising mix, or the different sources of funding available. In the second, we look at how tactics can be delivered from day to day.

It's been pointed out that it's not always clear where the distinction between strategy and tactics lies, with different articles and textbooks classifying strategy and tactics in different ways, so you may well see slightly different definitions in your wider reading.[1] For our purposes, strategy provides the broad principles which underlie your day-to-day fundraising activities and which enable you to achieve your objectives. Tactics, meanwhile, are the details of how you deliver that strategy on the ground.

How you approach developing your tactics is likely to depend, in part at least, on your position within the organisation and your ability to delegate to other team members. If you're a director of fundraising responsible for several members of staff (who are, in turn, responsible for delivering specific areas of fundraising) then you might choose to focus on selecting the optimal fundraising mix – a combination of different types of income – for your organisation. You might then delegate the writing of subplans for each element of the mix to the appropriate member of staff, who would address the detail of delivering the strategy. If this is the case for you, then the first part of this chapter ('Developing your fundraising mix') is likely to be the most relevant.

If, however, your strategy is focused on a specific area of fundraising, or you are responsible for the detail of fundraising delivery, then it might be more helpful to you to work through the tactical detail. In this case, the second part of the chapter ('Delivering your tactics') is likely to be the most relevant.

Developing your fundraising mix

This section explores the fundraising mix, describing each element and listing some of their overarching strengths and weaknesses. It is beyond the scope of this chapter to explore each element in its fullest detail: to find out more about each, you might like to refer to the other books in DSC's Fundraising Series, where the fundraising disciplines are examined in considerably more depth.[2]

Individual giving: Direct response, major gifts and legacies

Individual giving comprises a wide range of ways to give to charity and techniques used to raise funds. Individuals can give one-off gifts by post, telephone, face to face or online, or regular gifts via direct debit, standing order, debit or credit card, or their payroll. They can also leave gifts to charities in their will. According to NCVO, in 2017/18, £8.8 billion was given in donations and £4 billion in legacies – ultimately, 47% of the sector's £53.5 billion income came from the public, with half of that being from voluntary donations.[3]

The majority of people give in some way, with the Charities Aid Foundation (CAF) finding that 57% of people had given money to charity in 2018.[4] The median amount given in the four weeks prior to replying to the survey was £20, and the mean was £45 (suggesting the importance of fewer, larger gifts). CAF also found that women and older people were more likely to participate in charitable and social activities, and most people reported that they gave 'from time to time' (as opposed to 'weekly', 'monthly', 'rarely' or 'never').[5] The top five causes supported were children, animal welfare, medical research, hospitals and hospices, and homelessness.[6] Cash remained the most popular way of giving, followed by buying goods and buying lottery or raffle tickets.[7] The Chartered Institute of Fundraising (CIoF) found in 2013 that the return on investment (ROI) for regular giving was £6.44 for every £1 invested, while for direct marketing it was £1.53 for every £1 invested.[8]

Some individuals also give major gifts. What actually constitutes a major gift will vary from charity to charity. For some it may be a few hundred pounds, while for others it could be several hundreds of thousands. It is difficult, therefore, to put a precise figure on the value of major giving. However, Angela Kail, Stephanie Johnson and Matthew Bowcock, analysing giving data from around 2014, estimated a value of around £4.7 billion per year for giving by a combination of major donors and ultra-high-net-worth individuals.[9] Coutts found that £1.83 billion was given in donations of £1 million or more (across 310 donations) in 2016, with gifts to higher education and foundations dominating.[10] According to the CIoF, major gift fundraising has a typical ROI of £2.97 for every £1 invested.[11]

Finally, 6% of people leave a gift to charity in their will, with legators most commonly being female, aged 85, living in southern England and leaving gifts to three charities.[12] Legacy income is likely to grow in future decades, with Legacy Foresight estimating that the market will almost double to £5.2 billion per year.[13] Legacy fundraising also has an excellent ROI: as of 2013, it was £27.27 for every £1 invested.[14]

There are a number of advantages and disadvantages to investing in individual giving. Once established, individual giving can be a reliable, predictable source of often unrestricted income (i.e. money that does not come with any restrictions on how you spend it). However, for a charity starting from scratch, it can be expensive in the short term, with NFP Synergy stating that, as a rule of thumb, it's likely to take two years to recover the cost of recruiting a new supporter.[15] Alongside the costs of actually recruiting donors, you will need to ensure you have the necessary infrastructure in place (for example, a database or an online giving portal). You will also need to establish processes to ensure that individual-giving fundraising is carried out optimally (for example, your databases should be segmented effectively and Gift Aid should be claimed where possible) and, of course, legally (for example, ensuring you adhere to the requirements of the General Data Protection Regulation).

Developing relationships with supporters is a long-term commitment. However, on the positive side, as those relationships deepen over time, donors might begin to give in other ways, eventually potentially giving a major gift or pledging a legacy, which can be transformational for an organisation.

You should also be aware that the market is in a state of flux and that individual-giving practices are therefore subject to ongoing change (see chapter 11 and particularly page 180). Johnty Grey, Director of Mass Engagement at WaterAid, has argued that charities have to take action to avert a catastrophic decline in individual giving, created by a combination of regulation as well as changes in technology, customer expectations and product life cycles. He argues that to address this change, charities need to develop more innovative cultures and experiment with doing things differently.[16]

Community and events fundraising

Community and events fundraising can involve a whole range of activities. Some are high-profile national or international initiatives, such as Movember, Cancer Research UK's Race for Life and Macmillan Cancer Support's World's Biggest Coffee Morning. Other events are organised by third parties but spaces are bought by fundraisers, such as the London Marathon and the Great North Run. There are also volunteer-organised events, such as raffles and coffee mornings. An increasing number of events are virtual, for example the British Heart Foundation's MyMarathon, which encourages people to run a marathon over the course of a month.[17] Altogether, NCVO's analysis suggests that £4.7 billion is raised through these types of fundraising activity every year.[18] According to the CIoF, special events bring in a ROI of £2.38 for every £1 invested, while local fundraising brings in £2.06 for every £1 invested.[19]

A positive aspect of community and events fundraising is that volunteers can play an important role in either organising or staffing these activities, thereby helping to keep costs down. However, charities sometimes find that increasing amounts of staff time can be drawn into supporting activities which were supposed to be led by volunteers, which

CHAPTER SIX **CHOOSING YOUR TACTICS**

can, conversely, push costs up – you will need to manage your fundraising carefully to avoid this happening.

Events which take place in a local community can have the added benefit of enabling your organisation to tap into wider networks through volunteers or attendees. They can also raise your profile in an area, generating positive publicity. These activities don't come without risks, however. As weather patterns become increasingly unpredictable, the risk of cancellation of outdoor events will be higher. Similarly, people are increasingly wanting to tackle more challenging or unusual events,[20] so the risk of injury could increase, which could, in turn, generate negative publicity for your organisation. Of course, the COVID-19 pandemic also demonstrated how unexpected events can affect this type of fundraising.

Grants fundraising

According to NCVO, in 2017/18 voluntary sector income included £5.1 billion given through grants from charities to other charities, £0.6 billion from National Lottery grants and £15.7 billion from government (in both grants and contracts).[21] Typically, in this type of fundraising, fundraisers will seek to fund a specific project; research the available grant funding; apply through letter, a form or online; and then, if they receive a grant, monitor its success and report back to the funder.

Grants fundraising has a very good ROI, bringing in £9.56 for every £1 invested.[22] It can also bring in large gifts – often thousands of pounds – in a relatively short space of time. Grant-givers also sometimes fund innovative projects of which other donors (such as corporate or major donors) may be wary.

However, there are some downsides. Grants tend to be restricted to specific projects, which, for organisations that primarily rely on grants income, can make it difficult to fund core costs. This is especially the case if core costs aren't budgeted into the full costs of any work (which suggests the importance of budgeting for the full costs of projects when making applications, and scheduling in when these will be accepted by the funder). Grants can also be 'all or nothing': several months of work to tailor an application to a specific funder can result in a rejection, although it might well be possible to reuse the content elsewhere.

Corporate fundraising

NCVO estimates that the private sector contributes £2.7 billion to the voluntary sector's income each year,[23] although in 2018 CAF found that total donations among the FTSE 100 had dropped 26% since 2013.[24] Companies can give in a number of ways, from cash to stocks and shares to sponsoring activities such as events. Companies can also offer other kinds of support such as publicity, gifts in kind or staff time. Corporate fundraising has a reasonable ROI of £4.28 for every £1 invested.[25]

It's increasingly expected that companies will engage in philanthropic efforts.[26] However, there is some debate about whether corporate giving can ever be truly philanthropic or whether the company always receives some benefit. Instead, corporate giving could be described as enlightened self-interest, or even as a pure marketing activity, intended to improve the company's image.[27]

A positive side of building a relationship with a company is that it could result in a number of different forms of support, including the ability to raise your organisation's profile among staff and customers. If you build relationships effectively over time, you might be able to increase the type and level of support from a corporate partner. It can also be a win-win, offering benefits to both parties – for example, income for your organisation and an improved image for the company. Companies also have a tendency to give in the areas where their business is operating, which can reinforce the idea of partnership. The company gives back to the local community and the community members support the business.

However, there are some potential downsides of partnering with a company. There is the risk of negative publicity, for example if a corporate partner is accused of poor business practices. It's also not a quick win: NCVO estimates that it can take three to six months or longer to develop a relationship, and certain types of relationship, such as charity of the year, may need significant resources to manage.[28]

Ensuring a balanced portfolio

As well as considering each type of income separately, you should consider how well they fit together into a broader fundraising portfolio. In chapter 2 we discussed portfolio analysis, looking at internal ability and external attractiveness in the context of an existing fundraising portfolio (see page 32). A similar exercise could be carried out when assessing new investment decisions, considering which investment options are both internally and externally attractive. (However, it's wise not to look at existing and potential new income streams in the same analysis, as portfolio analyses tend to down-weight newer forms of income.)

Developing a balanced portfolio of different types of income can reduce the risks associated with fundraising, ensuring that your organisation isn't left vulnerable as circumstances change. You should consider developing forms of income that will deliver within different time spans, from activities such as local collections (which would deliver income in the short term) to activities such as legacy fundraising (which can take a number of years to bear fruit). Commonly, those types of fundraising that take longer to develop also have a higher ROI – but, of course, your organisation will almost certainly also need to invest in forms of fundraising which will deliver in the short term in order to continue operating.[29]

We have created a simple imaginary version of this portfolio thinking in table 6.1 as an example, but the reality will vary depending on the circumstances of your organisation.

TABLE 6.1 EXAMPLE OF PORTFOLIO THINKING

	Impact on our service user groups	Maturity in 2021	ROI in 2021	Maturity in 2025	ROI in 2025
Trusts and foundations	Medium	Mature	6.0	Mature	8.0
Corporate	Medium	Growth	1.5	Mature	3.0
Individual giving	High	Growth	0.8	Mature	2.5
Legacies	Low	Introduction	N/A	Growth	10.0
Community	High	Introduction	1.0	Growth	2.0
Sporting	Medium	Mature	3.0	Decline	2.0
Shops	Low	Mature	1.8	Decline	1.4
New product				Introduction	?
New product				Introduction	?

Similarly, consider fundraising products which balance risk and reward, as often those products that deliver higher ROI are riskier, while those that deliver lower ROI have less risk associated with them. Again, ideally you would have a mix of these different types of fundraising in your portfolio.[30]

Delivering your tactics

If you have individuals or even teams reporting to you, your consideration of tactics may end at this point, with your colleagues working through the detail of how they will be delivered. However, you might have responsibility for both deciding where to focus (i.e. the topic of the first part of this chapter) and determining how tactics will be delivered.

95

FUNDRAISING STRATEGY

In this section, therefore, we suggest a framework – illustrated in figure 6.1 – to help you work through your tactics in a thorough fashion. The framework starts with the donor, which ensures that you build your plans around your audience, and works logically through a set of tactical decisions in the order they're likely to occur, from the immediate gift you would like to receive to the longer-term journey on which you plan to take your donors. The framework should enable you to take a holistic look at how your fundraising is delivered, taking into account not only the obvious issues (such as how you'll promote your offering) but also the less obvious but nonetheless vitally important (such as ensuring that internal teams are briefed about your plans).

FIGURE 6.1 A FRAMEWORK FOR DELIVERING YOUR TACTICS

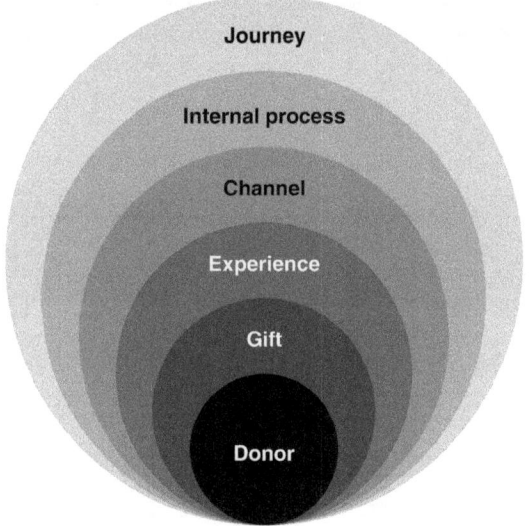

Donor

The first element to consider is the donor themselves. Depending on the level of detail in your audience segmentation (see chapter 4), you might want to take some time here to refine precisely who your focal donors will be for each element of your strategy. For example, if you were focusing on challenge events fundraising, you might have used a broad approach in your segmentation, focusing on demographics and geography. In contrast, in this section, you might like to focus on each of your events individually, discussing the focal audience for each. For example, you might have a women-only event focused on individuals living within a 30-mile radius of York, and a family event focused on people aged 25–45 and their children, living within a 30-mile radius of Edinburgh.

CHAPTER SIX **CHOOSING YOUR TACTICS**

Even if you fully detailed your various audiences in the earlier segmentation process, it would be sensible to take some time here to review your notes about your donors – even if this has been covered elsewhere and doesn't ultimately translate into additional written content for the plan. What do you know about who they are demographically? What motivates them? What are their needs? How have they developed a relationship with your organisation? How do they like to give? Having this information to hand as you progress through the rest of your tactics can help to ensure that you're designing the detail of your fundraising approach with your donors at its core.

Gift

The next element of your tactics to consider is the gift, or what precisely it is that you want the donor to give. As part of your thinking, you will need to balance what your organisation needs with what is likely to be the optimal level and type of gift for the donor.

Firstly, you could identify the *type* of gift you want your donor to give. Most obviously, as fundraisers, we seek to acquire monetary gifts, but donors could also give time or influence, share contacts, or offer items, land or shares. Once you know what type of gift you want them to give, consider how much and how often you want them to support you. Will you be seeking an annual commitment from a charitable trust or a one-off gift from an individual? Finally, how do you want them to give? Possibilities include a cheque, a bank transfer, an online donation, a text donation, a cashless payment or a gift in a will.

Experience

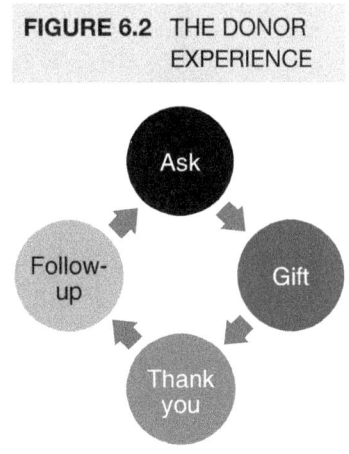

FIGURE 6.2 THE DONOR EXPERIENCE

Once you've clarified the details about your donor and what it is you want them to give, you can begin to think through the experience that you will offer them. We can break the donor experience down into four stages: the ask, the gift, the thank you and the follow-up (see figure 6.2). (It might be that you wish to adapt the stages to better suit your focal area of fundraising – if so, feel free.)

The ask

What ask will you make of the donor? We've identified four types of ask:

- **Proposition:** this is probably the most common type of ask, at least in individual donor fundraising. The fundraising proposition is essentially the

97

answer to the question 'why should I donate to you right now?' As discussed in the previous chapter (on crafting your message), a good proposition encompasses the need, the solution to that need and why a donor should give now. Figure 6.3 shows a classic example from Help the Aged. This ask clearly links the need (cataracts which leave people blinded and helpless) with the solution (a gift of £10, funding an operation) and the now (desperate need and the importance of prevention).

- **Product:** some asks could be classed as more like products. Rather than an ask for (at least seemingly) disinterested support of your organisation, there is a clear offer as to what the donor will get in exchange for their giving. Examples of fundraising products include offers to sponsor a child, adopt a needy animal or pay a nurse's salary in exchange for regular updates. Similarly, offers to join a friends' group or society could be classified in this way.

- **Project:** some asks are structured around a particular project, in which case commonly any income received is restricted to that project. This type of ask is most common in high-value fundraising, particularly with charitable trusts and foundations and with major donors, and also sometimes with corporate partners.

- **Proceeding:** this would be an invitation to donors to take part in an event, either physically (such as running a marathon or attending a charity ball) or virtually (such as Movember or Cancer Research UK's Dryathlon).

FIGURE 6.3 EXAMPLE PROPOSITION FROM HELP THE AGED[31]

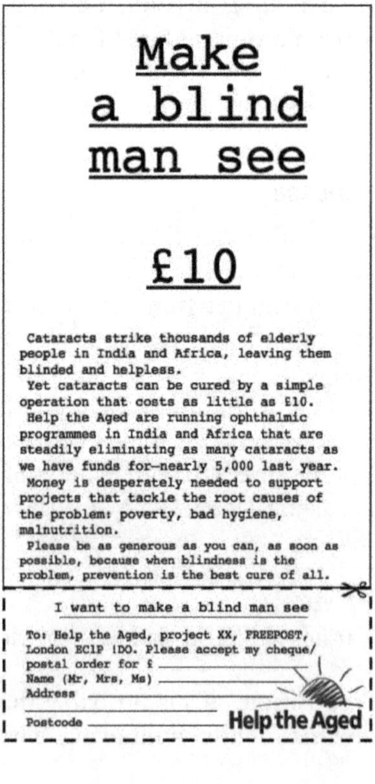

Whatever type of ask you choose to make, you can also take this opportunity to think through in some detail what will appear in front of the donor. What might they see or hear? And, in some cases, perhaps, what will they touch, feel or smell? For example, a charity working with people with sight loss might enable its supporters to touch some text in Braille, and it's now possible to impregnate direct mail with a range of scents, from fruits or flowers to ashtrays or dogs![32]

Case study: Mind's Pause box

Mind's Pause box is an interesting example of a fundraising product. It also picks up on themes discussed earlier in this book around learning from trends in the wider environment (see the information on completing an external audit in chapter 1).

Mental health charity Mind was able to tap into two growing trends from the wider environment with its Pause subscription box product: the trend in purchasing monthly subscription boxes and a growing interest in mindfulness.

Supporters can sign up to a monthly gift of £7.50 and, in return, receive a Pause box each month containing a mindfulness activity (such as origami, drawing or cross-stitch). The box is designed to encourage relaxation, creativity and reflection – enabling people to focus and, ultimately, improve their well-being. The box enables people to be part of Mind's mission of improving mental health while also supporting the charity financially.

The product has enabled the charity to reach out to a new group of younger supporters as well as taking advantage of referrals, with 20–30% of subscriptions being given as gifts.

The product's results seem to be strong. In the first year, digital sign-ups exceeded the target by 41%, with a cost per acquisition of less than £42.[33]

The gift

In the 'Gift' section above (see page 97), we talked about the importance of thinking through what it is you want a donor to give. You can also return to thinking about giving in this section; however, here, having already decided on the type of gift, you would focus on the *mechanism*. How can you make it as easy and as convenient as possible for your donors to give? How will they feel as they go through the process of making a gift? And how can you make them feel better as they do it?

The thank you

Once a donor has given a gift, how will you thank them? The thank you is a vital part of the donor experience but one that can receive too little attention, with donors receiving bland, generic responses or, even worse, sometimes receiving no thank you at all. Fundraising consultant John Grain says that in his charity mystery shopping exercises, the thank you is often dull and uninspiring, and there seems to be a lack of imagination in the ways that organisations thank their supporters.[34]

As well as providing a poor experience for the donor, this lack of focus on thanking could be costing charities future income. Indeed, evidence from a classic study suggests that providing a good thank you can help to raise more money in the future. Donors who received a thank-you call from a board member within 24 hours of receiving a gift gave 39% more than other donors the next time they were asked to give, and, a year later, were giving 42% more.[35]

In a ground-breaking study, fundraising professor Jen Shang and colleagues found that thank-you letters should be tailored according to the stage of the relationship between charity and donor:

- Early in the relationship, letters should focus on **the difference the gift has made**.

- Once donors have made a greater number of gifts than average, letters should focus on **the donor as a special person** and how much they mean to the charity.

The authors found that approaching thank yous in this way had the potential to increase both average donation and response rates.[36]

The follow-up

As well as the initial thank you, in most cases, it will be good practice to follow up with donors to tell them about how their donation was spent and the difference it made. Indeed, relationship fundraising guru Ken Burnett talks about the five Fs, or the importance of fundraisers becoming 'famous for fast, frequent, fabulous feedback'.[37]

Practically, this means developing good relationships with service delivery colleagues who can provide you with statistics on how you've performed, and, just as importantly, stories as to how individual lives have been impacted through your work. This is great feedback that will develop trust between organisation and donor, especially taking into account that trust is one of the key drivers of donor loyalty.[38]

> **Case study: Sue Ryder**
>
> One organisation that has been able to use follow-up particularly successfully is Sue Ryder. It was able to increase its income from trusts and foundations by 349% in a single year (2018/19), including an uplift of more than £1 million in giving from trusts and foundations. The organisation's approach was driven by treating trusts and foundations in a similar way to major donors – understanding and considering them as individuals.[39]

In order to treat trusts and foundations as individuals, it's important to get to know those involved. The team at Sue Ryder talked to trustees and staff on the phone whenever possible, met them in person and made sure they checked in with them regularly.[40] The team then sought to ensure that they offered trusts and foundation great experiences. For example, early on in the COVID-19 pandemic, they held a special webinar for trusts, foundations, corporates and major donors who had donated more than £100,000. One foundation whose grant manager attended was holding a trustees' meeting that evening to make a decision on a £100,000 grant; this was subsequently awarded to the charity.[41]

The team at Sue Ryder also recognised milestones in giving: some trusts and foundations were making what might have seemed like relatively small gifts each year, but these can add up significantly over time.[42] The overall approach was underpinned by building relationships within the charity, involving staff in thanking trusts and foundations and identifying personal connections with potential donors. In one case, it turned out that a staff member was in a book club with a couple who ran a large grant-making trust. That relationship led to a £250,000 gift over five years, despite previous applications having been unsuccessful.[43]

Channel

The channel is essentially the communications route or routes that you choose to reach the donor. The first thing to note is that the number of channels available has grown dramatically in recent years (see table 6.2). A fundraiser working in the mid-twentieth century would have been able to choose from a limited selection of analogue channels, such as advertising, post, telephone and face-to-face contact. Today's fundraiser, in contrast, has tens if not hundreds of options to choose from, from the traditional options listed above to email, social media, virtual reality, wearables (such as smart watches) and voice assistants (such as Amazon Alexa).

One way of choosing between the array of channels is to consider how your existing donors behave (for example, which channels they have responded to in the past) and their perceptions of the different channels. The CIoF and market research agency FastMap have examined donors' perceptions of commonly used fundraising channels, including direct response television (which invites donations via a text message or a call), direct mail and telephone. They also considered the profiles of different groups who are likely to engage with each channel and the actions they are likely to take. To give just one example, the study found that telephone is perceived as an authoritative channel, although it is less likely to be a donor's preferred channel.[44]

TABLE 6.2 GROWTH OF FUNDRAISING CHANNELS

Past	Today: established	Today: emerging
• Physical spaces (e.g. shops) • Post • Print • Radio • TV – two or three commercial channels • Outdoor advertising • Telephone	Everything from the past plus: • Websites • Digital advertising • Social media • Email • Digital television – hundreds of TV channels including Freeview, other commercial channels and streaming services • Contactless donation terminals • Messaging • Apps	Everything from the past and established channels from today plus: • Chatbots • Wearable technology (e.g. smart watches) • Influencers • Smart products (e.g. cars and fridges) • Augmented and virtual reality • Gaming • Voice assistants (e.g. Amazon Alexa)

However, although the insights from the study above may be useful when making decisions about which channels to use, you should be aware that any study that asks a donor what they think they are likely to do won't be as reliable as looking at actual behavioural data (see page 45 in chapter 3).

Alongside thinking about the characteristics of individual channels, you should also be aware that both donors and charities are increasingly likely to take a multi-channel approach. Ideally, supporters should have a joined-up experience, so that the tone, style and frequency of your communication does not vary too much, whichever channel they choose to communicate through.

> **Case study: Using Amazon Alexa to encourage giving**
>
> Voice assistants are an interesting emerging digital channel – one of the key assistants is Alexa. A number of charities have developed Alexa skills (a skill is a software programme designed for Alexa) to enable supporters to donate or fundraise via voice. For example, people can donate to the NSPCC by saying 'Alexa, open NSPCC' and going through a few simple steps to make a gift. Their donation is made via their Amazon account and passed on to the NSPCC.[45]

Similarly, Cancer Research UK's Stand Up To Cancer campaign has launched a fundraising quiz via Alexa, hosted by comedian Joe Lycett. Tiffany Hall, Cancer Research UK's Chief Information Officer, described how Alexa's unique qualities mean that organisers can focus on the fun aspects of the quiz, while the Alexa skill looks after the hard work of hosting.[46]

Internal process

Whatever fundraising method you are focusing on, you will need to make sure you have robust internal processes in place to support it. It's very easy to focus on the front end of fundraising, such as the channel and the messaging, and for the important processes underlying fundraising to be neglected in the planning stages.

The particular processes you will need to consider will vary from method to method. We've listed some common issues to consider in table 6.3, although the list is not comprehensive.

TABLE 6.3 COMMON PROCESSES UNDERLYING SOME FUNDRAISING METHODS

Fundraising method	Processes to consider
Trusts and foundations	• How will information on each funder be recorded? • How will you know when to apply to each? • How will you gather internal data from your organisation (for example, budgets and programme data)? • How will you know when to complete relevant reports?
Direct marketing	• Who internally will need to be briefed about communications? • How and when will you access donor data? • Who needs to sign off messages? How and when? • Are you set up to process Gift Aid? • How will you record donor communication preferences?

Fundraising method	Processes to consider
Major donors	• How will you record data about potential donors (in a legal and ethically appropriate way – see below)? • How will you record who is responsible for working with each donor?
Legacy giving	• Do you have processes in place to record non-financial actions, such as a commitment to leave a gift in the future? • How will you ensure that gifts received are dealt with in the appropriate legal manner?
Events	• How will donors buy tickets or sign up? • Is there a process for risk assessment? • How will volunteers and staff be briefed about their roles in an event? • What post-event actions need to be put in place (for example, to collect sponsorship money)?
Corporates	• How will you research which companies you might approach? • How will you decide which companies to actually approach? • How will you record the various relationships your staff and volunteers have with representatives of the companies?

It's vital across all forms of fundraising to have processes in place to ensure that your approach adheres to the Code of Fundraising Practice, and any other appropriate legal and ethical standards (see www.fundraisingregulator.org.uk/code). It would be appropriate at this point to ensure that you have processes in place to address this area.

Achieving the right balance between process and innovation

Although we've focused on the importance of getting the right procedures in place, it is important to make sure that your fundraising processes, and particularly how you make your decisions as an organisation, do not become unwieldy. Having too many layers of process can stifle innovation or even stop you taking advantage of opportunities in a timely way. Some important questions to ask yourself include:

- How will you react quickly to opportunities?

- How many stages of sign-off will you need when launching new fundraising opportunities?

- Are the right people focused on decisions on risk and opportunity rather than, for example, everyone focusing on the nitty-gritty of fundraising solicitations, based on their own personal and potentially inexpert opinions?

Journey

The final tactical consideration is the longer-term journey that your donor experiences, after making a gift or after taking the particular action that you're requesting. Indeed, in most cases, you will want to develop a longer-term relationship with a donor, rather than engage in a series of one-off transactions.

Academics Ian MacQuillin, Adrian Sargeant and Jen Shang have examined what the social psychology literature can tell fundraisers about how to develop relationships. They point out that after the initial gift, it's crucial that charities make donors feel rewarded. Similarly, not giving a second gift should feel like it might be a loss for donors (for example, if they feel they might miss out on a chance to make a difference).[47]

You should design donor journeys in such a way as to ensure that your donors are satisfied with their experience supporting your organisation, so they feel like they've made both tangible and intangible investments in it. In other words, as well as knowing they have made a monetary gift, they should feel that they have personally connected with your case for support. The donor journey should also demonstrate that your organisation is the best alternative in that donor's set of choices.

In order to develop commitment, the social psychology literature also suggests encouraging donors to reflect on how they might like to contribute to your organisation in the future. You can also prompt them to consider how much making an impact with their gift would mean to them.

Finally, MacQuillin, Sargeant and Shang point out that what is optimal in communications will change over time. In the early stages of a relationship, communications should focus on the charity (for example, highlighting its warmth and competence). However, as time goes on, the donor's focus of attention will shift to considering what needs the relationship will meet for them, and thus communications will need to develop accordingly.[48] Although applying psychological theory to fundraising in this way is relatively new, Sargeant and Shang have seen impressive results from their studies – in some cases, doubling or tripling income.[49]

> **Case study: Developing a new donor journey**
>
> A practical example of how journeys can affect the fundraising bottom line is given in this case study from Diabetes Canada and agency HJC.
>
> Diabetes Canada had hit a plateau with its overseas running event, Team Diabetes, where income and participant numbers were static. The charity worked with HJC to run a hands-on supporter journey session. As part of the process, they created three supporter personas, identified key problems and mapped out new supporter journeys. As a result of the process, the charity increased the number of participants from 143 to 223 in one year; money raised went up by more than 55%; the percentage of visitors to the event page who signed up for the event increased; and the percentage of signed-up participants who reached their fundraising goal also improved.
>
> Donna Dowsett, National Director of Team Diabetes, described how journey mapping enabled the fundraising team to work better together and to focus on the most important moments in a supporter's journey. However, as we explored in the earlier discussion of internal process (see page 103), it's also vital to put in place relevant processes, such as adapting your website's functionality and database to ensure that these journeys will work effectively. Journey mapping without the processes to support it is unlikely to be successful.[50]

Conclusion

In this chapter, we considered the tactical elements of a fundraising strategy at two levels. Firstly, we looked at what you might include in a plan if you are a director or head of fundraising with the ability to delegate delivery to different levels. Secondly, we considered what you might include if you are responsible for a single area of fundraising or for delivering the practicalities of a strategy.

In the following chapters, we move on to look at additional areas of how the strategy is operationalised, examining the devilish detail of timing and budgets.

Notes

1. Rajan Varadarajan, 'Strategic Marketing and Marketing Strategy', in *Handbook of Marketing Strategy*, edited by Venkatesh Shankar and Gregory Carpenter, Cheltenham, Edward Elgar, 2012, pp. 9–27.
2. This section provides return on investment (ROI) figures from the Chartered Institute of Fundraising's 2013 Fundratios report. If you are interested in this area, you may also wish to consult reports produced in 2019 and 2020 by the fundraising consultancy LarkOwl, which benchmarked the ROI of fundraising income streams, as discussed in chapter 2 (see page 25). See 'Benchmarking' [web page], LarkOwl, 2020, https://larkowl.uk/fundraising-benchmarking-2019, accessed 19 May 2021.
3. 'Never more needed' [web page], NCVO, 2021, https://data.ncvo.org.uk, accessed 19 May 2021.
4. *CAF UK Giving Report 2019* [PDF], Charities Aid Foundation, 2019, www.cafonline.org/docs/default-source/about-us-publications/caf-uk-giving-2019-report-an-overview-of-charitable-giving-in-the-uk.pdf, accessed 4 March 2021, p. 7.
5. *Ibid.*, p. 11.
6. *Ibid.*, p. 13.
7. *Ibid.*, p. 15.
8. 'Fundratios 2013: Overview of results' [web page], Centre for Interfirm Comparison/Chartered Institute of Fundraising, 2013, www.cifc.co.uk/Fundratios13.html, accessed 19 May 2021.
9. Angela Kail, Stephanie Johnson and Matthew Bowcock, *Giving More and Better: How can the philanthropy sector improve* [PDF], NPC and Hazelhurst Trust, 2016, www.thinknpc.org/resource-hub/giving-more-and-better, accessed 4 March 2021, p. 5.
10. 'Million Pound Donors Report 2017' [web page], Coutts, 2017, https://philanthropy.coutts.com, accessed 19 May 2021.
11. 'Fundratios 2013: Overview of results' [web page], Centre for Interfirm Comparison/Chartered Institute of Fundraising, 2013, www.cifc.co.uk/Fundratios13.html, accessed 19 May 2021.
12. *Legacy Trends 2018: Discovering potential through data* [PDF], Smee and Ford, 2018, https://spotlight.wilmingtononline.co.uk/docs/images/Legacy%20Trends%202018%20update_936.pdf, accessed 19 May 2021.
13. *Legacy Giving 2050*, London, Legacy Foresight, 2014.
14. 'Fundratios 2013: Overview of results' [web page], Centre for Interfirm Comparison/Chartered Institute of Fundraising, 2013, www.cifc.co.uk/Fundratios13.html, accessed 19 May 2021.
15. Joe Saxton, *Gimme, Gimme, Gimme! A guide for organisations new to fundraising or just starting out raising money* [PDF], NFP Synergy, 2011, https://nfpsynergy.net/gimme-gimme-gimme-guide-fundraising-small-organisations, accessed 19 May 2021.
16. See Rebecca Cooney, 'Change to avert "catastrophic decline" in individual giving, says WaterAid executive' [web article], Third Sector, www.thirdsector.co.uk/change-avert-catastrophic-decline-individual-giving-says-wateraid-executive/fundraising/article/1519498, 26 November 2018.
17. See 'MyMarathon' [web page], British Heart Foundation, 2021, www.bhf.org.uk/how-you-can-help/fundraise/mymarathon, accessed 19 May 2021.

18 *The UK Civil Society Almanac 2018* [PDF], NCVO, 2018, https://ncvo-app-wagtail-mediaa721a567-uwkfinin077j.s3.amazonaws.com/documents/ncvo-uk-civil-society-almanac-2018.pdf, accessed 19 May 2021.
19 'Fundratios 2013: Overview of results' [web page], Centre for Interfirm Comparison/Chartered Institute of Fundraising, 2013, www.cifc.co.uk/Fundratios13.html, accessed 19 May 2021.
20 Elizabeth Kessick, 'How MOB events are changing the events fundraising landscape' [blog post], JustGiving, https://blog.justgiving.com/how-mob-events-are-changing-the-event-fundraising-landscape, 8 July 2015.
21 'Where do voluntary organisations get their money from?' [web page], NCVO, 2020, https://data.ncvo.org.uk/financials/income-sources, accessed 19 May 2021.
22 'Fundratios 2013: Overview of results' [web page], Centre for Interfirm Comparison/Chartered Institute of Fundraising, 2013, www.cifc.co.uk/Fundratios13.html, accessed 19 May 2021.
23 'Where do voluntary organisations get their money from?' [web page], NCVO, 2020, https://data.ncvo.org.uk/financials/income-sources, accessed 19 May 2021.
24 *Corporate Giving by the FTSE 100: Bigger impact through better business*, London, Charities Aid Foundation, 2018.
25 'Fundratios 2013: Overview of results' [web page], Centre for Interfirm Comparison/Chartered Institute of Fundraising, 2013, www.cifc.co.uk/Fundratios13.html, accessed 19 May 2021.
26 Abi Rimmer, 'Most consumers favour companies that support charities, says study' [web article], Third Sector, www.thirdsector.co.uk/consumers-favour-companies-support-charities-says-study/fundraising/article/1183955, 28 May 2013; '73% of Americans consider companies' charitable work when making a purchase' [web article], Mintel, www.mintel.com/press-centre/social-and-lifestyle/givingtuesday-73-of-americans-consider-companies-charitable-work-when-making-a-purchase, 23 November 2018.
27 Arthur Gautier and Anne-Claire Pache, 'Research on Corporate Philanthropy: A review and assessment', *Journal of Business Ethics*, vol. 126, no. 3, 2015, pp. 343–69.
28 *Corporate Fundraising: Resource sheet* [PDF], NCVO, 2014, http://culturehive.co.uk/wp-content/uploads/2014/06/Corporate-Fundraising.pdf, accessed 19 May 2021.
29 Joe Saxton, *Gimme, Gimme, Gimme! A guide for organisations new to fundraising or just starting out raising money* [PDF], NFP Synergy, 2011, https://nfpsynergy.net/gimme-gimme-gimme-guide-fundraising-small-organisations, accessed 19 May 2021.
30 *Ibid.*
31 Ken Burnett, 'Help the Aged: "make a blind man see" press advertisement' [web article], The Showcase of Fundraising Innovation and Inspiration (SOFII), https://sofii.org/case-study/help-the-aged-make-a-blind-man-see-press-advertisement, 14 May 2008.
32 See, for example, www.webmartuk.com/print-technology/innovation-in-print-scented-varnishes.
33 Caroline Appleton, 'Mind Pause box' [web article], The Showcase of Fundraising Innovation and Inspiration (SOFII), https://sofii.org/case-study/mind-pause-box, 5 September 2019; 'Mind: Launching the Mind Pause subscription box' [web page], Equimedia, www.equimedia.co.uk/our-work/mind-pause-subscription-box, accessed 19 May 2021; 'Pause' [web page], Mind, https://pauseformind.org.uk, accessed 19 May 2021.

34 John Grain, 'CDE Project 4: Thank you and welcome' [web article], The Showcase of Fundraising Innovation and Inspiration (SOFII), http://sofii.org/article/cde-project-4-thank-you-and-welcome, 1 May 2017.
35 Penelope Burk, *Donor-Centered Fundraising*, Chicago, Cygnus Applied Research, 2003.
36 Jen Shang, Adrian Sargeant, Kathryn Carpenter and Harriet Day, *Learning to Say Thank You: The role of donor acknowledgements*, Plymouth, UK, Philanthropy Centre, 2018.
37 Ken Burnett, 'Pure Gold: The 34 fundamental foundations of fundraising' [blog post], www.kenburnett.com/Blog65foundationsoffundraising.html, 26 April 2016.
38 Adrian Sargeant, *Donor Retention: What do we know and what can we do about it?* [PDF], 2008, www.academia.edu/25237004/Donor_Retention_What_Do_We_Know_and_What_Can_We_Do_About_It, accessed 19 May 2021.
39 Andy Watts, 'How changing our relationships with trusts led to a huge spike in income at Sue Ryder' [web article], Chartered Institute of Fundraising, https://ciof.org.uk/events-and-training/resources/how-changing-our-relationships-with-trusts-led-to, 24 April 2019.
40 *Ibid.*
41 Rob Woods, 'Episode 32: Andy Watts – The trust fundraising approach that increased income by 349%' [podcast], Bright Spot, www.brightspotfundraising.co.uk/podcast/episode-32-andy-watts-the-trust-fundraising-approach-that-increased-income-by-349, accessed 19 May 2021.
42 Andy Watts, 'How changing our relationships with trusts led to a huge spike in income at Sue Ryder' [web article], Chartered Institute of Fundraising, https://ciof.org.uk/events-and-training/resources/how-changing-our-relationships-with-trusts-led-to, 24 April 2019.
43 Rob Woods, 'Episode 32: Andy Watts – The trust fundraising approach that increased income by 349%' [podcast], Bright Spot, www.brightspotfundraising.co.uk/podcast/episode-32-andy-watts-the-trust-fundraising-approach-that-increased-income-by-349, accessed 19 May 2021.
44 *'Fundraising Media DNA'* [PDF], Chartered Institute of Fundraising/Fastmap, 2017, www.fastmap.com/fundraising-campaigns, accessed 19 May 2021.
45 Amazon Pay Team, '"Alexa, Open NSPCC": UK charity finds help in their crusade from Alexa Skills and Amazon Pay' [web article], Amazon, https://pay.amazon.co.uk/blog/alexa-open-nspcc, 20 February 2019.
46 Joe Lepper, 'Joe Lycett Hosts Stand Up to Cancer Quiz on Amazon Alexa' [web article], Charity Digital, https://charitydigital.org.uk/topics/topics/joe-lycett-hosts-stand-up-to-cancer-quiz-on-amazon-alexa2-6192, 26 September 2019.
47 Ian MacQuillin, Adrian Sargeant and Jen Shang, *Relationship Fundraising: Where do we go from here? Volume 2: Review of theory from social psychology* [PDF], Centre for Sustainable Philanthropy, Plymouth University, 2017, www.plymouth.ac.uk/uploads/production/document/path/11/11913/RF_-_Where_do_we_go_from_here_Vol_2.pdf, accessed 19 May 2021.
48 *Ibid.*
49 'Home' [web page], Institute for Sustainable Philanthropy, 2021, www.philanthropy-institute.org.uk, accessed 19 May 2021.
50 'Case Study: Customer experience (CX) journey mapping' [web page], HJC, 2021, www.hjcnewmedia.com/casestudies/customer-experience-cx-journey-mapping, accessed 19 May 2021.

CHAPTER SEVEN
Scheduling and budgeting for your fundraising

Introduction
In the previous three chapters, we began to look at how to put your strategy into practice – who you talk to (audience) and what you say (message), as well as the particular route(s) you take (tactics). In this chapter, we move on to the level of operations and how to plan out the specific actions you'll need to take to deliver your tactics. We begin by focusing on scheduling and move on to budgeting.

Scheduling
Scheduling has been defined as being about the optimal allocation of resources to particular activities over time. It probably won't surprise you to learn that research shows that projects frequently run over, in both cost and time.[1]

Pulling together a schedule is therefore a vitally important part of your overall fundraising strategy. Its most obvious benefit, as alluded to above, is ensuring that you have enough time and resources to deliver your plan, but it also has a number of other benefits. A schedule can:

- be a tool to measure and monitor progress against;

- help to avoid clashes between activities;

- identify interdependencies, so that you can see how a change in one part of your plan may affect other areas;

- act as a communications tool to enable others to see what's planned to happen, where their role fits into the broader picture and, ultimately, whether the plan is on track.

> ### Effective time management for fundraisers
> Time management is often a struggle for fundraisers, particularly those in smaller organisations, who might manage multiple income streams and get involved in everything from opening the post to organising events to meeting major donors. However, there are a

number of tips which you may find useful both when planning your fundraising and on a day-to-day basis.

Admittedly, it's easy to say and harder to do, but a number of authors stress the importance of focusing on the most important tasks. NCVO, for example, discusses the importance of the Pareto Principle, which suggests that 80% of your results will come from 20% of your actions.[2] Try, therefore, to understand and then focus on the key elements of your role, and consider whether there are aspects that could be delegated to others or even eliminated altogether.

Alongside the broader fundraising plan discussed in this chapter, you could consider planning your work on a daily basis, making sure that you address the most challenging tasks at a time that works best for you. As part of the daily planning process, fundraising consultant Pamela Grow recommends batching: putting tasks you do regularly into one or two spans of time. She recommends, for example, checking email and your organisation's social media once or twice a day – perhaps towards the beginning and end of your daily working hours.[3]

Writing for the Charity Village website, consultant Lorraine Arams points out the importance of managing your own stress and well-being. She recommends ensuring that you take regular breaks, eat lunch outside your workspace, and eat and sleep well.[4]

The first stage in scheduling your fundraising is to collect the information that you will need. This might include:

- **calendars:** for the individuals involved, for the organisation and for the project overall;

- **project summary:** information about what it is that you're trying to achieve, the constraints you need to work within (for example, budget), and key details such as start and end dates;

- **risks:** details which will help you to ensure that you factor in enough time (see page 132 in chapter 8 for more detail on risk);

- **activities:** your fundraising broken down into its key component tasks.[5]

Once you have the information you need, there are various ways in which you could schedule your activities (you might find it helpful to use specialised software such as Microsoft Project to support this process). The simplest way is likely to be a calendar which shows when key activities are happening (such as events taking place or direct marketing campaigns landing on doormats). This might be helpful in giving a broad overview of what's happening when, but it's less likely to be helpful in ensuring that the various actions that need to be completed in advance are

FUNDRAISING STRATEGY

running to schedule. A basic to-do list setting out the various actions could therefore be more useful in the run-up to your activities, but it might not make clear the interdependencies between actions (for example, in a direct mail campaign, data must be obtained a certain period before the materials for an appeal can be printed).

Gantt charts

For most fundraising plans, the most useful and effective scheduling tool will be a Gantt chart, which lays out visually when different activities in a project will be happening, mapping the various activities down the vertical axis against time periods across the horizontal axis. It can also show dependencies (marked by connecting arrows) – activities that must be completed before others can begin. A simplified Gantt chart for a direct mail campaign is illustrated in figure 7.1.

FIGURE 7.1 A GANTT CHART FOR DEVELOPING A DIRECT MAIL APPEAL

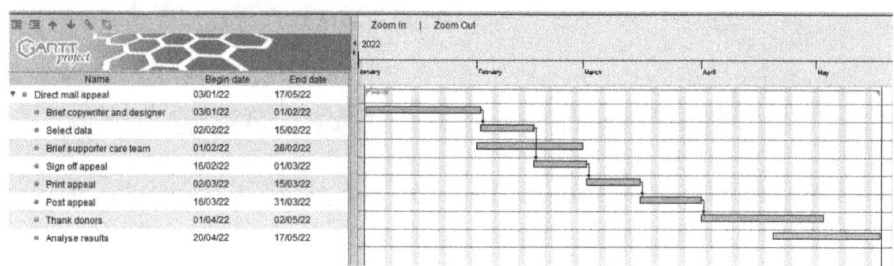

Image reproduced under the GNU General Public License version 3 as published by the Free Software Foundation

Although the principles of the Gantt chart date back to the late nineteenth century, the chart as we know it today was developed and popularised by Henry Gantt in the early 1900s. It saw its first substantial use during the First World War. Henry Gantt had been hired to help the US Army prepare for the war by ramping up its production of armaments. He designed his Gantt chart as a project management tool to facilitate that process.[6] Gantt charts are most relevant to projects – that is, tasks with defined beginnings, middles and ends. Although we might not explicitly refer to them as projects, most fundraising activities will fit that mould.

> ### When a Gantt chart might not be needed
>
> Some types of fundraising (for example, running events and developing campaigns) lend themselves very well to working with Gantt charts, while others may not need that level of complexity. For example, a single person or team working on a less linear project

> might not need to use a Gantt chart, especially if the project does not have dependencies that can be shown clearly in this way. Instead, managing the process of applying to grant-makers and then timetabling reporting and relationship-building milestones might be more easily managed using a calendar-based system or timetabling tasks within a database record. It could, however, still be helpful to use a Gantt chart to plan an approach to a major funder, or if you need to factor in the work of a different department to write the proposal or report back on progress.

The first decision to make when constructing a Gantt chart is whether you're going to plan backwards or forwards. In other words, do you want to start from the date you want a key activity in your project to happen and work backwards through the various planning stages, or begin from the current date and work out how long each stage will need to take, thus coming to the ultimate date your key activity should happen? This decision might be made for you, depending on whether activities are already planned in around specific dates. In such cases, it will probably be sensible to work backwards from the date your key activity needs to be delivered. Additionally, working backwards can be a good way to make sure that crucial elements of the project aren't missed, because at each stage you can check what needs to have been completed for the activity to be possible.

Once you've identified the particular activities you will need to complete, you can consider how long each one will take and the relationships between them. You should consider which activities are parallel (i.e. tasks that can be completed at the same time as each other) and which are dependent on each other (i.e. dependencies). For instance, artwork for a mailing could be completed at the same time as the data is selected (parallel activities), but the letter can't be printed until the data has been selected (dependent activities).

This process also enables you to consider the critical path for your project, by which we mean a series of activities that have to happen in a particular order for your plan to stay on track. The critical path is the longest series of interrelated activities. This is an important concept to be aware of and track, because if one activity in the critical path is delayed, then the whole project will be delayed. Understanding your critical path can also help you to see where the flexibility or slack is in the plan – which activities could be rescheduled without affecting the project's end date.

Figure 7.2 shows the critical path (patterned bars) for the simplified Gantt chart we looked at above. You can see that while most activities form part of the critical path, the exact date when the supporter care team is briefed is flexible. As long as it happens in advance of the mailing being sent, it could potentially happen in either February or March. Similarly, as long as sufficient time is left for responses to be received, the results could be analysed in May or pushed out by several weeks.

FIGURE 7.2 A GANTT CHART FOR DEVELOPING A DIRECT MAIL APPEAL, WITH A CRITICAL PATH

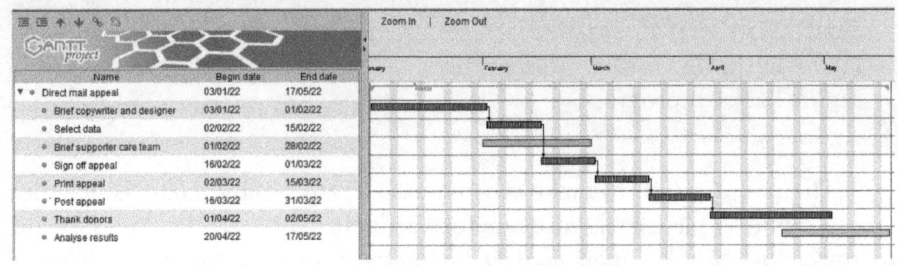

Image reproduced under the GNU General Public License version 3 as published by the Free Software Foundation

As fundraising projects become larger and involve more people and resources, the planning process is also likely to become more complex. Planning activities for yourself can be a relatively simple process. However, if you also need to involve other members of the team or the wider organisation, you will have to take into account their workloads and availability, particularly where their input might have an impact on the critical path.

In longer or more complex projects like these, you can use milestones to break down your work into chunks or phases. Milestones aren't necessarily activities; instead, they are the most important elements of a plan, key indicators that the project is progressing as planned, or points at which you're likely to stop to assess whether your project is on track. They might include start and end dates, the date a piece of copy is signed off, the date of an event or the date of a meeting with a donor. As one project manager says, milestones can function as signposts, showing that a project is progressing to plan.[7]

Budgeting

As well as allocating time for your fundraising, you will need to allocate monetary resources and clarify how much money your activities are likely to bring in. Developing a budget is important for a number of reasons. Budgeting ensures that:

• you have enough money to deliver the fundraising activities you have planned;

• your organisation has enough money to deliver its services;

CHAPTER SEVEN **SCHEDULING AND BUDGETING FOR YOUR FUNDRAISING**

- you know when money will be coming in and going out;

- your fundraising activities will – eventually – make a profit for your organisation.

Like your schedule, your budget can be a communications tool that you share with the wider organisation to illustrate how much money a particular activity is likely to cost, when those costs may be incurred and how much is likely to be raised.

It is almost impossible to give a generic answer to the question of how much, or what percentage of its income, an organisation should spend on fundraising. Fundraising spend commonly differs between size and type of charity, subsector (for example, education or health), level of fundraising development and the type of fundraising undertaken. One universal, though, is that if the COVID-19 pandemic taught us anything, it is the importance of diversity of income rather than focusing on single high-yield fundraising streams.

A thorough audit (see chapters 1 and 2) should have given you some helpful indicators around fundraising spend, potentially in terms of both your organisation's historical income and spending, and trends in the wider market or among your competitors. As a very rough guideline, NCVO finds that, overall, around 14% of organisations' total spending goes on raising funds.[8]

As in other areas of strategy development, the budgeting process might vary depending on your role. A director of fundraising looking after a number of teams might, for example, produce a high-level budget allocating overall figures to teams. In contrast, a fundraiser who looks after one stream of income might produce a more granular budget, showing detailed line-by-line costs.

Importantly, overarching fundraising budgets must take account of how much the organisation needs to run its services: how much needs to be raised both gross (before costs) and net (after costs). However, organisations should also take account of what fundraisers believe it will be possible to raise and reduce their expenditure accordingly rather than piling additional monies into the income line.[9] Ultimately, it's important that overarching fundraising budgets are developed in conversation with the wider organisation.

A key point for charity directors, or anyone setting budgets (and ultimately targets) for others, is how individuals and teams will be affected by those budgets. You should consider whether targets are to be set for individual fundraisers – in which case, individuals should be consulted as part of the process – or whether they are to be set at a team level, which can help to avoid silo-working or fighting over donors.[10]

Similarly, measuring fundraisers on short-term or yearly income can affect their behaviours (for example, by incentivising fundraisers to bring

115

forwards or hold back income to fit budget cycles). This could result in less optimal results – for example, a fundraiser might make an immediate ask of a major donor when, with patience, a larger gift could have been achieved.[11] This is also important because if your first donation from a donor or funder is much lower than they are able to give, there is a risk that, however much you upgrade their support through good relationship-building, your support from them will always be 'anchored' to that lower starting point.

There are various ways to allocate an overall fundraising budget. However, in most cases, the ideal method would be the task method. This means working through the strategy to assess how much each planned activity will cost. However, in reality, organisations might base their fundraising budgets on other methods, including:[12]

- relying on figures from the previous year's spending, perhaps plus or minus a certain percentage;
- allocating a percentage of budgeted donations;
- using beliefs about what competitors do;
- allocating what's left after other activities are accounted for;
- allocating what it's believed can be afforded.

Investing in fundraising

Many donors are concerned about charities 'wasting money' on fundraising, instead preferring to see their donations going to 'the cause' or directly to the service users. These external pressures, combined with an internal culture of under-investment, can result in fundraisers wanting to deliver their work as cheaply as possible.[13] While delivering fundraising cheaply may be well intentioned, it's been argued that under-investment is a serious issue which may encourage corners to be cut, stifle innovation and ultimately lead to less income being raised for the cause.[14]

One way of addressing these issues is to see fundraising as an investment rather than a cost – and, indeed, to present it to donors as such. Rather than, for example, showing how out of every £1 donated, only 20p is spent on fundraising, you might instead show how investing £1 in fundraising might generate an additional £4 for the cause. Indeed, it's been pointed out that fundraising offers excellent returns when compared to other forms of investment. If you invested £1 million in developing regular giving, then you would likely get back around £3 million in ten years. If you were to invest the same amount in bonds, your return would only be £300,000. You could also spend more or less on fundraising depending on how favourable the wider environment is likely to be, reducing your risk.[15]

There are a number of examples of charities which have invested in fundraising and seen significant results:

- Guide Dogs demonstrated that its return on investment from fundraising would bring in 16 times the results of investing in stocks and shares.[16]

- Since 2010, animal charity Battersea has invested heavily in fundraising with the aim of growing a significant individual donor base, developing its major giving programme, and increasing its events and community fundraising activity. The investment has increased its income more than ten-fold.[17]

- In the US, author Dan Pallotta famously recounts how, in 1993, the Los Angeles LGBT Center (Los Angeles Gay and Lesbian Center at the time) invested $50,000 to test AIDSRides (a series of sponsored bike rides in support of people with AIDS). That $50,000 was used to attract another $120,000 from a corporate sponsor, and the event netted just over $1 million in its first year – 20 times the original investment. A similar event for breast cancer awareness cost $350,000 and netted $4.2 million – a return of 12 times the investment.[18]

Of course, not every investment in fundraising will show such dramatic returns – and, indeed, not every investment will result in a positive return at all, with failure being an important element of innovation. Naturally, too, fundraisers should still work as carefully as possible through investment scenarios and seek to manage their costs. However, the above examples show that investing in fundraising can ultimately increase the amount of money that makes its way to a cause, and which donor wouldn't want to invest in that?

The task method of budgeting

Having discussed some overall principles of budgeting, in the rest of this chapter, we'll consider the task method.[19] A useful starting point for this approach could be the schedule you created previously: you can consider the costs associated with each activity identified there. It can also be useful to categorise your costs into two types:

- What are the **direct costs** associated with each activity (i.e. the actual expenses required to carry out each action, such as printing, postage, online advertising or venue hire)?

- What are the **indirect costs** associated with each activity or the overall project (i.e. expenses not directly attributable to a solicitation method, such as staff salaries or computer equipment)?

You could also consider whether your costs are fixed or variable:

- **Fixed costs** will be the same regardless of output. For example, designing a poster is likely to be a fixed cost, as it will not be affected by how many posters you ultimately print.

- **Variable costs** will change according to output. For example, printing is likely to be a variable cost depending on how many copies you require.

It's good practice, where possible, to consider staff time alongside the direct costs of an activity. Some activities can look profitable when only direct costs are considered; however, if they take up a disproportionate amount of staff time, they might prove to be unprofitable. A classic example might be a community fundraising activity where the plan is to deliver it using volunteers but where it becomes apparent that, for the activity to succeed, it will need large amounts of support from paid staff members.

It can also be helpful (both as a reminder for your own purposes and as a tool for communicating with others) to show how you calculated your budget. As an example, rather than just stating a print cost of '£500 for leaflets', you could include '£500 (25,000 leaflets at 2p each)'. In other words, you're showing how you have worked out the cost, or keeping your method to hand as a reminder.

Using our earlier schedule as a starting point, then, your budget might look something like table 7.1.

TABLE 7.1 EXAMPLE BUDGET

	Direct costs	**Indirect costs**
Brief copywriter and designer	Copywriting: £500 Design: £2,000	2 hours of staff time: £24
Select data	–	3 hours of staff time: £36
Brief supporter care	–	1 hour of staff time: £12
Sign off appeal	–	1 hour of staff time: £12

CHAPTER SEVEN SCHEDULING AND BUDGETING FOR YOUR FUNDRAISING

	Direct costs	Indirect costs
Print appeal	10,000 × £0.50: £5,000	–
Post appeal	10,000 × £0.50: £5,000	–
Thank donors	–	16 hours of staff time: £192
Analyse results	–	6 hours of staff time: £72

Once you have established your budget, it's also a good idea to add in some contingency funds to cover unforeseen costs, necessary overspends or unanticipated price increases. Your organisation might have a set policy on this; if not, 5–10% might be a sensible contingency to include.

Alongside expenditure, you should also consider the income each activity will bring in. This is a good opportunity to consider income multipliers – i.e. ways to maximise income. For example, as well as selling tickets to an event, you could sell refreshments, raffle tickets and merchandise, and also claim Gift Aid on any donations that are made.

Once you know what income you are likely to receive and what expenditure you're likely to make, you can consider timings to illustrate when income will come in or go out. This is likely to be particularly important in a small organisation where margins can be tight. A helpful way to keep track of incoming and outgoing resources is a cashflow figure. Figure 7.3 shows a simple example of what it might look like.

FIGURE 7.3 AN EXAMPLE OF A CASHFLOW FIGURE

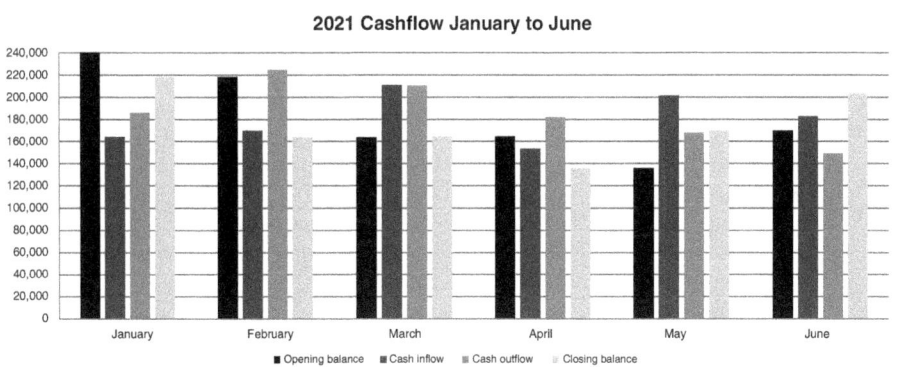

	Jan-21	Feb-21	Mar-21	Apr-21	May-21	Jun-21
Opening balance	**£240,000**	**£218,300**	**£163,637**	**£164,266**	**£135,700**	**£169,647**
Events and community income	£64,000	£28,963	£35,869	£47,630	£50,600	£82,900
Direct marketing income	£57,300	£101,400	£86,500	£58,200	£100,502	£81,376
Legacies	£43,042	£39,483	£88,548	£47,587	£50,456	£18,560
Fundraising costs	£102,050	£137,744	£123,523	£95,218	£80,846	£59,614
Salaries	£83,992	£86,765	£86,765	£86,765	£86,765	£89,500
Closing balance	**£218,300**	**£163,637**	**£164,266**	**£135,700**	**£167,647**	**£203,369**

Conclusion

This chapter looked at how best to schedule fundraising projects by bringing together several fundamental pieces of information: the key activities that need to be delivered, the overall project deliverables and the availability of staff. We suggested using a Gantt chart to do this (but you can also use another format that's appropriate for your project). We then considered how to develop a budget, focusing particularly on the task method, or working through a plan to assess how much each activity will cost, and illustrating both income and expenditure for any given activity.

A budget which includes both income and expenditure enables you to track the return on investment of your fundraising and, ultimately, the lifetime value of your donors. We discuss these concepts in more detail in the following chapter, which considers how to monitor and control your fundraising activities.

Notes

1. Willy Herroelen, 'Project Scheduling: Theory and practice', *Production and Operations Management*, vol. 14, no. 4, 2005, pp. 413–32.
2. 'Time management' [web page], NCVO, 2017, https://knowhow.ncvo.org.uk/your-team/your-development/professional/time/time, accessed 19 May 2021.
3. Pamela Grow, 'Time management for the one-person nonprofit fundraising office' [web article], www.pamelagrow.com/1900/time-management-for-the-one-person-nonprofit-fundraising-office, 28 November 2011.
4. Lorraine Arams, 'Fifteen time management tips for nonprofit professionals' [web article], Charity Village, https://charityvillage.com/fifteen_time_management_tips_for_nonprofit_professionals, 20 September 2010.
5. 'Project schedule development: Planning the timing and sequence of project activities' [web page], MindTools, 2018, www.mindtools.com/pages/article/newPPM_71.htm, accessed 19 May 2021.

6. Nathan Black, 'A brief history of time(lines): Henry Gantt and his revolutionary chart' [blog post], OnePager, https://www.onepager.com/community/blog/a-brief-history-of-the-gantt-chart, 14 October 2014.
7. Brett Harned, 'How to use milestones in project management' [blog post], TeamGantt, www.teamgantt.com/blog/the-how-and-why-of-using-milestones-in-your-project-plan, 5 November 2018.
8. 'How do voluntary organisations spend their money?' [web page], NCVO, 2020, https://data.ncvo.org.uk/financials/spending, accessed 19 May 2021.
9. Simone Joyaux, 'Fundraising on a budget and understanding the fundraising budget' [web article], *Nonprofit Quarterly*, https://nonprofitquarterly.org/2016/09/08/fundraising-on-a-budget-and-understanding-the-fundraising-budget, 8 September 2016.
10. Valerie Morton, 'Targets for fundraisers work best when accompanied by good management and a realistic timescale' [web article], Third Sector, www.thirdsector.co.uk/targets-fundraisers-work-best-when-accompanied-good-management-realistic-timescale/fundraising/article/1222674, 6 January 2014.
11. Kate Sayer, 'Can a fresh approach to budgeting cure charities' fundraising woes?' [blog post], NPC, www.thinknpc.org/blog/can-a-fresh-approach-to-budgeting-cure-charities-fundraising-woes, 11 August 2015.
12. Adrian Sargeant and Elaine Jay, *Fundraising Management: Analysis, planning and practice*, London, Routledge, 2014.
13. David Ainsworth and Andrew O'Brien, *Being Honest and Telling the Truth Well about Fundraising Costs: Project 20 fundraising investment* [PDF], The Showcase of Fundraising Innovation and Inspiration (SOFII), 2017, https://sofii.org/images/Articles/The-Commission-on-the-Donor-Experience/Project-20.Fundraising-investment.pdf, accessed 19 May 2021.
14. Ken Burnett, 'The "less cost is best" fallacy' [blog post], www.kenburnett.com/Blog35Lesscostisntbest.html, 26 March 2013.
15. *Beyond Reserves: How charities can make their reserves work harder* [PDF], ACEVO/Chartered Institute of Fundraising/Charity Finance Group, 2012, https://cfg.org.uk/userfiles/documents/CFG%20resources/CFG%20Publication/SV_Reserves_Final.ashx.pdf, accessed 19 May 2021.
16. Ken Burnett, 'Should charities invest in fundraising rather than in stocks, shares and bonds? Or is this really the wrong question?' [blog post], www.kenburnett.com/Blog74Investment.html, 27 February 2017.
17. 'Third Sector Awards 2015: Fundraising team – winner: Battersea Dogs & Cats Home' [web article], Third Sector, https://www.thirdsector.co.uk/third-sector-awards-2015-fundraising-team-winner-battersea-dogs-cats-home/fundraising/article/1365257, 23 September 2015.
18. Dan Pallotta, 'You say you want impact' [web article], *Harvard Business Review*, https://hbr.org/2010/11/you-say-you-want-impact.html, 22 November 2010.
19. Adrian Sargeant and Elaine Jay, *Fundraising Management: Analysis, planning and practice*, London, Routledge, 2014.

CHAPTER EIGHT
Monitoring and controlling your fundraising performance

Introduction

By this point, you should have a good idea of how to develop a strategy and plan for its delivery. In this chapter, we consider how you know whether your plan is on track and how you might plan for when something – almost inevitably – doesn't go as expected. This can be done through a form of performance management. Performance management is a series of processes which enable organisations to optimise their strategy.[1] It is part of a sequence encompassing goal-setting, performance measurement, performance diagnosis, and identifying risk (and taking corrective action).[2] Having already discussed goal-setting in previous chapters, this chapter focuses on the remaining three elements.

Performance measurement

When planning performance measurement, it is important to be clear what will be measured and why. Consider precisely what needs to be measured. Having too few measures can mean that important information or trends are missed. Similarly, having too many can mean that important information is lost in the noise and that valuable resources are used up in unnecessary measurement.

> **Case study: Operation Smile**[3]
> Digital channels lend themselves particularly well to testing different approaches and easily and clearly tracking results. Operation Smile, a charity which provides cleft palate surgery worldwide, worked with digital agency Manifesto to recruit new donors across Facebook, paid search, Google Ad Grants and the Google Display Network.
>   Operation Smile and Manifesto focused on raising the average value per gift by recruiting high-value donors. They then developed an extensive testing plan, which started by focusing on the charity's landing page. They looked at the optimum content, length and structure of the page, and refined the donation journey. This testing increased the percentage of people giving by 114% compared with the year-to-date average.

> They then focused on testing different images and descriptions of patients. Using Facebook's A/B testing tool in its Ad Manager toolbar (which allows you to run two different versions of an advert concurrently) to test copy featuring different patients increased the return on advertising spend by 9% from the year-to-date average, while testing the advertising copy increased the average conversion rate by 173% from the year-to-date average.

Once you've decided what to measure, you can choose which metrics will be your key performance indicators (KPIs). In fundraising, KPIs are the most important metrics. They most closely track or predict your overall fundraising performance and, therefore, link to the objectives you've already set. For example, if your strategy is to become more customer-centric, you might use a customer satisfaction index as a basic metric to identify high customer satisfaction, and then choose high customer satisfaction as one of your KPIs.[4]

There are likely to be two types of KPI you need to consider:

- **Leading KPIs** are those that you can examine to understand whether you're on track to meet your objectives.

- **Lagging KPIs** are those that show you whether you've achieved your objectives.

For example, if you have an objective to increase your event income by 10%, then event registration is likely to be a leading KPI that will indicate whether you are going in the right direction. However, events income will be a lagging KPI that shows you whether, ultimately, you have achieved your objective.

Ideally, the experience of completing your audit (see chapters 1 and 2) and the early stages of developing your fundraising strategy (see chapter 4) should have helped to highlight which metrics are likely to be the most important to your future success and thus should become KPIs.

Good KPIs have 12 key characteristics. They should be:

- **Aligned:** they should fit into your broader strategy.

- **Owned:** an individual or team will be accountable for the outcomes.

- **Predictive:** they should ultimately predict value for your organisation.

- **Actionable:** they should provide data that will allow action to be taken.

- **Few in number:** they should provide quality rather than quantity of information.

- **Easy to understand:** they should not be based on obscure internal calculations.

- **Balanced and linked:** they should reinforce rather than contradict each other.

- **Able to trigger changes:** as well as being actionable, they should be capable of triggering further changes.

- **Standardised:** they should be based on standardised rules and calculations.

- **Context driven:** they should enable people to track progress over time by including targets and thresholds.

- **Reinforced with incentives:** they may link to organisational reward systems.

- **Relevant:** they should be regularly renewed and refreshed to make sure that they are still relevant.[5]

There's also the old adage that what gets measured gets done. Your choice of metrics and KPIs can affect your – or your colleagues' – fundraising practice. So, for example, if your fundraising is only measured against the number of donors recruited, then the temptation might be to recruit as many donors as possible without thinking about whether they are likely to continue to give to your organisation over the longer term, or indeed how much they might give in the future.

When choosing metrics, you should therefore think about which ones will truly add value to both your donors and your organisation. A wide range of metrics are used by different organisations and types of fundraising, but some examples include:

- the number of donors making a second gift;
- donor retention over multiple years;
- trusts and foundations making a larger gift;
- companies that want to extend partnerships with your organisation.

Case study: Arkansas Children's Foundation[6]

Arkansas Children's Foundation provides a great example of how to develop and then carefully review activity metrics which support an organisation's wider fundraising programme.

The foundation (which raises funds to support two children's hospitals, a research facility, clinics, and state-wide outreach programmes in the USA) took a strategic look at its fundraising success

CHAPTER EIGHT **MONITORING AND CONTROLLING YOUR FUNDRAISING PERFORMANCE**

as it planned for a large fundraising campaign. It was obvious that to support the growth of its work, the foundation needed to continue to develop its fundraising practice.

With talented leadership and staff, strong donor relationships, a committed board and a track record of success, Arkansas Children's Foundation saw that in order to continue growing, it needed to formalise its system of tracking and analysing metrics.

When the foundation began the process of developing its metrics, gift officers and the leadership tracked many key performance indicators that have since been fine-tuned or reconsidered. Once a metrics-tracking habit had been built among staff and a set of data was available to analyse, gift officers and the leadership looked at the effects of metrics measurement on fundraising, the efficacy of the tracking systems, and the efficiency of the process and applications. The philosophy of the leadership at the time was to first focus on activity, then zero in on the *right* activity. Through this deep work, they identified five key individual metrics and three key team metrics related to fundraising activity which are still tracked today. The individual metrics were: number of prospects added to the pipeline, number of contacts, number of face-to-face visits, number of solicitations submitted and total revenue. The team metrics were: solicitations of $1 million or more, total revenue from gifts of $1 million or more, and cost per dollar raised as a foundation.

Back at the beginning, when Arkansas Children's Foundation embarked upon a revamp of its metrics-tracking, everyone involved had understood that this work would be a key driver for increased philanthropic revenue. And they were right. Looking at averages over six years, the foundation saw a 53% increase in revenue during one period and another 51% increase during the next period, bringing them to the success they see today.

Metrics are ingrained into the culture of the foundation to the point where staff at all levels are versed in departmental goals and participate in metrics-related conversations. The board expects continued success and stays up to date on progress through the story told by metrics.

Two metrics to be particularly aware of in the fundraising context are return on investment (ROI) and lifetime value (LTV). ROI expresses the ratio between how many pounds you have raised or will raise for every pound you have spent or will spend on any given fundraising activity. For example, breaking even on any given activity gives you a ROI of 1.0. (See page 25 in chapter 2 for more detail on the importance of ROI in fundraising data.) LTV is the income raised from a donor over their lifetime with an organisation, minus the cost of servicing that donor – essentially, their net contribution.

Often, LTV will be a more appropriate metric to use, or at least to consider in conjunction with ROI. For example, if you're recruiting new donors to your organisation, you'll often lose money in the process. If donor recruitment (often referred to as 'acquisition') were considered purely in terms of ROI, you wouldn't do it – but eventually you'd be in trouble, as your organisation would have no new supporters to replace those who, for whatever reason, stop supporting you. Similarly, it could be argued that ROI, when considered on its own, encourages you to think in a way that prioritises short-term results – focusing on the outcome of each activity rather than thinking about how it might affect the longer-term relationship with the donor. Therefore, a blend of both methods may well be appropriate.

Return on investment and lifetime value

Calculating return on investment

You can calculate your return on investment (ROI) for an income stream, project or product by dividing its income by its full costs, including, for example, associated salary costs. For instance, if you raise £150,000 from charitable trusts and foundations in a financial year and the cost of doing so (your trust fundraiser, its associated costs and other central costs) is £30,000, your ROI for trust fundraising is £150,000 divided by £30,000, which is £5, so your ROI is 5.0.

Calculating lifetime value

Lifetime value (LTV) is a predictive measure used to determine a supporter's donations over their giving lifetime minus the costs of serving them. LTV calculations also discount future income. We apply discounting because money in the hand is worth more than anticipated income in the future – so, £100 today is worth more than £100 in a year's time and much more than £100 in, say, five years' time. The analysis also allows you to compare potential future income with how you might alternatively invest that money. For instance, if you took £150 and invested it at a 10% interest rate, you would have £165 in a year's time. The example that follows shows how the calculation is made.

Consider a group of event participants who support your organisation for an average of three years each. During that time, they might (again, on average) participate in three events at a value of £200 per year, purchase Christmas cards at £25 per year and participate in your annual raffle at £15 per year. The gross value to your organisation of each of these supporters over the average time they support you is therefore £720, or £240 per year. The cost of raising these funds over the three-year period then needs to be subtracted to identify the total net value of this supporter type. This would include the cost of all communications, such as newsletters, fundraising packs, merchandise and solicitations. The cost of these activities might be £90 per year, making the annual net value of each supporter £150. See table 8.1 for a summary of this scenario.

However, it becomes more difficult to predict costs and revenue the further ahead you look, because of factors such as inflation, risk and estimating accuracy. The value of £150 in three years' time may be less in real terms than it is today, so you need to apply a discount to the projected future income. In order for your comparisons to be valid, you must use the same discount rate for all supporters. The formula for this calculation is:

$$LTV = \sum_{i=1}^{n} C_i (1 + d)^{-i}$$

Although it might look daunting at first, the formula is relatively easy to apply. It calculates the net value (C, which stands for revenue minus cost) of each future year's fundraising activities and then applies a discount rate (d) that increases the further away you are from the present day (i represents the number of years into the future up to n, which stands for the expected duration of the relationship in years). You can see the resulting analysis in table 8.2.

TABLE 8.1 EXAMPLE DATA FOR A LIFETIME VALUE CALCULATION

	Year 1	Year 2	Year 3	Total over three years
Income				
Event sponsorship (including Gift Aid)	£200	£200	£200	£600
Raffle	£15	£15	£15	£45
Christmas cards	£25	£25	£25	£75
Total income	**£240**	**£240**	**£240**	**£720**
Costs				
Event recruitment and support	£75	£75	£75	£225
Raffle mailing and fulfilment	£2	£2	£2	£6

FUNDRAISING STRATEGY

	Year 1	Year 2	Year 3	Total over three years
Christmas card mailing and fulfilment	£4	£4	£4	£12
Annual newsletter	£2	£2	£2	£6
Annual thank-you phone calls	£5	£5	£5	£15
Email updates	£2	£2	£2	£6
Total costs	**£90**	**£90**	**£90**	**£270**
Net value	£150	£150	£150	£450

TABLE 8.2 EXAMPLE LIFETIME VALUE CALCULATION

	Year 1	Year 2	Year 3	Total over three years
Discount rate formula (This shows how the discount factor in the row below is derived, based on a 10% discount.)	n/a	=1/(1.1)^1	=1/(1.1)^2	
Discount factor	1.00	0.909	0.826	
Discounted value of 10% per year (net value × discount factor)	£150	£136.36	£123.97	£410.33

Note: the number in the formula in brackets is the discount rate (in this case 10%) applied to each year. The carat symbol (^) is the power function and that relates to the number of years you are projecting ahead. Year 1 is not discounted because it is your baseline starting point, year 2's discount rate is to the power of 1 because it is one year on from that starting point and year 3's discount rate is to the power of 2 because it is two years on from that starting point.

After you're clear about what you will measure, you should also consider:

- **Who will measure it?** Ensure that measurement is stipulated within appropriate roles and that everyone is clear about their responsibilities to help the process of measurement run smoothly.

- **How will it be measured?** Make sure that you have systems and processes set up before your strategy is implemented, or early in the implementation, to enable you to measure progress quickly and easily.

- **Where will it be measured?** Establish where your data will be stored and how measurements will be communicated to the relevant people. Depending on the systems available in your organisation, you might be able to set up a fundraising dashboard (see figure 8.1 for an example of a fundraising performance dashboard, based on an agreed scale of 0 to 10 for each of the metrics) or management information system which would display KPIs and progress towards them. It may be helpful for internal communication and staff motivation to consider how you will portray this information so that it is not just a series of numbers in tables. Graphs and charts can be particularly helpful.

- **When will it be measured?** Collect measurements at the appropriate times so that you are able to take appropriate actions as and when needed. Conversely, don't measure too often, as this can become a waste of resources. Over-measurement – looking at the data daily just because it's there, for example – can be dangerous. Analysing KPIs monthly or quarterly smooths out peaks and troughs and tells a clearer story.[7]

FIGURE 8.1 FUNDRAISING PERFORMANCE DASHBOARD

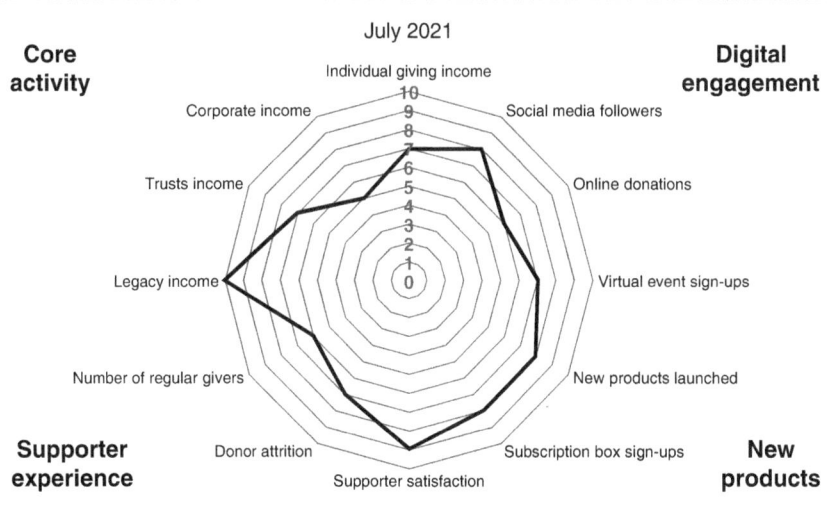

Tracking retention of fundraising staff

One metric you might not immediately think of as being important to your fundraising success is fundraising staff retention. However, it's a metric you may want to consider tracking. A survey by well-being specialist Claire Warner found that the average amount of time fundraisers had been in their role was two years and eight months, and only 40% saw themselves as still working in the same organisation in two years' time.[8] High levels of turnover in fundraising teams can be surprisingly costly – a study in the USA estimated that the cost of losing a fundraiser was 117% of their annual salary. The calculation included the obvious costs, such as recruitment advertising, but also the sometimes hidden costs associated with someone being less productive in their first year of employment as they learn the ropes, and the initial support that their colleagues need to give them as they're getting started.[9] Moreover, regular turnover of fundraising staff is likely to be particularly problematic when trying to maintain relationships with donors, which are often crucial to the role. With those issues potentially arising every couple of years, the costs of high fundraiser turnover for non-profit organisations are likely to run into the millions.

So why is turnover so high? Findings from the USA suggest that the top three reasons fundraisers leave their role are, firstly, money, with many leaving to obtain a higher salary; secondly, lack of opportunity to progress their careers; and, finally, a clash of culture, with many fundraisers feeling under pressure to bring in money now as opposed to developing longer-term relationships.[10] In the UK, pay isn't commonly cited as the key reason; instead, fundraisers note few opportunities for development, lack of training, a need for flexible working and wanting a new challenge as the most common reasons for moving on.[11]

Therefore, given potential losses associated with high fundraising turnover, you could not only track fundraiser retention but also monitor levels of staff satisfaction, explore reasons for leaving and, wherever possible, put in place solutions to mitigate any issues that are revealed.

Performance diagnosis

Once you've started to collect your metrics, you can consider *why* these results occurred, particularly in relation to those metrics that you've identified as KPIs. While of course you'll want to understand why targets haven't been met, it can be equally (if not more) useful in your future planning to understand why they've been exceeded.

Understanding what's causing a problem – or leading to a success – is a vital part of the process. Indeed, it's been said that solving a problem is easy: it's identifying what caused it in the first place that's difficult. As well as considering obvious issues, such as people forgetting to take a particular action, technical issues and so on, you can look at problems in the context of five different areas:

- **Mission and goal:** how well does your goal (or the objective you are trying to achieve) fit within the context of the macro-environmental forces you have identified (see page 11)?

- **System design:** do your organisational systems support the goal?

- **Capacity:** does your organisation have the leadership, people and infrastructure necessary to achieve the goal?

- **Motivation:** do your policies, culture and reward systems support the goal?

- **Expertise:** do you have people with the expertise to deliver the goal?[12]

One of the abilities that distinguishes great fundraising leaders is the quality of thinking they apply when dealing with problems. They are able to move from seeing specific pieces of information (data) to identifying broader trends or patterns to understanding the fundraising or broader organisational systems that might be driving those patterns.[13] When confronting problems, therefore, it can help to take a step back to consider how those problems might interrelate with other issues, and what can be done to address the root cause rather than always jumping in to address the surface-level issue.

Case study: How Unicef uses complaints to alter behaviour

As well as understanding why particular results have been achieved, organisations need to take action as a result. Vicky Johnson, Head of Supporter Care at Unicef UK, explains how the organisation not only monitors data but also analyses it and uses it to change behaviour:

> We use metrics to track complaints. Through text giving and follow-up phone calls we were getting a lot of complaints about too many calls and people not liking being called. We started to closely monitor trends to alter our behaviour accordingly. Using complaints management to spot trends and alter behaviours has led to less complaints. As every complaint is tracked we record this against things like the telephone agency used, the geographical location of the supporter, the type of fundraising etc. If we receive more than three complaints on a specific topic this triggers more specific investigation into that issue. We increased the detail of reporting which allowed us to see if, for example, complaints were triggered by an increase in calls being made or just the perception of this. This led us to change certain behaviours such as only doing one call per day and leaving a message.

> We **measure** supporter satisfaction though ratings left on live chat, online ratings on Facebook and we are going to start measuring on telephone and text too.
>
> We use three categories of **measurement** – compliments, comments and complaints.[14]

Identifying risk (and taking corrective action)

Before you launch your fundraising strategy, it's sensible to think about what might go wrong and put measures in place to either avoid the risks altogether or minimise their impact. This process is often referred to as risk management. The first stage in the process is to understand what the risks might be. In order to be thorough in your risk assessment, it may help to consider the following types of risk:

- **Strategic:** might the world you're operating in change and thus invalidate your approach? For example, are you equipped to cope with changes in technology or downturns in the economy?

- **Financial:** might costs be higher than you have planned for? Or income lower than you've budgeted?

- **Logistical:** might it be difficult to deliver projects on time? Is there a risk that your processes might not be adequate?

- **Reputational:** is it possible that your reputation or brand might be damaged?

- **Relational:** might relationships with key stakeholders be affected?

- **Compliance and/or ethical:** are you fully compliant with laws and codes of practice? Are these likely to change? Do you have a clear ethical fundraising policy in place?

- **Other:** for example, weather conditions or chances of injury.

You can record risks using a simple template like the one in table 8.3.[15] The template contains columns for you to record the results of an evaluation of each risk. It can be sensible to do this according to how likely each risk is to occur and how severe its impact might be (giving a score out of, say, 5 for each). The total score is derived from multiplying the likelihood score by the impact score. (You may come across alternative methods of scoring risks, for example where extra weight is given to impact.) You can then use each risk's total score to plot it on a matrix like the one shown in figure 8.2, which places each risk into one of the established categories. Note that some of the risks that get the same total score might end up in different categories, depending on the levels of likelihood and impact. For example, a risk that is highly probable yet insignificant would be considered less serious than a risk that is remote but has extreme/catastrophic impact.

You might decide that for risks that are minor or insignificant, you do not need to take any action (although of course things do change, and it's worth revisiting each risk regularly). However, for those issues that are more likely to occur and/or have a higher potential impact, you might want to put contingencies in place to mitigate or avoid the risk altogether. These contingencies can go in the 'Actions' column of the template.

TABLE 8.3 EXAMPLE RISK TEMPLATE

No.	Risk event	Cause(s)	Impact	Owner	Score			Actions
					Likelihood	Impact	Total	
1	Garden party event called off	Bad weather	Loss of income	Fundraising manager	3	4	12	Make marquee available
2								

FIGURE 8.2 EXAMPLE RISK MATRIX

Impact							
	Extreme/catastrophic	5	5	10	15	20	25
	Major	4	4	8	12	16	20
	Moderate	3	3	6	9	12	15
	Minor	2	2	4	6	8	10
	Insignificant	1	1	2	3	4	5
			1	2	3	4	5
			Remote	Unlikely	Possible	Probable	Highly probable
			Likelihood				

■ major or extreme/catastrophic risks;   ▨ moderate or major risks;   ▢ or ░ minor or insignificant risks.

Risk registers and your board

Guidance from the Charity Commission for England and Wales, *Charities and Risk Management (CC26)*, advises trustees on how they should think about, and of course mitigate, risk in their organisations.[16] Further guidance – 'Charity governance, finance and resilience: 15 questions trustees should ask' – helpfully provides questions that trustees should ask regarding finance and resilience.[17]

There is a danger, though, in assessing potential fundraising activity merely through a lens of risk: the board may not balance the risk assessment with a good understanding of the potential benefits of the activity.[18] Conversely, good risk management and controls from your board should actually enable your organisation to innovate and take risks appropriately, as set out in robust guidance from accountancy firm Sayer Vincent and the Charity Finance Group.[19]

We recommend that it is best to operate a 'no surprises' policy, which means looking at these issues with your board on a regular basis and encouraging them to focus at a strategic level, rather than on operational detail.

Contingency planning

You could seek to mitigate the risks you identify in four ways:[20]

• For minor or unlikely risks, you might decide to **tolerate** them – i.e. do nothing unless the risk level changes.

• For the most serious risks, you might **terminate** them – i.e. decide that the risk is so high, you'll stop the activity.

• For medium risks, you could either **treat** them, perhaps by having a contingency plan in place or by taking actions to lessen them, or **transfer** them, perhaps by using an insurance policy to transfer the risk to a third party.

Given the risk of things going wrong with your plan, it's sensible to have a contingency plan – a plan B – in place which would state what you might do to address the risks you have identified as treatable. Indeed, a lack of adequate contingency planning and trouble-shooting mechanisms has been argued to be the most important factor in predicting project failure.[21]

The first step in contingency planning is to decide when a contingency plan would need to kick in. You could do this by setting appropriate tolerances in your metrics: for example, it might be acceptable for expenditure to go over budget by 10% before corrective action needs to be taken.

Once you know what would trigger the contingency plan, you can lay out who would need to do what and when, and who would need to be kept informed of progress.

The type of contingency plan needed will vary from charity to charity and from fundraising activity to fundraising activity. However, as a general principle, it can be sensible to build in some contingency time and financial resources. Therefore, as part of this exercise, it can be helpful to revisit your schedule and budget (see chapter 7).

Conclusion

In this chapter, we focused on monitoring and controlling fundraising performance. In order to monitor performance, we considered what needed to be measured (or metrics) and why, focusing on KPIs as the most important metrics in fundraising success. We also discussed two commonly used metrics – ROI and LTV – and the particular importance of LTV in giving a fuller, longer-term picture of success. Alongside using metrics to define what has happened, we discussed the importance of diagnosing why it happened so that appropriate changes can be implemented. Finally, we discussed how understanding the different types of risk will allow you to take appropriate risks (in order to move your fundraising forwards) and take appropriate action to mitigate avoidable risks.

Once you've determined how you will monitor performance, diagnose problems and control risk, you've essentially completed the process of developing your strategy. The next challenge is to implement it effectively, a process discussed in the next chapter.

Notes

1. Mark Frolik and Thilini Ariyachandra, 'Business Performance Management: One truth', *Information Systems Management*, vol. 23, 2006, pp. 41–8.
2. Michael Morris, Leyland Pitt and Earl Honeycutt, *Business-to-Business Marketing: A strategic approach*, London, Sage, 2001.
3. Based on 'Recruiting new donors with data driven strategy' [web page], Manifesto, 2020, https://manifesto.co.uk/our-work-examples/recruiting-new-donors-with-data-driven-strategy, accessed 19 May 2021.
4. Mark Frolik and Thilini Ariyachandra, 'Business Performance Management: One truth', *Information Systems Management*, vol. 23, 2006, pp. 41–8.
5. Harold Kerzner, *Project Management, Metrics, KPIs and Dashboards*, Hoboken, Wiley, 2011.
6. Based on Lindsay Doerr, '"If you can't measure it, you can't manage it": Using metrics to strengthen your fundraising program' [blog post], CCS Fundraising, https://ccsfundraising.com/if-you-cant-measure-it-you-cant-manage-it-using-metrics-to-strengthen-your-fundraising-program, 10 October 2019.
7. Zach Shefska, 'Fundraising metrics for beginners: How and when to measure' [web page], Causevox, 2017, www.causevox.com/blog/fundraising-metrics-beginners, accessed 19 May 2021.

8   Claire Warner, 'How well are your charity's fundraisers?' [web article], Civil Society Media, www.civilsociety.co.uk/fundraising/how-well-are-your-charity-fundraisers.html, 8 June 2020.
9   'Staff turnover: The 3 reasons fundraising professionals leave' [blog post], Sumac, www.sumac.com/blog/nonprofit-management-and-hr/penelope-burk-on-the-3-reasons-fundraising-professionals-leave, 19 August 2013.
10 *Ibid.*
11 Claire Warner, 'How well are your charity's fundraisers?' [web article], Civil Society Media, www.civilsociety.co.uk/fundraising/how-well-are-your-charity-fundraisers.html, 8 June 2020.
12 Adapted from Richard Swanson, *Analysis for Improving Performance: Tools for diagnosing organizations and documenting workplace expertise*, San Francisco, Berrett-Koehler, 2007.
13 Adrian Sargeant and Jen Shang, *Great Fundraising* [PDF], Clayton Burnett, 2013, https://www.philanthropy-institute.org.uk/reports-sign-up, accessed 19 May 2021.
14 Commission on the Donor Experience, 'CDE project 16 section 2: Case examples, tips and links' [web page], The Showcase of Fundraising Innovation and Inspiration (SOFII), https://sofii.org/article/cde-project-16-section-2-case-examples-tips-and-links, 30 April 2017.
15 Rebecca Bowry and Alyson Pepperill, *Risk Management for Charities: Setting your risk appetite – supplementary guidance,* Institute of Risk Management, 2016, www.theirm.org/media/4519/irm-charities-sig-setting-risk-appetite-final-updated-051016.pdf, accessed 19 May 2021.
16 *Charities and Risk Management (CC26)* [PDF], Charity Commission for England and Wales, 2010, www.gov.uk/government/publications/charities-and-risk-management-cc26/charities-and-risk-management-cc26, accessed 19 May 2021.
17 See 'Charity governance, finance and resilience: 15 questions trustees should ask' [web page], Charity Commission for England and Wales, 2012, www.gov.uk/government/publications/charity-trustee-meetings-15-questions-you-should-ask, accessed 19 May 2021.
18 Nicola Pritchard, 'Trustees and risk taking' [blog post], NPC, www.thinknpc.org/blog/trustees-and-risk-taking, 24 May 2019.
19 See *Rethinking Risk: Beyond the tick box* [PDF], Sayer Vincent/Charity Finance Group, 2016, www.sayervincent.co.uk/wp-content/uploads/2016/06/Rethinking-Risk.pdf, accessed 19 May 2021.
20 Rebecca Bowry and Alyson Pepperill, *Risk Management for Charities: Setting your risk appetite – supplementary guidance,* Institute of Risk Management, 2016, www.theirm.org/media/4519/irm-charities-sig-setting-risk-appetite-final-updated-051016.pdf, accessed 19 May 2021.
21 Jeffrey Pinto and Samuel Mantel, 'The Causes of Project Failure', *IEEE Transactions on Engineering Management*, vol. 37, no. 4, 1990, pp. 269–76.

CHAPTER NINE
Getting internal buy-in and managing change

Introduction
You've worked through a thorough process of crafting a strategy, from assessing your organisation's environment (chapters 1 and 2) to identifying key audiences and messages (chapters 4 and 5) to planning out exactly what will happen and when (chapters 6 and 7) and how you'll know whether you have been successful (chapter 8). But two other key aspects of implementing your strategy are to ensure others buy into it and to manage any changes the strategy requires. This involves the following elements:

- **Leadership:** are the right people in place to facilitate delivery of the strategy?

- **Culture:** does the strategy align with the dominant culture of your organisation?

- **Resources:** are the finances and staff available to deliver the strategy?

- **Structure:** does the team structure facilitate the strategy? Is there a good mix of people with the skills to deliver?

- **Control:** are there processes in place to make sure what needs to happen actually happens?

- **Skills:** are the right skills in place for delivery?

- **Development:** do the right people know about and accept your strategy? Is there a commitment to it as a living document that will be adapted as time moves on and things change?

- **Information systems:** are there systems in place to supply the relevant management information to the relevant people at the relevant times?[1]

You will have already explored these issues when you completed the internal analysis part of your audit; however, you may wish to check that circumstances haven't changed. This chapter begins by examining how to get internal buy-in and then moves on to consider different types of change and how to implement them.

Getting internal buy-in

The successful implementation of your strategy will probably rely to some degree on the actions of different people from across your organisation, such as the finance team to process donations, the communications team to share messages and service delivery colleagues to generate case studies. Therefore, you're likely to need the buy-in of various individuals and teams. Indeed, a survey from the business world found that companies that made above-average profits achieved buy-in for their strategy from all levels of the organisation.[2]

If you're a director of fundraising or are solely responsible for fundraising, you might need buy-in from a whole range of stakeholders: the trustees, the CEO, fellow directors, staff and volunteer team members to name just a few. If you're responsible for a particular area of fundraising, there might be fewer people you need to engage (for example, your senior manager and the people you manage), but it's unlikely that you'll be delivering your strategy without input or support from anyone else. It will be helpful, therefore, to identify who those key stakeholders might be and to consider their likely reactions to your plans.

We would recommend conducting a stakeholder mapping exercise to identify how to communicate with different internal audiences (see figure 9.1).[3] Essentially, this matrix enables you to consider your stakeholders in terms of their power over your work and their interest in it at this moment in time (you may want to try to 'move' them once you've done your analysis):

- **High power and high interest:** these people need to be managed closely. In practice, this might mean that you will need to engage with someone like the chair of trustees throughout the process of strategy development and implementation.

- **Low power and low interest:** these people only need to be monitored. An example might be a member of an advisory group focusing on service delivery (rather than fundraising) who has not yet shown any interest in your fundraising work.

- **High interest and low power:** these people need to be kept informed. An example might be a more junior member of staff (say, a service delivery team member) who has shown a keen interest in your organisation's fundraising work.

- **High power and low interest:** these people need to be kept satisfied. For example, another member of the board whose primary interest is around service delivery might require enough information to feel confident that the process of developing a fundraising strategy is being completed professionally and ethically, but they may be less interested in the detail of the strategy.

FIGURE 9.1 STAKEHOLDER MAPPING[4]

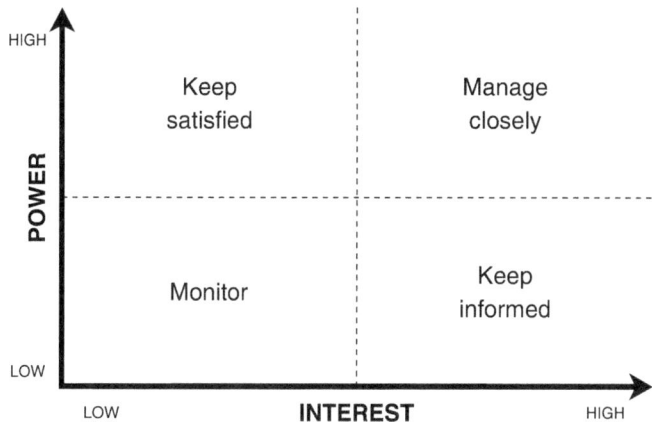

It is also likely that your strategy will involve some element of change, whether small tweaks to the way things are done now, experimenting with new fundraising channels or a radical overhaul of your fundraising approach. It is therefore advisable to consider the magnitude of change your strategy is likely to bring and how that can be managed successfully.

Relatively minor changes involving a small number of people are likely to be fairly easy to implement – although do consider whether a change that feels small to you might feel much bigger to someone else (for example, if you're removing a responsibility that they particularly enjoy). In contrast, strategies that require larger-scale changes – however carefully thought through – can be much more difficult to implement and are likely to be met with considerably more internal resistance. The following sections consider how you might achieve buy-in from various stakeholders in your organisation and how you might go about implementing change successfully.

Involving others

As mentioned in the introduction to this book, one element of achieving buy-in is to make sure stakeholders feel genuinely involved in the process of strategy development. Indeed, co-creation is essential in allowing people to feel invested in the outcome of a strategy. It is prudent not to present your important internal stakeholders with the finished article of a fundraising strategy. They will almost certainly not buy in to it if you do so, especially if you would like them to change anything about the way they do things. Essentially, the process of developing your fundraising strategy is just as important, if not more so, than any document you produce as a result of it.

There are a number of ways you could achieve this involvement. For example:

- interviews with key stakeholders, ensuring that you incorporate their language into the strategy;
- holding a strategy workshop;
- giving key individuals ownership of different elements of the strategy;
- holding regular meetings to discuss implementation.[5]

Communicating your strategy

Poor communication of a strategy, particularly where it affects a large number and/or wide range of people, can hinder effective implementation. Indeed, lack of communication has been cited as one of the key reasons that strategy implementations fail.[6] The suggestions below bring together expert insights into communicating about strategy:

- **Communicate the core of your strategy.** The process of strategy development, as you've seen, involves the collection and consideration of a large amount of information. It's unlikely that many of your colleagues will want to engage with every bit of detail, so it's important to be able to communicate the really key information succinctly. Single-page diagrams, charts or infographics can be especially helpful in conveying the essence of what you're trying to do.

- **Share the underlying insights.** Although not everyone will want to engage with all of the detail, there may well be core insights – for example, research into donors' needs or feedback from key supporters – which will help to powerfully make the case for your strategy. Identifying and sharing those insights can help people to understand the rationale for the strategy.

- **Avoid vague statements.** It's easy for vague statements such as 'we need to grow our fundraising' to be misinterpreted. It works better to use wording such as 'we need to increase the number of donors giving by direct debit by 25%'. Being clear and concrete can help people to understand and buy in to the approach – and, ultimately, use it to guide their own decisions and actions.

- **Share stories.** As seen in fundraising communication more generally, stories can be a powerful means of sharing your message. Framing elements of your strategy (such as 'why change is needed') as a story can make communication about it more effective.

- **Use a variety of channels.** Using multiple channels to communicate your strategy internally can help you to reach different people and reinforce your message. You might, for example, attend colleagues' meetings, add information to your intranet and make sure you mention progress in more casual conversations.[7]

These general insights can be considered alongside the sections below, which discuss how to achieve buy-in from various audiences and how to manage change successfully.

Getting leadership buy-in

In order to progress a strategy, it's normally vital to get agreement from senior people in your organisation, whether trustees, senior management or your line manager. Researchers Susan Ashford and James Detert carried out a study into obtaining internal buy-in from senior management and found that a combination of seven tactics was particularly effective in getting senior people to buy in to a new idea. The seven tactics are:

- **Tailor your pitch to the receivers.** Understand managers' goals, values and knowledge and tailor your messages accordingly.

- **Frame the issue.** Think about how to package the idea that you're presenting for the audience. For example, show how your ideas would help your organisation to meet its wider strategic goals (i.e. beyond fundraising).

- **Manage emotion.** Manage your own emotions when presenting ideas and think about how those ideas might affect others emotionally. For example, you might feel angry or frustrated about a challenging internal situation – but expressing those negative emotions might make your pitch feel like a complaint rather than a solution. Do your best to present ideas in a way that can mitigate negative emotions.

- **Choose the right time.** A good time to present your idea might be when wider organisational priorities change or when a new staff member joins (for example).

- **Involve other people.** Think particularly about those who might help you in building a compelling case or who might be trusted by the audience you're trying to convince.

- **Adhere to norms.** For example, present information in the way that is preferred within your organisation.

- **Suggest solutions.** Be prepared to offer an answer whenever problems are highlighted.[8]

Ashford and Detert found that using all seven tactics accounted for 40% of the difference between gaining senior management buy-in and not gaining it. They point out that the tactics draw on three types of knowledge: strategic (understanding broader organisational goals), relational (understanding the key players in the decision and how they might react) and knowledge of organisational norms (for example, how the organisation presents information). If you're a fundraiser seeking to implement change, then doing your best to understand the wider strategy, the people you're working with and the norms at play in your organisation could be a very sensible move.

Managing change
Assessing change

As well as needing to get buy-in from senior management, you are likely to have to make the case for change with your colleagues. The first stage of managing change is to understand why people might be opposed to it. Why might you encounter resistance when drawing up and implementing your fundraising strategy, and what can you do about it? It can be helpful to consider whether your stakeholders are in any of the following overlapping 'camps':

- **'I don't get it'**: essentially, there is an information gap here. How can you improve communication with them and check that you understand each other?

- **'I don't like it'**: there is an emotional or values gap between you. How can you build excitement about the project and remove fear of it?

- **'I don't trust you/the organisation'**: in this case, you probably need to address a relationship gap. To do so, you will need to consider how to build or rebuild mutual trust and repair damaged relationships.

It can also be helpful to step back and assess the type and level of change you are proposing. Change can be mapped onto a matrix like the one shown in figure 9.2.[9] The first step is to consider how radical the proposed change will be. Is it likely to be an evolution (for example, an adaptation of existing processes) or a revolution (for example, the introduction of a new fundraising team)? The second consideration is whether the change is core or peripheral – in other words, whether it will affect colleagues' perceived core roles.

As figure 9.2 illustrates, changes which are radical and affect core work are likely to cause considerably more disturbance and risk than those which are incremental and affect peripheral aspects of a role. Where your change falls on this continuum will suggest the level of internal effort necessary to implement it.

FIGURE 9.2 CHANGE MATRIX

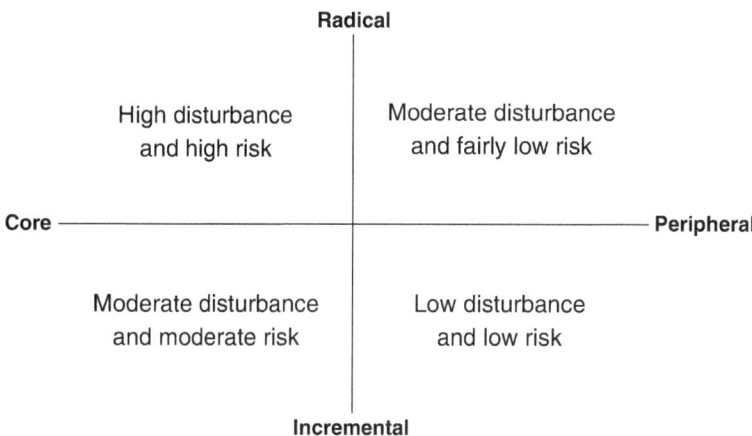

Achieving small-scale change

If you want to introduce a relatively low-risk and low-disturbance change – for example, tweaking an existing process in your team – this might be relatively straightforward to achieve. It will also likely be easy to resolve issues that colleagues are already keen to see addressed. However, it still may be worth considering how such changes are framed to achieve a straightforward implementation.

The Behavioural Insights Team is an organisation which considers how behavioural science might be applied in areas of public policy. It has produced a simple framework for applying behavioural approaches, and this framework could also be applied in framing messages around change. The framework is known as EAST, which stands for:

- **Easy:** make something the default option, reduce the difficulty of taking part and simplify messages.
- **Attractive:** make something attractive (for example, colourful and rewarding).
- **Social:** show how other people take part and make the action social.
- **Timely:** prompt people at the right time and demonstrate the immediate benefits.[10]

For example, following the EAST acronym, you could communicate how a change in the process of sending out thank-you letters might make someone's role easier (easy/attractive), has already been adopted by another team (social) and can be implemented when other work is quieter (timely).

Case study: Getting buy-in from digital teams at St Mungo's[11]

Legacy fundraising is one area where buy-in from other teams can be challenging to achieve, with concerns about raising the twin taboos of death and money. However, homelessness charity St Mungo's provides a good example of how its legacy and digital teams worked together.

In 2011, a survey conducted by the Office for National Statistics found that only 52% of people aged 65–74 had used the internet in the past three months. By 2019, this figure had grown to 83.2%.[12] With growing numbers of older people using digital channels, legacy fundraisers will increasingly need to have conversations in the digital space. However, legacy fundraisers can often find it challenging to engage colleagues working in digital communications and fundraising, often because of the taboos mentioned above.

Despite this, digital and legacy staff at St Mungo's worked together successfully to increase engagement with legacy supporters through digital channels. Their top tips for a successful partnership include:

- **Involve digital teams in planning from the outset.** At St Mungo's, the digital team often has insights from other campaigns that are equally applicable to legacy campaigns and will be able to provide valuable insight. It's also helpful for them to feel that they have equal involvement in a legacy campaign.

- **Respect each other's expertise.** Both parties bring useful skills and knowledge to the table. The digital team was particularly able to advise around testing different adverts, audiences and strategies.

- **Build your skills – and your profile.** Working together on the campaign was a great opportunity for the legacy team members to build their digital skills. And working so closely with digital colleagues was helpful in building relationships across the wider fundraising and communications team.

- **Make use of testing.** Using digital channels enabled the legacy team to make tweaks to its campaign in real time. The digital team was an invaluable part of this process, supporting the legacy team in maximising return on investment and making the case for additional future investment.

- **Keep the relationship going.** The teams took time at the end of the campaign to reflect on the results and to consider what they would do differently next time.

Achieving broader internal change

For larger changes, or for changes where people may be more resistant, you may need to develop what is essentially a complementary internal plan to sit alongside your strategy. The point of this plan is to 'sell' the strategy to an internal audience. John Kotter, a leading authority on leadership and change, has developed an eight-step process for leading change. You may find this a useful structure if you are attempting to implement larger-scale changes:

1. **Create a sense of urgency.** Communicate how important it is to act as soon as possible – for example, does your organisation have a limited time to act on an opportunity that you've identified? You could communicate urgency by sharing compelling new evidence, such as donor testimonies about their experience.

2. **Build a guiding team.** Bring on board the right people to lead the change within your organisation.

3. **Get the vision right.** Rather than presenting a set of numbers and reams of analysis, paint a clear picture of the desired future so that stakeholders can see where the strategy will take your organisation.

4. **Communicate for buy-in.** Ensure that everyone in your organisation can see why change is needed and what it might involve. Enable people to ask questions and put forwards their ideas as part of the process.

5. **Empower action.** Remove any barriers (such as organisational processes) that are stopping people from embracing the change.

6. **Create short-term wins.** Focus on some easy wins so people can see examples of change working.

7. **Don't let up.** Keep the changes happening until the vision is achieved.

8. **Make change stick.** Seek to reinforce the new way of doing things – for example, by celebrating successes and showing how results are linked to new behaviours.[13]

Implementing larger-scale change can be challenging, so it may be worth exploring the wider literature on change management in more detail, particularly if you anticipate internal resistance or other challenges to implementing your approach.[14]

Case study: Growing internal participation and a culture of giving at the University of Arkansas at Little Rock[15]

Alongside appeals to potential external supporters, some institutions reach out to their internal staff as potential donors. In the university world, demonstrating high levels of internal participation in giving can be a way to leverage gifts from other individuals and foundations.

The University of Arkansas at Little Rock ran a campaign that increased staff participation in giving from 6.5% to 42% over three years. The university began by forming a campaign committee involving representatives from across the organisation. Members were chosen strategically – for example, a professor of marketing and people with experience in working with or volunteering for non-profits.

The committee began by focusing on the goals of the internal campaign and quickly agreed that the focus should be on participation, rather than money raised, with everyone asked to donate according to their means. The campaign was timed to run from September – the start of academic year – through to Thanksgiving, an appropriate date to be able to thank participants. However, gifts would continue to be accepted until December (the end of the calendar year but also an important time for giving).

The committee set up tables outside the university's opening assembly and outside the all-university luncheon (a regular event) where they could talk to people about the campaign and hand out pledge cards. The chancellor also profiled the campaign in his speech, demonstrating senior-level support.

All units across campus (academic as well as administrative) selected an ambassador who solicited employees in their unit for campaign contributions. The committee additionally hosted a kick-off breakfast for all campaign ambassadors to motivate them and provide some guidance on what they could do practically to support the campaign. Another event was held halfway through the campaign to re-energise people and enable them to discuss and share ideas with colleagues digitally.

People who took part in the campaign were enabled to donate to whatever aspect of the university's work mattered most to them. Often that meant projects which were taking place in their own department.

Communication was an important part of the campaign. The wider university was informed about progress against the participation goals as the campaign developed. At the close of the campaign, a celebratory event was held to thank everyone who had given, with all donors being given tickets to a basketball game. All donors were given a lapel pin which, as well as recognising their contribution, made the campaign visible to a wider audience.

Of course, when we're thinking about internal buy-in in fundraising, we're not generally talking about staff giving – much more commonly, we're considering wider staff support of the process of developing and implementing a strategy. And indeed, many organisations will feel uncomfortable about asking staff members to give. However, this case study provides good examples of how several of John Kotter's principles can be used in practice.[16]

Conclusion

The process of strategy development and implementation is never simple, and success can never be guaranteed. In terms of actually delivering the strategy on the ground, a number of the challenges you encounter may be internal, as you try to implement new ways of approaching fundraising within your organisation. However, if you can ensure that colleagues in fundraising and the wider organisation are on board with your plans, and put in place appropriate processes to ensure that change is managed successfully – following the advice in this chapter – then your fundraising strategy will be more likely to succeed.

Notes

1. Graeme Drummond, John Ensor and Ruth Ashford, *Strategic Marketing: Planning and control*, Abingdon, Butterworth Heinemann, 2008.
2. 'Mindsets: Gaining buy-in to strategy' [web page], BTS, 2020, www.bts.com/news-insights/articles/mindsets/mindsets-gaining-buy-in-to-strategy, accessed 19 May 2021.
3. The exercise was originally developed by Aubrey Mendelow and later adapted using a range of dimensions, including power and interest combination introduced by academics Colin Eden and Fran Ackermann. See Aubrey L. Mendelow, 'Environmental Scanning: The impact of the stakeholder concept', in *International Conference on Information Systems Proceedings*, Association for Information Systems, 1981, http://aisel.aisnet.org/icis1981/20, accessed 19 May 2021; and Colin Eden and Fran Ackermann, *Making Strategy*, London, Sage, 1998.
4. Based on Colin Eden and Fran Ackermann's adaptation of Aubrey Mendelow's matrix, see Colin Eden and Fran Ackermann, *Making Strategy*, London, Sage, 1998.
5. Ted Jackson, 'Strategy implementation: How to get leadership buy-in' [web page], ClearPoint Strategy, 2017, www.clearpointstrategy.com/strategy-implementation-leadership, accessed 19 May 2021.
6. Erica Olsen, 'Strategic implementation' [web page], On Strategy, 2021, https://onstrategyhq.com/resources/strategic-implementation, accessed 19 May 2021.

7   Susan Ashford and James Detert, 'Get the boss to buy in' [web article], *Harvard Business Review*, https://hbr.org/2015/01/get-the-boss-to-buy-in, January–February 2015; Georgia Everse, 'Eight ways to communicate your strategy more effectively' [web article], *Harvard Business Review*, https://hbr.org/2011/08/eight-ways-to-energize-your-te, 22 August 2011.
8   Susan Ashford and James Detert, 'Get the boss to buy in' [web article], *Harvard Business Review*, https://hbr.org/2015/01/get-the-boss-to-buy-in, January–February 2015.
9   Gus Pennington, *Guidelines for Promoting and Facilitating Change* [PDF], LTSN Generic Centre, 2003, https://s3.eu-west-2.amazonaws.com/assets.creode.advancehe-document-manager/documents/hea/private/id296_promoting_and_facilitating_change_1568036853.pdf, accessed 19 May 2021. © 2003 Advance HE. All rights reserved.
10 *EAST: Four simple ways to apply behavioural insights* [PDF], Behavioural Insights Team, 2015, www.bi.team/wp-content/uploads/2015/07/BIT-Publication-EAST_FA_WEB.pdf, accessed 19 May 2021.
11 Based on Howard Lake, 'How legacy and digital fundraising teams can work together more effectively' [blog post], UK Fundraising, https://fundraising.co.uk/2018/04/05/legacy-digital-fundraising-teams-can-work-together-effectively, 5 April 2018.
12 'Internet users, UK: 2019' [web page], Office for National Statistics, 2019, www.ons.gov.uk/businessindustryandtrade/itandinternetindustry/bulletins/internetusers/2019, accessed 19 May 2021.
13 John Kotter, *Leading Change*, Boston, Harvard Business School Press, 1996.
14 See, for example, John Kotter, *Leading Change*, new edition, Boston, Harvard Business School Press, 2012 and Chip Heath and Dan Heath, *Switch: how to change things when change is hard*, London, Random House, 2011.
15 Based on Jamie Byrne, 'Forming a Culture of Giving: A case study in successful university internal fundraising', *Urban and Metropolitan Universities in Tomorrow's Economy*, vol. 16, no. 4, 2005, pp. 71–84.
16 John Kotter, *Leading Change*, Boston, Harvard Business School Press, 1996.

CHAPTER TEN
Fundraising ethics

Introduction

A key part of both developing and implementing a fundraising strategy is making sure that your approach is legal and ethical. The concept of legality is a relatively easy one: it means ensuring that fundraising is carried out in a way that is permitted by law. On the other hand, ethics – or the moral principles that influence our behaviour – is a more difficult concept.

In his white paper on fundraising ethics, Ian MacQuillin, director of the fundraising think tank Rogare, says that ethics tell us how to live a good life and also outline our rights and responsibilities. Importantly for fundraising practitioners, ethics help us to discuss and decide what is right and wrong and to make moral decisions: differentiating between good and bad.[1] MacQuillin also points out that ethics can operate at three levels:

- **meta-ethics:** where ethical judgements come from;
- **normative ethics:** ethical theories of how to live;
- **applied ethics:** the application of ethical theories to specific issues – in our case, fundraising.

In this chapter, we concentrate on ethical theories (normative ethics) and what they might mean in practice (applied ethics).

> **How did regulation in England and Wales change after 2015?**
>
> Following investigations into fundraising practice in 2015, new requirements (covering England and Wales) were introduced via the Charities (Protection and Social Investment) Act 2016.
>
> The first requirement states that where a charity uses a professional fundraiser or commercial participator to raise funds, the compulsory written agreement must include:
>
> - the scheme for regulating fundraising or recognised fundraising standards that will apply to the professional fundraiser or commercial participator in carrying out the agreement;
> - how the professional fundraiser or commercial participator will protect the public, including vulnerable people, from unreasonably

> intrusive or persistent fundraising approaches and undue pressure to donate;
>
> - how charities will monitor the professional fundraiser or commercial participator's compliance with these requirements.[2]
>
> The second requirement states that charities must include the following information about their charity in their trustees' annual reports:
>
> - approach to fundraising;
> - work with, and oversight of, any commercial participators/ professional fundraisers;
> - fundraising conforming to recognised standards;
> - monitoring of fundraising carried out on [the charity's] behalf;
> - fundraising complaints;
> - protection of the public, including vulnerable people, from unreasonably intrusive or persistent fundraising approaches, and undue pressure to donate.[3]

Ethical theory and the fundraising profession

MacQuillin argues that there is a lack of ethical theory available to fundraisers to support their ethical decision-making. He points to a relative lack of academic articles and books which deal directly with fundraising ethics, particularly when compared to commercial marketing.[4] He argues that this is a problem on several levels:

- It may lead to poor practice, such as the UK fundraising crisis of 2015 (see the case study on page 188).

- Ethical practice is an important part of being a 'profession', so a perceived lack of foundational ethics could damage fundraising's claim to 'profession-hood'.

- There is a lack of a firm foundation from which fundraising can push back against what might be seen as inappropriate regulation.[5]

The Fundraising Regulator and the Fundraising Preference Service

The Fundraising Regulator

The Fundraising Regulator took over the regulation of fundraising in 2016. It is an independent organisation which regulates fundraising in England, Wales and Northern Ireland (see www.fundraisingregulator.org.uk). In Scotland, fundraising regulation is overseen by the Scottish Fundraising Standards Panel (see www.goodfundraising.scot).

The Fundraising Regulator was set up following a review into the self-regulation of fundraising by Sir Stuart Etherington, then chief executive of NCVO. The review sought to identify what measures were required to rebuild public trust in charity fundraising. The regulator is funded through a voluntary levy on charities which spend £100,000 or more each year on fundraising.

The regulator:

- has responsibility for setting the fundraising standards outlined in the Code of Fundraising Practice;
- investigates complaints from the public about fundraising when complaints can't be resolved by the charities themselves;
- runs the Fundraising Preference Service (described in more detail below);
- publishes a directory of all the organisations that have registered with it.[6]

The Fundraising Preference Service

The Fundraising Preference Service allows people to manage the fundraising communications they receive from charities registered in England, Wales or Northern Ireland. People can use the service via telephone or a website to select the specific charity or charities with whom they want to manage their communications as well as to choose the communication channels they wish to stop.

The Code of Fundraising Practice says that charities must stop sending direct marketing communications to individuals once a request has been received (either directly from an individual or via the Fundraising Preference Service). If a charity repeatedly ignores a request, then the Fundraising Regulator may:

- name that charity on its website as being in breach of the code;
- notify the Information Commissioner's Office of a breach of the Data Protection Act 2018;
- notify the Charity Commission for England and Wales of a governance issue.[7]

Ethical dilemmas and the role of regulation

It is likely that during the process of developing a fundraising strategy, and almost inevitably when delivering that strategy, you will be faced with an ethical dilemma. An ethical dilemma is where you have to choose between two courses of action where the following three statements are all true:

- Both are permissible.
- Both have potentially good consequences.
- Both have potentially bad consequences.[8]

To give an example commonly used in discussions of fundraising ethics, you may be offered a donation where you have an ethical concern about the (perfectly legal) business practices of the donor. The donation might help your service users by funding the services you deliver, but it might also harm your organisation – and in the longer term your service users – through negative PR.

At the most fundamental level, when considering ethical dilemmas, charities must adhere to the relevant law (which may differ across England and Wales, Scotland and Northern Ireland). Across the UK, charities must also follow the standards outlined in the Fundraising Regulator's Code of Fundraising Practice and the Chartered Institute of Fundraising's rulebooks for street and door-to-door fundraising.[9] In some cases, making a decision on an ethical challenge can be relatively easy – for example, in the UK, if you were asked to include misleading information in fundraising materials, you could decline as that course of action would be specifically prohibited by the Code of Fundraising Practice.[10] Indeed, if we use the definition above, this wouldn't even really count as an ethical dilemma, as it's not permissible.

Examples of legislation that affects fundraising

This is a small snapshot of some of the legislation which, most commonly, fundraisers need to be aware of:

- **Street collections:** if you want to collect money on the street or in a public place, you'll need a street collection licence (England and Wales), a public charitable collection permit (Scotland) or a permit from the Police Service of Northern Ireland.

- **Gambling:** fundraising from gambling (raffles, lotteries, etc.) must be undertaken in line with the Gambling Act 2005. For example, if you run a lottery that has proceeds which exceed £20,000 for a single draw or aggregated proceeds which exceed £250,000 in a calendar year, then you will need a licence from the Gambling Commission.

- **Data protection:** the General Data Protection Regulation came into effect in May 2018. Fundraisers must ensure they are using personal data in line with one of the legal bases for processing personal data: most commonly in fundraising, legitimate interest or consent.

- **Licensing:** selling alcohol at a charity event is likely to need a licence from the local authority.

However, many issues which fundraisers will need to address in their day-to-day fundraising practice fall into greyer areas: they are difficult or troubling but are not specifically addressed within law or existing codes of practice. Additionally, as MacQuillin points out, the UK's Code of Fundraising Practice can sometimes be vague. For example, it states that charities must not fundraise in a way that places undue pressure on a person to donate, but it doesn't clearly lay out what amount or type of pressure is 'undue'.[11]

In practice, what often happens in fundraising is that we consider each ethical dilemma as and when we encounter it. Making important decisions in these circumstances may well be challenging, however, as emotions may be running high, your organisation may be under pressure to bring in funding, available time may be limited and it might be challenging to access the evidence needed to support decisions.

Alternatively, therefore, you could develop a policy or guidelines by considering in advance what might happen in specific scenarios. For example, should you take a major donor's preference into account when developing a specific service? Would it be appropriate to seek out a relationship with a particular company? Is it OK to use a specific image of a service user? Should you only contact a donor if you have their consent, even if consent is not required by law?

However, the difficulty of thinking this way about ethics is that, given the enormous variety of charities and the way the world is rapidly changing, it's virtually impossible to come up with a full list of all possible scenarios, which means that every new situation could throw up a new set of ethical questions. As a first step, therefore, relatively early in the fundraising strategy planning process, it can be helpful to extrapolate from these individual scenarios into a set of higher-level or overarching ethical questions that are likely to cover a much broader range of circumstances. Then, you can consider each through the lens of ethical theory, as explained in the next section.[12]

Categorising ethical dilemmas

Ethical questions are likely to fall into one of three key areas: *who* is approached, *how* people are approached, and individual versus organisational ethics. Although it is unlikely to be exhaustive, considering the list of higher-level questions below should cover many eventualities:

1. **Where are our red lines on who we approach or receive resources from for our cause?**

   - How do we decide whom we cannot (proactively) approach?

   - How do we decide whom we cannot (reactively) accept money from for our cause?

   - Underpinning both of the above decisions, how do we decide how far we should enquire into potential donors' assets and income? For example, what if, several hundred years ago, an individual donor's family assets were increased through investments in slavery?

   - How are the above decisions affected by the type of donor? For example, does it make a difference whether a donor is giving a gift while alive or has left a legacy? Are there different considerations when receiving support from a company, an individual and a charitable trust?

   - How are the above decisions affected by the requirements of donors, such as anonymity or benefits requested?

2. **Where are our red lines on how we approach people for resources for our cause?**

   - When asking for support, how do we balance the rights of non-donors, potential donors, donors and service users?[13] This could include the right not to be asked versus the right to receive a charity's services, and how donors and service users should be described, referenced, acknowledged and credited.

   - When asking for support, how do we balance the needs of current and future service users?[14] For example, this may affect decisions on investing in long-term and short-term sources of income.

   - When crafting our asks, how do we balance the needs of our charity with those of the wider sector? For example, suggesting we spend nothing on fundraising could benefit our charity but make others' ratio of spending on the cause versus fundraising appear comparatively poor.

- How do we decide what other factors should be considered in ethical decisions (for example, privacy, choice, dignity and capacity to make an informed choice)?

3. **How do we balance the morality/ethics of internal stakeholders (for example, fundraisers, trustees and volunteers) with the morality/ethics of the organisation?**

- How do we balance fundraising which conflicts with a staff member's or volunteer's sense of morality/ethics but does not directly conflict with the morality/ethics of the charity?

- How do we recognise when internal stakeholders' sense of morality and/or ethics is emotional (a reaction based on their current state of mind) and when it is rational (an established moral case based on considered arguments)?

Considering ethical standpoints

Once you have considered challenges like the ones in the above list, you can start to examine them through the lens of ethical theory. In doing this, it's helpful to consider which ethical theory would be most appropriate as a basis for your organisation's fundraising practice. In a 2016 paper on fundraising's ethical landscape, MacQuillin analyses previous writing on fundraising ethics.[15] He first suggests that, at their heart, fundraising's ethical theories fall into two camps:

- **Consequentialist:** this is about acting in the way that produces the overall best outcome.

- **Deontological:** this is about doing the right thing according to a point of moral principle, regardless of outcome.

Sitting underneath those headings are three theories specific to fundraising: trustism, donor-centrism and service of philanthropy. To these MacQuillin adds a fourth theory – rights-balancing.

Trustism

Trustism says that fundraising should be conducted in a way that maintains public trust. MacQuillin points out that protecting public trust is likely to be one of the first things a fundraiser will think about in practice. It is one of the underlying reasons for the existence of codes of conduct and it plays an important role in giving to charities. This is a consequentialist idea as it means the ethics of an action should be judged according to the action's effect on public trust.

According to MacQuillin, trustism says that 'a fundraising act would be ethical if it promoted, sustained, protected or maintained public trust, and unethical if it damaged these things'.[16]

Donor-centrism

In the donor-centrist approach, donors are put at the heart of charity communications. This could be because doing so raises more money for an organisation or because the organisation believes that it is the right thing to do. MacQuillin therefore gives two similar but distinct meanings of donor-centrism, both equally valid:

- Fundraising is ethical when it 'gives priority to the donor's wants, needs, desires and wishes, provided that this maximises sustainable income for the nonprofit'.

- Fundraising is ethical when it 'gives priority to the donor's wants, needs, desires and wishes'.[17]

The first is a consequentialist idea, because the ethics is contingent on the fact that focusing on the donor's wants and needs actually does raise more money. The second version is deontological, because it says fundraisers should focus on donors as a point of principle.

> ### The Community-Centric Fundraising movement
>
> Often (incorrectly, in our view) portrayed as diametrically opposed to donor-centric fundraising models, Community-Centric Fundraising (see https://communitycentricfundraising.org) centres on the community that an organisation serves rather than its donors. The movement, based in Seattle, USA, has developed ten principles through which its followers 'aspire to transform fundraising and philanthropy, so that they are co-grounded in racial and economic justice'.[18] These principles are set out in chapter 11 (see page 172). We believe that this is a helpful challenge to more 'traditional' views of fundraising which risk perpetuating rather than challenging the power structures that are in place and which can be damaging for the communities that charitable organisations exist to serve. We suggest that any discussion of fundraising ethics needs to consider these issues particularly carefully.

Service of philanthropy

The service of philanthropy approach suggests that ethical fundraising enables donors to give in a way that's meaningful to them. MacQuillin therefore says that according to this ethical theory, 'fundraising is ethical when it brings meaning to a donor's philanthropy'.[19] This is a deontological notion – it's the right thing to try to bring meaning to a donor's philanthropy (even if you are ultimately unsuccessful).

Service of philanthropy is an important ethical principle to be aware of but is less helpful than the other two theories in practice. Therefore, it is not considered further in this chapter.

Rights-balancing

MacQuillin goes on to argue that the various pre-existing ethical theories related to fundraising miss out one of fundraising's key stakeholders, whom fundraisers owe an important duty to: the charity's service user, who will be disadvantaged if an organisation's fundraising is not successful. He points out that many ethical dilemmas in fundraising are about balancing the needs of donors with what fundraisers need to do on behalf of their service users, yet the pre-existing theories don't deal directly with that tension. He therefore proposes a new theory of fundraising ethics – rights-balancing.[20]

According to MacQuillin's rights-balancing theory, 'fundraising is ethical when it balances the duty of fundraisers to solicit support on behalf of their beneficiaries, with the right of the donor not to be subjected to undue pressure to donate'.[21]

In order to use the theory in practice, MacQuillin argues that you should acquire the best available evidence about any dilemma and then seek to strike a balance that works in the best interests of your service users over the longer term while considering the rights of donors. He gives the example of telephone fundraising and argues that if the evidence suggests that people dislike the practice because of poor fundraising practice, then the theory might argue that improving practice (for example, through training) would be in the best interests of service users.[22]

> ### Why all this theory?
>
> Although it might seem like there's a lot of theory in this chapter, it's impossible to 'do' ethics without theory. Take, for example, the ethical question 'Is it ever acceptable to make people feel guilty about not giving?' In a discussion among a group of fundraisers, someone might say it's wrong to make people feel bad. Whether they realise it

or not, that person is applying a set of general principles or, in academic terms, a theory (in this case, the theory of donor-centrism). If someone then adds that making someone feel guilty will hurt their charity's reputation, that's trustism. If someone else counters that donors don't feel so bad compared to the good the money does, then that's rights-balancing ethics. In our day-to-day practice, we might not realise that applying these general principles is how we make ethical decisions; however, by making this process conscious, we can make better decisions in a more efficient way.

Spending time early on engaging with ethical theory is ultimately likely to be a time-saver for you. If you can establish the underlying principles of your ethical decision-making, it'll make actually taking those decisions a lot easier. Sometimes discussions about dilemmas can go around in circles with people each bringing their individual subjective points of view. For example, if you were to debate accepting a gift from a company, the finance director might come at the decision from the perspective of providing income to deliver services, the CEO might focus on public trust and the fundraiser on the impact on relationships with donors. These different ways of focusing can ultimately make it very challenging to come to a final decision, as there will be strong arguments in different directions. However, if you've established an underlying ethical position (for example, 'we base our ethical decisions on what's most likely to enhance public trust'), then you have a set of criteria against which you can weigh arguments. Like other management theories, ethical theories are ultimately designed to help you make better, more objective decisions.

As well as saving time, engaging with theory can help you to make ethically consistent decisions. Choosing a theory-based underlying ethical position means that you will weigh up each decision against the same criteria. Without that underlying theory, there's a risk that individual arguments will be drowned out by those voices that speak the loudest or the individuals who have the most power.

Earlier in this chapter, we suggested some overarching ethical questions which, we hope, will encompass the majority of the ethical decisions you need to make (see page 154). Engaging with these overarching questions can enable you to consider key decisions ahead of when ethical dilemmas actually occur – and therefore make better decisions. If you wait until ethical dilemmas actually arise to engage with ethical thinking, then you're likely to end up making decisions under time pressure, clouded by emotions and without the opportunity to gather data to support your decisions. Spending some time in advance to work through how you might address these questions in your specific organisation can mean that you're equipped to deal with individual dilemmas as and when they arise.

Examples of ethical positioning

Returning to the core questions we outlined above (see page 154), once your organisation has considered the ethical theory which will underly its fundraising practice, it can begin to explore each question through the lens of that theory.

The following sections consider the question 'How do we decide whom we cannot (reactively) accept money from?' through the lenses of trustism, donor-centrism and rights-balancing. It's important to stress, however, that the ideas explored below are not necessarily the absolute right considerations – there's no such thing as 'right' in ethics – and it will be down to your organisation to consider each question from your own perspective. It's also key to remember the importance of gathering the best available evidence in each case – by thinking through each issue in advance, it might be possible for your organisation to undertake research among your donors and other stakeholders where evidence is sparse.

Trustism

As described above, trustism would suggest that fundraising is unethical when it damages public trust. However, the challenge with its application as an ethical theory is that it is difficult to correlate public trust with specific fundraising acts.[23] In considering the question above, you would need to attempt to use the best available evidence to ascertain whether the risk of accepting gifts from certain sources would result in enough public outcry to stop others giving. Perhaps – if there is no better evidence – this could be done by considering how publicly noteworthy acceptance or rejections of donations have played out in the past.

To give just one example, in 2015 the Girl Scouts of Western Washington returned a donation of $100,000 which specified that it couldn't be used to support transgender girls. The gift arguably conflicted with the organisation's statement that the Girl Scouts are for every girl. The Girl Scouts set up a crowdfunding campaign to replace the lost money, and this raised more than three times the original donation.[24] Although a simplification, it could be argued that the rejection of the original gift bolstered public trust (if we see the replacement giving as a proxy for trust) and, therefore, that organisations may have a good argument for rejecting gifts which conflict with their core approach.

Donor-centrism

Donor-centrism focuses on the donor's needs and wants. Considering who an organisation cannot accept money from through this lens may, at first, seem relatively simple: if we are putting the donor first, then it could be argued that rejecting a donation would cause hurt and upset. Therefore, the vast majority of donations should be accepted. Similarly, fundraisers should usually adopt the fundraising practices that most appeal to their donors and not do the things that irk them (such as using 'intrusive' methods of fundraising or using a proportion of their gift to fund overheads).

However, the issue may be more complex when we consider not just the donor making the donation but the wider donor base. Using the Girl Scouts example above, it could be argued that the majority of existing donors would subscribe to the organisation's approach – and, therefore, that accepting a donation which goes against this might cause upset to that majority (and, in the consequentialist version of this theory, lead to a loss of donations). The hurt and upset caused to one rejected donor might therefore be outweighed by the hurt and upset caused to the wider base of existing or potential donors if their donation were accepted.

Rights-balancing

The rights-balancing approach seeks to balance the rights of donor and service user. Sticking with the Girl Scouts example, when considering the rights of the donor, the donor-centrist analysis above would suggest that it would be right to return the donation, given the potential hurt and upset caused to the wider donor base. However, if we adopted a rights-balancing approach, we would also need to consider the impact on the organisation's service users. Accepting this donation could have a positive impact on service users by enabling additional services to be provided. However, we would also need to consider the negative impact on a sub-group of service users – transgender girls – who wouldn't be able to access those services. In this case, the Girl Scouts organisation decided that the negative impact of having to adopt a discriminatory approach to a group that already often suffers societal discrimination outweighed the potential positives of accepting the donation.

In practice, many rights-balancing ethical dilemmas may be less nuanced than this, being simple trade-offs between what donors want and what service users need. For example, donors might not want a certain proportion of their gift spent on overhead costs. However, since an organisation cannot run without its overhead costs being met by donors, it is in service users' interests that donors contribute to overheads. Therefore, the (claimed) right to have all of a donation go to funding projects is counterbalanced by the service users' needs for a functional, sustainable organisation working on their behalf.

Ethical fundraising policy

Once your organisation has considered its core approach to ethics and worked through the overarching questions we outlined in the previous section (and any others relevant to your particular situation), you may wish to create an ethical fundraising policy. This can help to communicate your organisation's ethical position both internally (to staff and volunteers) and externally (to your wider audiences).

Some of the issues your policy might cover include:

- **The core principles that underlie your approach to fundraising:** the British Library, for example, says that its fundraising will always be truthful, accurate in how it describes the library's activities and the intended use of funds, and respectful of the dignity and privacy of its users.[25]

- **What you will and won't do in terms of fundraising:** in its ethical policy, Farleigh Hospice states that its fundraising will comply with relevant legislation, that it won't pay commission to anyone fundraising on its behalf and that it won't pass on personal information to a third party.[26]

- **Who you will and won't take money from:** for example, animal charity Wild Welfare says that it won't accept donations from anyone who might use their relationship with the charity to deflect criticism from their own involvement in animal welfare issues.[27]

- **Commitments to your donors:** in its ethical policy, the University of Bath lays out a number of commitments to its donors, including their right to information, right to a choice over how they're contacted and right to anonymity (if requested).[28]

Applying your approach and dealing with tricky cases

The final step when considering your organisation's approach to ethics is to apply your agreed approach as and when real-life ethical dilemmas occur. Having worked through the issues above, you should, we hope, have addressed the ethical scenarios that you are most likely to confront. However, it's very possible that other dilemmas might arise, not foreseen or included here, or that the particular circumstances will require more in-depth consideration.

In those circumstances, it might be helpful to work through MacQuillin's decision-making model (see figure 10.1).[29] The model first asks whether a proposed activity is legal and code compliant. If not, it shouldn't be attempted. If the answer is a very clear 'yes', you will be fine to go ahead. If it's unclear, then you face an ethical dilemma.

If you're faced with an ethical dilemma, the model recommends firstly considering your organisation's overarching ethical theory (as described above) and secondly considering the different stakeholders or issues involved – service users, donors, public trust, and any others. Each of those should be weighted, compared and balanced, and a decision made (which could also be a decision *not* to do something). That decision can

FUNDRAISING STRATEGY

then be evaluated and tested for its impact on the stakeholders or issues described above. If it still holds up, you can go ahead with the course of action. Any decision you make should be occasionally re-evaluated to make sure it continues to hold up as and when circumstances and/or stakeholders change.

FIGURE 10.1 ROGARE'S DECISION-MAKING MODEL

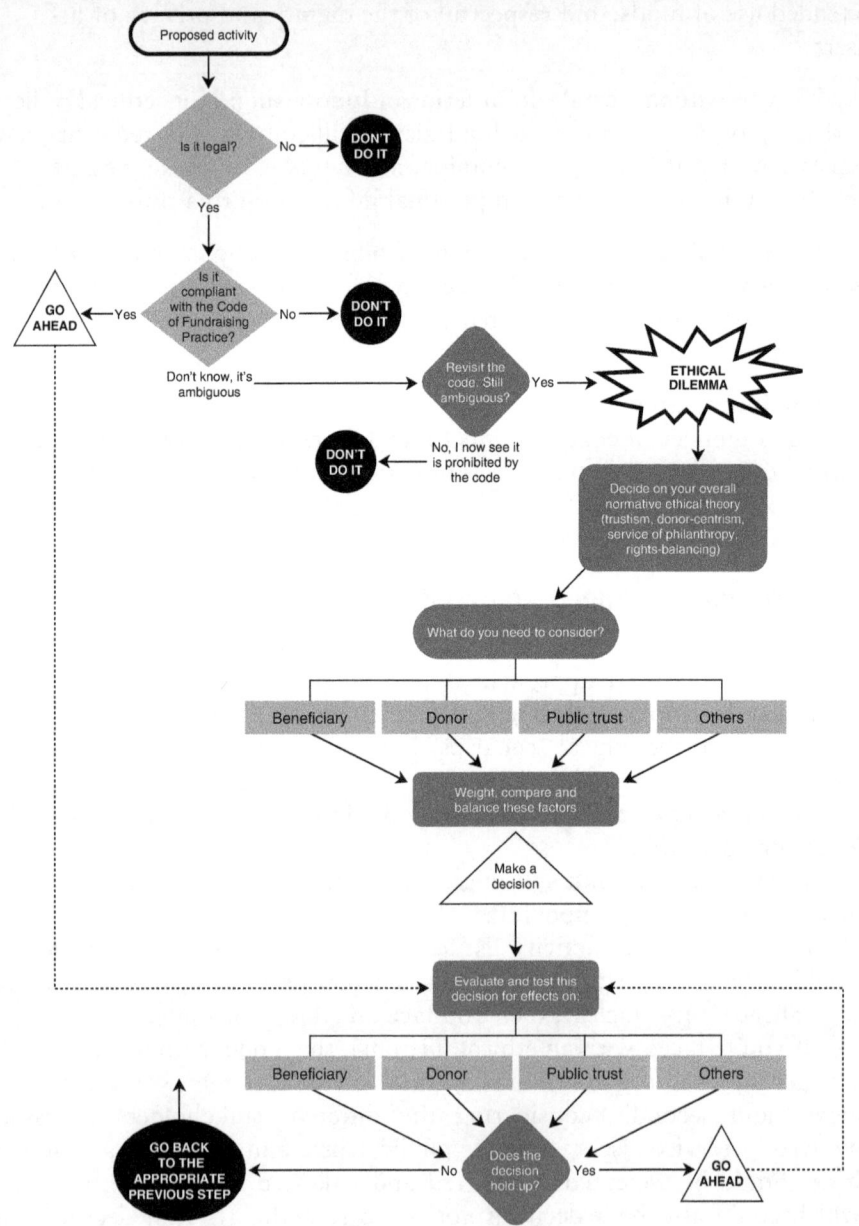

Fundraising complaints

If a member of the public has a complaint about a charity's fundraising practice, they should initially raise the issue with the charity concerned. If the complaint cannot be resolved, it can be taken to the Fundraising Regulator (for charities registered in England, Wales or Northern Ireland) or to the Scottish Fundraising Standards Panel (for charities registered in Scotland).

Every quarter, the Fundraising Regulator publishes summaries of its investigations, and decisions around the most serious complaints are published in full.[30] The Fundraising Regulator also publishes an annual complaints report. In 2018/19, it received 737 complaints and carried out 82 investigations (a number of complaints were outside the regulator's remit or raised prematurely). In more than half of these cases, the regulator identified a breach of the Code of Fundraising Practice.

The report also includes details of complaints handled by charities themselves. Charities reported 20,541 complaints, 6% lower than the previous year. Analysis showed that addressed direct mail, door-to-door fundraising and outdoor events were the types of fundraising that generated the most complaints.[31]

Conclusion

As argued throughout this chapter, it is important to ensure that fundraising is carried out legally and ethically. It's arguable that, in the past, fundraisers may have been hampered in their ethical decision-making by a lack of solid ethical theory, which is particularly important where ethical dilemmas fall into a grey area not specifically addressed by law or the Code of Fundraising Practice.

In recent years, MacQuillin has codified the pre-existing theory and also suggested a new theory: rights-balancing fundraising ethics.[32] You can draw on these theories when pulling together a strategy. As described in this chapter, it may be helpful when developing a strategy to consider overarching ethical questions before you even encounter specific ethical dilemmas. Your organisation may then like to pull together an ethical values statement, informed by this thinking. Finally, as and when ethical dilemmas are encountered, MacQuillin's decision-making framework can provide a process for thinking through the key issues and coming to an informed ethical conclusion.[33]

In the next chapter, we discuss some of the key contemporary issues affecting fundraising. Along with any ethical considerations, these issues should be taken into account when drafting, reviewing and updating your strategy.

Notes

1. Ian MacQuillin, *Rights Stuff: fundraising's ethics gap and a new theory of fundraising ethics* [PDF], Rogare, 2016, https://df618d67-1d77-4718-ac14-01d78db8f9d0.filesusr.com/ugd/8bc141_c83e86ee3ec1450eb0177cbb8f345433.pdf, accessed 19 May 2021.
2. 'Charities Act 2016: New fundraising rules' [web page], Charity Commission for England and Wales, www.gov.uk/government/news/charities-act-2016-new-fundraising-rules, 1 November 2016.
3. *Ibid*.
4. Ian MacQuillin, 'Fundraising ethics: Raise more money while keeping your donors happy. What could be simpler? Part one' [web article], The Showcase of Fundraising Innovation and Inspiration (SOFII), https://sofii.org/article/fundraising-ethics-raise-more-money-while-keeping-your-donors-happy, 14 February 2019.
5. Ian MacQuillin, *Rights Stuff: fundraising's ethics gap and a new theory of fundraising ethics* [PDF], Rogare, 2016, https://df618d67-1d77-4718-ac14-01d78db8f9d0.filesusr.com/ugd/8bc141_c83e86ee3ec1450eb0177cbb8f345433.pdf, accessed 19 May 2021.
6. 'The Directory' [web page], Fundraising Regulator, 2021, www.fundraisingregulator.org.uk/directory, accessed 19 May 2021.
7. 'Fundraising Preference Service code breaches' [web page], Fundraising Regulator, 2021, www.fundraisingregulator.org.uk/fundraising-preference-service/breaches, accessed 19 May 2021.
8. Ian MacQuillin, 'Fundraising ethics: Raise more money while keeping your donors happy. What could be simpler? Part one' [web article], The Showcase of Fundraising Innovation and Inspiration (SOFII), https://sofii.org/article/fundraising-ethics-raise-more-money-while-keeping-your-donors-happy, 14 February 2019.
9. See www.fundraisingregulator.org.uk/code; *Institute of Fundraising Compliance Rule Book: Street fundraising (regular giving)* [PDF], Chartered Institute of Fundraising, 2019, https://ciof.org.uk/IoF/media/IOF/Compliance/public-fundraising-rules-for-street-regular-giving-(2).pdf, accessed 19 May 2021; *Institute of Fundraising Compliance Rule Book: Door to door (direct debit and lottery) fundraising* [PDF], Chartered Institute of Fundraising, 2019, https://ciof.org.uk/IoF/media/IOF/Compliance/public-fundraising-rules-for-door-to-door-direct-debit-lottery.pdf, accessed 19 May 2021.
10. 'Behaviour when fundraising' [web page], Fundraising Regulator, 2021, www.fundraisingregulator.org.uk/code/all-fundraising/behaviour-when-fundraising, accessed 19 May 2021.
11. Ian MacQuillin, *Rights Stuff: fundraising's ethics gap and a new theory of fundraising ethics* [PDF], Rogare, 2016, https://df618d67-1d77-4718-ac14-01d78db8f9d0.filesusr.com/ugd/8bc141_c83e86ee3ec1450eb0177cbb8f345433.pdf, accessed 19 May 2021.
12. Claire Routley, Cherian Koshy, Lucy Lowthian, Meredith Niles, Roewen Wishart, Michael J. Rosen, Heather Hill, Ligia Peña and Andrew Watt, *The Ethics of Legacy Fundraising during Emergencies* [PDF], Rogare, 2020, www.rogare.net/legacy-ethics, accessed 19 May 2021.

13 See 'But what about potential donors and non-donors?' in Cherian Koshy, 'The fundraiser's duty to ask: A philosophical rationale' [blog post], Critical Fundraising, https://criticalfundraising.com/2017/01/30/new-ideas-the-fundraisers-duty-to-ask-a-philosophical-rationale, 30 January 2017.
14 See Cherian Koshy, 'Charitable giving and emergency situations: Striking the balance between urgent need and long-term solutions' [blog post], Rogare, https://criticalfundraising.com/2020/04/01/new-ideas-charitable-giving-and-emergency-situations-striking-the-balance-between-urgent-need-and-long-term-solutions, 1 April 2020.
15 Ian MacQuillin, *Rights Stuff: fundraising's ethics gap and a new theory of fundraising ethics* [PDF], Rogare, 2016, https://df618d67-1d77-4718-ac14-01d78db8f9d0.filesusr.com/ugd/8bc141_c83e86ee3ec1450eb0177cbb8f345433.pdf, accessed 19 May 2021.
16 *Ibid.*, p. 12.
17 *Ibid.*, p. 14.
18 'Prioritize communities: Reimagine fundraising' [web page], Community-Centric Fundraising, 2021, https://communitycentricfundraising.org, accessed 19 May 2021.
19 Ian MacQuillin, *Rights Stuff: fundraising's ethics gap and a new theory of fundraising ethics* [PDF], Rogare, 2016, https://df618d67-1d77-4718-ac14-01d78db8f9d0.filesusr.com/ugd/8bc141_c83e86ee3ec1450eb0177cbb8f345433.pdf, accessed 19 May 2021, p. 15.
20 *Ibid.*
21 *Ibid.*, p. 16.
22 *Ibid.*
23 Claire Routley, Cherian Koshy, Lucy Lowthian, Meredith Niles, Roewen Wishart, Michael J. Rosen, Heather Hill, Ligia Peña and Andrew Watt, *The Ethics of Legacy Fundraising during Emergencies* [PDF], Rogare, 2020, www.rogare.net/legacy-ethics, accessed 19 May 2021.
24 'Girl Scouts is #ForEVERYGirl' [web page], Indiegogo, 2015, www.indiegogo.com/projects/girl-scouts-is-foreverygirl, accessed 19 May 2021.
25 'Fundraising ethics' [web page], British Library, 2021, www.bl.uk/about-us/governance/policies/fundraising-ethics, accessed 19 May 2021.
26 'Ethical fundraising policy' [web page], Farleigh Hospice, 2021, www.farleighhospice.org/ethical-fundraising-policy, accessed 19 May 2021.
27 'Ethical fundraising policy' [web page], Wild Welfare, 2021, https://wildwelfare.org/ethical-fundraising-policy, accessed 19 May 2021.
28 *Ethical Fundraising Policy* [PDF], University of Bath, 2021, www.bath.ac.uk/publications/ethical-fundraising-policy/attachments/ethical-fundraising-policy.pdf, accessed 19 May 2021.
29 Ian MacQuillin, *Ethical Decision-Making Framework for Fundraising*, London, Rogare, 2019.
30 See 'Investigations' [web page], Fundraising Regulator, 2021, www.fundraisingregulator.org.uk/complaints/investigations, accessed 19 May 2021.
31 *Complaints Report 2018/19* [PDF], Fundraising Regulator, 2020, www.fundraisingregulator.org.uk/sites/default/files/2020-02/Complaints-report-201819.pdf, accessed 19 May 2021.

32 Ian MacQuillin, *Rights Stuff: Fundraising's ethics gap and a new theory of fundraising ethics* [PDF], Rogare, 2016, https://df618d67-1d77-4718-ac14-01d78db8f9d0.filesusr.com/ugd/8bc141_c83e86ee3ec1450eb0177cbb8f345433.pdf, accessed 19 May 2021.
33 Ian MacQuillin, *Ethical Decision-Making Framework for Fundraising*, London, Rogare, 2019.

CHAPTER ELEVEN
Contemporary issues in fundraising

Introduction

This chapter looks at several issues that it is important to consider in the current context of fundraising practice and strategy development: equality, equity, diversity and inclusion (EEDI) in both recruitment and fundraising practice; digitisation; the changing consumer; and donor fatigue. These are key issues related to ethical decision-making (see chapter 11) and your audits, both external (see chapter 1) and internal (see chapter 2).

Equality, equity, diversity and inclusion

Equality, equity, diversity and inclusion in fundraising recruitment

Research carried out by the Chartered Institute of Fundraising in 2019 has highlighted that the fundraising sector is facing a number of issues when it comes to EEDI. The research showed that Black, Asian and minority ethnic fundraisers are under-represented at all levels within fundraising, with only 9% of fundraisers being from minority ethnic communities (as opposed to 13% of the UK population). People with disabilities are also under-represented, with 3% of fundraisers reporting that they have a disability versus 18% of working-age people and 18% of charity sector employees. The research points out that although the fundraiser profession is in the majority female (76%), women are under-represented in senior roles. The mean pay gap suggests that, on average, men in the charity sector earn almost 11% more than women, while the median gap suggests that, on average, men earn 9% more.[1]

There is, of course, a moral case for addressing these issues. Not only should everyone be able to fulfil their potential, but also the principle of diversity and equality of opportunity aligns with the moral and ethical framework in which charities operate.[2] However, there are also practical benefits of EEDI, such as being better able to tap into the increasing spending power of diverse communities.

There are other benefits too. In his book about diversity of thinking, journalist, author and broadcaster Matthew Syed describes how, in today's environment, problems are often too complex to be solved by individuals and, therefore, in lots of different working environments, problem solving is becoming increasingly team-based.[3] The more complex a problem, the less likely it can be solved by one person alone. Syed describes how, for teams to function as effectively as possible, they need to be cognitively diverse – that is, take differing approaches to thinking through problems.

He argues that a team can be composed of very intelligent individuals, but if those individuals all think in the same way – and thus approach problems in the same way – then the collective intelligence of the team won't be optimal. When a team comprises people who think differently, they will have different perspectives on a problem: they will use different frames of reference, have a smaller chance of being vulnerable to blind spots and, ultimately, benefit from a more thorough view of the whole issue.

Syed argues, therefore, that cognitive diversity is increasingly viewed as a key source of competitive advantage and the best path to innovation and growth. He references a number of studies in support of his argument: for example, a McKinsey study showed that companies in the top quartile for gender and racial or ethnic diversity offered financial returns that were better than the industry average, while those in the lowest quartile were less likely to perform well.[4] Of course, demographic diversity and cognitive diversity are not one and the same thing, but Syed points out that the two often overlap, with people from different backgrounds – who've had different life experiences – often able to form different perspectives on an issue.[5]

So, what can charities do practically to increase EEDI within their fundraising workforces? The Change Collective at the Chartered Institute of Fundraising has produced helpful guidance on recruitment.[6] Below we share some tips based on that guidance, although this is by no means a comprehensive list.

Before the recruitment process starts:

• Take time to understand the current situation at your organisation. For example, if staff members are leaving, why is this? Are there any aspects of the role that could be improved? Or anything about the broader working environment that may be causing unhappiness? And are there any patterns emerging over time?

• Think carefully about the internal culture you want to create and how you can make it as inclusive as possible.

• Have an EEDI policy and statement in place, incorporating your organisational values.

• Ensure that all policies and procedures are fit for purpose from an EEDI perspective. Although some policies may not, on the face of it, be directly related to EEDI, might they have a disproportionate impact on people with disabilities, people from particular socio-economic backgrounds or specific genders? For example, a policy that requires travel at short notice might disadvantage women, who are more likely to have caring responsibilities.[7]

CHAPTER ELEVEN **CONTEMPORARY ISSUES IN FUNDRAISING**

- Ask anyone involved in recruitment to complete reputable EEDI and unconscious bias training.

When trying to attract candidates:

- Think carefully about essential and desirable criteria for applicants. For example, do applicants genuinely have to be educated to degree level?

- Is it possible for the role to be advertised as flexible and for home-working options to be offered?

- Consider where you advertise roles – are you reaching groups that are under-represented in your organisation?

- Review the language in the advert and job description. Might it, for example, be seen to be stereotypically gendered? For example, research suggests that words such as 'compassionate', 'pleasant' and 'polite' are stereotypically associated with women.[8] Try to avoid unnecessarily gendered language.

- Do you publish job advertisements with transparent salaries? Not doing so can increase the gender pay gap and lead to inequities.

- Do the images that you share of your organisation feature people from a range of backgrounds?

- Is information available to candidates in alternative formats, such as large print?

When assessing candidates:

- Introduce recruitment processes without any identifying details, such as name, age, ethnic background or gender. Removing such details from candidates' applications can minimise unconscious bias.

- Ensure that a scoring system is developed to assess candidates against the same criteria – potentially one that enables people to draw on a variety of experiences including paid work, volunteering and lived experience. Disregard information that isn't related to those criteria.

- Ask candidates about adjustments they may need (for example, an accessible venue for the interview).

- Consider using positive action to address diversity issues. This might include targeted advertising or guaranteeing an interview to people with a disability who meet a minimum standard. (However, do be aware that while they can take positive action, employers cannot positively discriminate – for example, by appointing someone to a role just because they are from a certain background.)

- Take steps to limit the amount of attention you give to less definable qualities, such as perceived organisational 'fit', and instead focus on specific areas, such as skills and experience.

> **Case study: Cancer Research UK's equality, equity, diversity and inclusion strategy**
>
> Cancer Research UK launched its three-year equality, equity, diversity and inclusion strategy in January 2021.[9] While the strategy focuses on the organisation as a whole, for example looking at 'inequalities in science and research funding', it is a good example of how to publish shared commitments and being clear about how the organisation can achieve them. Each of the five strategic priorities, listed below, is linked to core areas of focus and key initiatives. These explain the charity's commitment and proposed activity in each area. Priorities 3, 4 and 5 are particularly pertinent to fundraising. Cancer Research UK aims to:
>
> 1. Reduce cancer inequalities through its work and in partnership with others
> 2. Develop a more diverse and inclusive research community through the research it funds
> 3. Build an inclusive and diverse culture for all its people so they can succeed and feel like they belong
> 4. Achieve diversity across its governance, advisory and leadership structures making sure decisions are made in an inclusive way
> 5. Engage with people in ways that are inclusive, relevant and accessible[10]

Equality, equity, diversity and inclusion in fundraising practice

Fundraising in a legal and ethical way has long been an important issue within fundraising. In the UK, for example, the Code of Fundraising Practice (see www.fundraisingregulator.org.uk/code) was first developed in 2005 and summarises the standards to which professional fundraisers need to adhere.

However, more recently, both philanthropy and fundraising have been critiqued as having a role in perpetuating and cementing injustices, including sexism (for example, inappropriate sexual behaviour of donors and donor dominance),[11] racism (such as funding sources being tied to wealth derived from slavery)[12] and class inequalities (for example, very wealthy individuals having power over what is funded).[13] These issues have been thrown into relief in the wake of movements such as #MeToo and the Black Lives Matter protests.

It should be noted that this critique isn't universal. Academic Beth Breeze pushes back at recent critiques arguing that they may be damaging to the sector and its service users at a time when we need to encourage more, not less, giving. She points out that for giving and asking to be successful, people have to feel that they are taking part in a practice that is valued by society. She argues that critiques which assume philanthropists are homogeneous in their approach are incorrect: philanthropists are a diverse group with different motivations and practices, and mass collective giving far outweighs that of mega-donors.[14]

A particular criticism has been directed at the donor-centrism approach to fundraising (see chapter 10), which places the donor at the centre of an organisation's work. Vu Le, writer, speaker and former Executive Director of RVC (an organisation set up to support leaders and organisations of colour), argues that, at its worst, the donor-centrist approach:

• can drive competition between non-profits rather than encouraging them to work collectively;

• reinforces the idea that some people are there to be saviours and others to be saved;

• can make the people that non-profits support seem to be different from the donors by presenting them as somehow 'other' and silencing their voices;

• doesn't encourage donors to consider the difficult issues of systemic injustice (i.e. how disparities and inequality in, say, criminal justice or educational systems might be benefiting the donor but contributing to the very problems they are hoping to address through their giving);

• can further marginalise small charities that don't have access to the resources of larger organisations to thank and recognise their donors;

• reinforces money as the key measure of people's worth, as people who give more receive a greater standard of service;

• minimises the contribution of other people, such as volunteers;

• makes charities seem transactional: telling donors exactly what their money has bought can deny the holistic nature of non-profit work;

• prevents honest conversations with donors about issues which affect communities;

• ultimately, doesn't deliver authentic relationships with donors.[15]

Le therefore argues that rather than always necessarily being a social good, fundraising may be causing harm to society.[16] Alongside other fundraisers of colour, Le founded the Community-Centric Fundraising movement. The movement has developed a set of core principles which aim to ground fundraising in racial and economic justice. The principles are:

1. Fundraising must be grounded in race, equity and social justice [and so for example] must move toward sometimes uncomfortable discussions regarding race and wealth disparities.

2. Individual organizational missions are not as important as the collective community.

3. Nonprofits are generous with and mutually supportive of one another.

4. All who engage in strengthening the community are equally valued, whether volunteer, staff, donor, or board member.

5. Time is valued equally as money.

6. We treat donors as partners, and this means that we are transparent, and occasionally have difficult conversations.

7. We foster a sense of belonging, not othering.

8. We promote the understanding that everyone (donors, staff, funders, board members, volunteers) personally benefits from engaging in the work of social justice – it's not just charity and compassion.

9. We see the work of social justice as holistic and transformative, not transactional.

10. We recognize that healing and liberation requires a commitment to economic justice [and] this involves... grappling with and addressing the root causes of inequity, including the destructive effects of capitalism and how we may be complicit in furthering them through our practices.[17]

Not all organisations and not all fundraisers will agree with the arguments outlined above. However, it's likely to be increasingly important to engage meaningfully with these issues and have a position on them within your organisation.

Service user portrayal

Dr Haseeb Shabbir, Reader in Marketing at the University of Huddersfield, has written and spoken extensively about developing inclusive communications.[18] In a presentation for Pyrotalks, he describes how, historically – and arguably still today – fundraising communications (from international development charities in particular) would typically de-humanise service users, and especially Black people.[19]

Indeed, when conducting an analysis of 622 UK TV commercials, Shabbir found that charity advertising was among the most likely to portray Black people as inferior to White people.[20] This, he argues, happened because since colonial times the charity sector has become conditioned to the use of an entrenched communications formula – the use of unidimensional frames in portraying service users. A unidimensional frame consistently portrays a group of people in a particular way: for example, recurrently showing Black children in Africa as hungry, sick or living in a dirty environment. This can lead to that group being stereotyped in a particular way and even de-humanised, by having their varied and complex human attributes stripped away. Therefore, while in the short term such images may stir motives for giving (for example, through activating guilt, sympathy or pity), in the long term they may also lead to negative stereotypes becoming entrenched. This long-term effect may reduce support for efforts to resolve the structural inequalities which may have led to the plight of the service user in the first place.

In response to this critique, however, charities may ask how they can rectify the needs of particular communities if they don't highlight the problems those communities face. Shabbir suggests moving away from the unidimensional frame to conveying information in a multidimensional way (i.e. to humanise portrayals).[21] Humanisation has been shown to be central to activating empathy.[22]

Shabbir suggests that one of the most powerful ways to do this is through the use of story-telling.[23] There has been significant interest in story-telling in fundraising in recent years, with many fundraisers arguing that it is both a powerful way to engage an audience and a way to increase donation income.[24]

When you are specifically aiming to create inclusive communications, story-telling can introduce a more nuanced and developed picture of the people your organisation supports – in technical terms, moving from a unidimensional to a multidimensional frame respects the dignity and human essence of the service user. Rather than de-humanising a service user in order to gain monetary support, Shabbir argues that it's time fundraisers adopted a multidimensional approach to characterising their service users so that their lived experiences and lives can be captured in a more complete and therefore inclusive manner.[25]

Case study: Comic Relief

One organisation that has been very much in the spotlight around equality, equity, diversity and inclusion (EEDI) issues is Comic Relief. The critique and the charity's revised approach may provide some lessons for those grappling with similar issues.

In 2020, Comic Relief announced that it would stop sending celebrities to film in African countries after criticism that the approach reinforced 'White saviour' stereotypes.[26] In 2019, for example, the charity was criticised by Member of Parliament David Lammy for perpetrating 'tired stereotypes' and failing to show the wider picture of progress in Africa.[27] Going forwards, Comic Relief will focus on sharing everyday stories from local filmmakers and photographers. Sir Lenny Henry, a Comic Relief co-founder, described how times had changed. Instead of telling African people's stories for them, the campaign wanted to offer them more agency and a partnership. Ruth Davison, the charity's CEO at the time, commented that she was proud to be leading the organisation at a time when it was developing its approach and shifting power.[28]

Case study: The Presidents Club

In recent years there have been a number of reports of sexism and inappropriate behaviour in fundraising.[29] One of the most notable was the Presidents Club scandal in 2018. While – we hope – an extreme example, it may again offer lessons for other charities around being aware of the actions of those who are raising funds in aid of their work.

For 33 years, the Presidents Club hosted an annual men-only charity dinner and auction, raising over £20 million for children's charities over this period. These events were attended by high-powered men from the business community and elsewhere.

In 2018, the event was attended by undercover *Financial Times* reporters who were hired among 130 female hostesses to work at the event. The hostesses were recruited for being tall, thin and pretty and were asked to wear skimpy outfits and high-heeled shoes, and to do their hair and make-up as if they were going to a 'smart sexy place'. A number of women who worked at the event reported being inappropriately touched, sexually harassed and propositioned.[30]

After the revelations came to light, the Presidents Club was disbanded. The Fundraising Regulator and the Charity Commission for England and Wales (CCEW) both completed investigations and found that the charity was in breach of regulations, and CCEW determined that the Presidents Club had failed to protect women at the event.[31] While, before the revelations, the charities the Presidents Club supported hadn't been aware of exactly how the funds were raised, once the allegations came to light they were faced with difficult questions about whether to keep the funds or return them. Notably, the majority of the public believed that the charities should keep the funds.[32]

How then might such problems be avoided in the future? Alongside adhering to relevant laws and codes of practice, and having robust policies, Peter Kellner, former chair of NCVO, suggests that charities that raise a significant amount of money from events organised by others should ensure that they understand the full details of such events.[33]

Digitisation of fundraising

Despite the digitisation of many aspects of life, digital giving has, historically, made up a relatively small percentage of all charitable giving. Indeed, it's been argued that with only around 10% of fundraised income coming through digital channels, no digital revolution has taken place in charities.[34] Reinforcing this argument, the 2019 *UK Giving* report by the Charities Aid Foundation (CAF) found that while 53% of people had donated cash, only 19% had given via a website or an app and 7% had donated via text.[35] However, the COVID-19 pandemic beginning in 2019 appears to have led to significant change, with cash donations being very low compared to previous years, and website and app donations increasing significantly (although it remains to be seen whether this trend will continue into the longer term).[36]

As well as increasingly being used by donors, it seems that interest in digital fundraising is growing among charities themselves. According to the Chartered Institute of Fundraising and Blackbaud, during the pandemic in 2020, 60% of respondents organised some form of virtual fundraising, with more than 75% of those using it for the first time. Overall, the report found that 64% of respondents considered virtual fundraising to be a good way of attracting new supporters. Notably, survey respondents whose fundraising was performing well were more likely to be optimistic about and open to embracing virtual fundraising. Looking forwards, the majority of respondents also believed that online giving was likely to increase in the short term. Respondents who had used virtual fundraising were also likely to report that they planned to continue various forms of virtual fundraising – from 'give as you shop' (97%) to social media giving (94%) to team virtual events (84%).[37]

The impact of artificial intelligence on fundraising

There has been plenty of speculation as to how artificial intelligence (AI) is likely to revolutionise our lives, from driverless cars to dystopian views of a future ruled by robots! But how is AI likely to affect fundraising both now and in the future? You might be surprised to realise that fundraisers are already using AI. Tools such as machine learning (software which learns as it acquires new data) are routinely used to improve the effectiveness of advertising on digital channels,[38] while a number of charities are using chatbots (computer programmes that are programmed to simulate conversation) to communicate with supporters on their websites.

Digital experts Allison Fine and Beth Kanter have argued that we're at a tipping point in the sector-wide adoption of AI.[39] They share examples of AI being used to analyse large amounts of supporter data, matching donors with causes that may interest them, advising philanthropists on strategic giving, and automating supporter stewardship (for example, by flagging donors who might need additional contact). They report how, in one charity, software that recommended the right content to include in appeals – as well as the right number of communications and the intervals between them – was able to increase the conversion of one-off to monthly donors by 866%.[40] Perhaps counter-intuitively, Fine and Kanter argue that one of the key benefits of AI is likely to be more human interaction with donors – by freeing up time that fundraisers might be spending on routine tasks, AI could help fundraisers to spend more time communicating with supporters directly.

As well as many benefits, there are, however, several issues with AI that fundraisers will need to consider. Fine and Kanter point out that AI could, in fact, make bad fundraising worse – for example, by bombarding the most generous people with fundraising asks. They also point out that there are ethical issues to be addressed, such as transparency around the use of data and whether people are aware that they are communicating with AI as opposed to a real-life representative of the charity.[41] Importantly, too, you should be aware that AI can encode the biases of its developers, such as racial or gender stereotypes. You will need to put in place measures to mitigate this possibility, such as auditing the results that AI produces.[42]

As well as affecting the obvious front end of how donors engage directly with charities, digital technology can play an important role behind the scenes. The development of increasingly sophisticated database technology can enable organisations to create personalised appeals and donor journeys for their supporters.[43]

Although the previously mentioned figures look positive, there are still issues to be overcome in charities' use of digital technology. According to the *Charity Digital Skills Report* in 2019, over half of charities didn't have a digital strategy, a figure that appeared to have remained more or less static since 2017. The report also found that 87% of the charities that responded said their understanding of what digital technologies were and how to apply them was fair or poor. In terms of digital fundraising specifically, 78% said their understanding was fair or poor, although 59% said they wanted to grow their digital fundraising, with 41% rating it as a key priority for the next year. However, one of the biggest barriers appeared to be money, with 37% saying that they didn't have the income to invest in digital development.[44]

Tactics which can be used in digital fundraising

When we think of the term 'digital fundraising', our immediate reaction might be a donation portal on a charity's website, but there is a whole range of digital tactics which can be applied within a fundraising strategy. Some of these are listed here to give a sense of the range of opportunities:

- donating via a third-party platform, such as JustGiving;

- giving by text;

- social media fundraising and giving – for example, through Facebook's charitable giving tools;

- search engine marketing;

- email fundraising;

- 'give while you shop' – for example, AmazonSmile;

- taking part in a virtual challenge event;

- participating in a live stream – for example, a concert or quiz;

- giving via a virtual assistant – for example, Amazon Alexa;

- Gaming for Good (an organisation that promotes gaming events which raise money for charity at the same time – for example, through the livestreaming platform Twitch);

- crowdfunding;

- virtual and augmented reality (using the technology to improve donors' interactions and experiences with the organisation);

- blockchain (there may be more opportunities to use this technology to track expenditure in the future).

Although having the money to invest in digital tools can be an issue, many of these options can be used either for free or comparatively cheaply compared to offline channels.

The case study below brings together two themes from this chapter – the potential of using digital to engage with supporters in an innovative way, and the potential to give agency to a service user through the use of story-telling.

Case study: WaterAid's Untapped campaign

WaterAid has made innovative use of digital channels – for example, enabling its supporters to experience life in a village in Sierra Leone via a Facebook Messenger chatbot. It also has a dedicated website offering a 360-degree view of the village and YouTube tutorials from residents sharing recipes and dance moves.[45]

The chatbot enabled people to 'talk to Sellu', a virtual recreation of Sellu, a real-life resident of the village. He took people through the experience of life in the village (from language to food to the challenges the community faces with dirty water), sharing text, videos and GIFs before gently introducing the option to donate. Around 25% of users went on to donate. The campaign was also designed to give agency to the service user and enable Sellu to tell his own story – to generate empathy rather than sympathy by bringing people closer to someone else's experience.[46]

Dan Gray, WaterAid Digital Engagement Manager, said:

> At the moment, the predominant use of chatbots is for service handling, with bots trained to learn answers to basic FAQs, or use machine learning to comb the internet for content. We decided to take a different approach, and work within the limitations of the technology to create some good, old-fashioned storytelling; immersing our digital audiences in the life of Sellu – a farmer, fisherman father-of-three from Tombohuaun, Sierra Leone.
>
> The ability to continuously interact with large cohorts of engaged digital users makes the chatbot a powerful tool for awareness, activation and retention all in one and we hope people will be encouraged to donate to our winter fundraising appeal, Untapped.[47]

The changing consumer

Various studies in recent years have shown that consumer behaviour has been changing. Some of the emerging trends include:

- **A tendency for consumers to value experiences over things (or possessions)**: some 76% say they would rather spend their money on experiences. The most common responses around what people want from brands are 'inspiration' and 'meaning'.[48] This could present a particular opportunity for investment in community and events fundraising, with charities able to offer experiences that, by their very nature, offer participants a sense of meaning.

- **A growing lack of customer loyalty**: only 8% of people consider themselves to be committed loyalists to their favourite brands and 46% say they would be more likely to try new brands than five years ago.[49] It's unlikely that charities will be immune to these trends, which means that donors may be increasingly likely to switch their support to another charity. Charities are likely to have to work harder to retain donors through offering excellent supporter experiences.

- **A growing interest in equity and the values that brands embody**: we might imagine that charities are already seen as organisations with strong values, but, as already discussed in this chapter, the evidence shows that charities still have work to do on the EEDI front – and donors may be increasingly likely to ask questions about such issues.[50]

- **The growth of new, engaging digital experiences**: again, as already discussed, charities will need to invest in digital fundraising to stay up to date with their donors' expectations.[51]

Of course, many trends that were already starting to emerge have been brought forwards by the COVID-19 pandemic. For example, online sales in Europe in April 2020 were up by 130% on 2019.[52] As consumer expectations continue to evolve, charities will need to keep a close eye on their donors' needs and ensure that they grow and change to meet them.

There's an argument that some of the change in consumer attitudes is driven by digital technology – or, more specifically, the investment that companies have made in providing excellent digital experiences (which have been characterised as requiring digital functionality, cohesive service and experiences across channels, convenience, personalisation and enjoyment).[53] Consumers now expect to receive excellent experiences, and indeed 33% would consider switching to another company after one bad experience.[54]

This seems to translate into the charity sector, with research suggesting that 57% of people will stop supporting a charity if another organisation provides a better experience.[55] It has been argued that digital consumers and donors want their experience to be quick, easy and tailored to them. In the charity sector specifically, they want to be part of something bigger than themselves – potentially, to join a movement for change.[56] Indeed, they often want to give spontaneously – for example, in response to something they have seen on the news – and expect that experience to be as streamlined as possible.[57] It's also been suggested that accountability will become increasingly important – that new generations of donors want to clearly see the impact that organisations have on their service users, and expect to be able to do so through a charity's digital channels.[58]

Donor fatigue

Perhaps in part linked to how consumers are changing, there is some evidence to suggest that the percentage of people giving to charity may be falling. CAF's *UK Giving 2019* report suggested that the percentage had dropped from 61% to 57% over three years. However, the amount given seemed to be stable at £10.1 billion annually, which suggests that while fewer people are donating, those who do give are donating larger amounts. CAF also found a decline in the percentage of people who found charities trustworthy, with this number falling from 51% to 48%.[59] Perhaps even more concerning is longer-term research which suggests that younger people are less likely to participate in giving: since 1980, the giving rate among the under-30s has decreased from 23% to 15%, and in the 30–44 age group it has decreased from 34% to 25%.[60]

It could be argued that this is a symptom of donor fatigue, defined as the declining response from donors to continued requests for support.[61] It is possible that donor fatigue could be related to the representation of need that people are continuously exposed to via traditional news sources and, increasingly, digitally. In his masters dissertation on donor fatigue, Aaron Warwick points to studies which show that too much exposure to bad news can lead people to try to avoid the issue. He points to the importance of finding a happy medium where people are exposed to difficult issues enough to encourage them to feel empathy and take an action, but not so much that they become overwhelmed. He also points out that there is a correlation between fatigue and hopelessness: potential donors need to know there is a solution to the problems presented.[62]

Looking at charity appeals specifically, experimental research from Philipp Süssenbach suggests that exposure to multiple charity appeals leads to moral fatigue, which he describes as a breakdown in responding and intent to help.[63] In a study of charity switching behaviour, academic Roger Bennett found that straightforward boredom can account for people changing their giving decisions.[64] You should therefore avoid sending excessive volumes of poor communications that create boredom and over-familiarity. Instead, send different communications and messages at different times in a donor's journey, and highlight new, unique aspects of your organisation over time.

It has been argued that donor fatigue is a myth, or indeed a cop-out used to explain poor fundraising practice.[65] Indeed, it's possible that the decline in the percentage of people giving might not be caused by donor fatigue; instead, there might be a simpler cause: less asking by charities since the introduction of the General Data Protection Regulation in 2018. More fundamentally, however, people may still care but support causes differently – as demonstrated by the responses to causes such as Extinction Rebellion or the calling out of sexual harassment. Instead, it may be that the way people are expressing their care is changing.[66] Similarly, people now have access to a wide range of ways to make change, outside giving and volunteering, from shopping ethically to supporting individuals through services like GoFundMe.[67]

There are a number of tried-and-tested ways to combat perceived donor fatigue. For example:

- **Focus on one person:** several studies suggest that focusing appeals on a single service user rather than on a group increases giving.

- **Encourage people to feel:** it may be that people are reluctant to support groups because considering the needs of a larger group can be emotionally overwhelming. However, one study showed that encouraging people to feel those emotions (the researchers explicitly told participants to let themselves feel their emotions rather than try to get rid of them) led to them feeling the same levels of compassion for a group as for an individual.

- **Link giving and identity:** when people see a connection between generosity and who they are, they are more inclined to be generous. For example, if you're an environmental charity, encouraging your supporters to see themselves as environmentalists is more likely to prompt support.

- **Consider timing:** allowing people to make the decision to give now but actually pay their gift later can encourage them to give.

- **Show the impact of giving:** giving can increase when charities show the impact that giving will have through how it will be spent or the impact it will have on others' lives.

- **Make people feel happy:** reinforcing a positive feedback loop between giving and happiness can increase future giving.

- **Make people feel like they've put in hard work:** in the world of events, those where people feel they've had to put in effort to raise money are likely to encourage higher levels of giving.

- **Encourage people to feel awe:** feeling that they are in the presence of something that transcends their understanding can encourage people to behave generously. For example, one study asked people to take pictures of awe-inspiring nature scenes and found that they felt more connected to others.

- **Tailor appeals by wealth:** one study suggested that showing wealthy people the *personal* difference they could make and less wealthy people the *communal* difference they could make encouraged giving.

- **Use social norms:** there is lots of evidence that we are influenced by other people's giving, so it can help to show that other people are supporting your cause.[68]

Conclusion

At the time of writing, the issues included here were at the centre of important debates in fundraising. By the time you read this chapter, new issues may well have arisen to complement the ones above, and there may have been other unexpected developments in fundraising practice. However, whatever the size of your organisation or the type of cause you support, it's important to consider what these and other emerging key issues are likely to mean for your approach to fundraising now and in the forthcoming years. It's also helpful to engage with charity sector media and conferences to help you understand what key issues are arising and to consider what implications these issues may have for your fundraising strategy. Engaging with such issues can help to address any threats to your fundraising practice and ensure that you take advantage of opportunities as they arise.

Notes

1. Change Collective, *Who Isn't in the Room? Equality, diversity and inclusion in the fundraising profession* [PDF], Chartered Institute of Fundraising, 2019, www.ciof.org.uk/IoF/media/IOF/Equality,%20Diversity%20and%20Inclusion/Change%20Collective/Change-Collective-Who-Isn-t-In-The-Room.pdf?ext=.pdf, accessed 19 May 2021.
2. 'Case for equality, diversity and inclusion' [web page], Chartered Institute of Fundraising, 2020, https://ciof.org.uk/about-us/what-we-re-doing/equality,-diversity-and-inclusion/case-for-equality,-diversity-and-inclusion, accessed 19 May 2021.
3. Matthew Syed, *Rebel Ideas: The power of diverse thinking*, London, John Murray, 2019.
4. Vivian Hunt, Dennis Layton and Sara Prince, 'Why diversity matters' [web article], McKinsey & Company, www.mckinsey.com/business-functions/organization/our-insights/why-diversity-matters, 1 January 2015.

5   Matthew Syed, *Rebel Ideas: The power of diverse thinking*, London, John Murray, 2019, ch. 1.
6   Change Collective, *Guide to Recruitment for Hiring Managers* [PDF], Chartered Institute of Fundraising, 2020, https://ciof.org.uk/IoF/media/IOF/Equality,%20Diversity%20and%20Inclusion/Change%20Collective/The-Change-Collective-Guide-to-Recruitment-for-Hiring-Managers-(download).pdf?ext=.pdf, accessed 19 May 2021.
7   'Indirect discrimination' [web article], Citizens Advice, www.citizensadvice.org.uk/law-and-courts/discrimination/what-are-the-different-types-of-discrimination/indirect-discrimination, 22 February 2020.
8   Steve Warnham, 'How to identify unconscious gender bias in job adverts' [web article], Totaljobs, www.totaljobs.com/recruiter-advice/how-to-identify-unconscious-gender-bias-in-job-adverts, 28 January 2020.
9   'Our EDI commitment' [web page], Cancer Research UK, 2021, www.cancerresearchuk.org/about-us/charity-jobs/working-with-us/equality-diversity-and-inclusion/our-commitment, accessed 19 May 2021.
10 'Cancer Research launches its EDI strategy' [press release], Cancer Research UK, www.cancerresearchuk.org/about-us/cancer-news/press-release/2021-01-29-cancer-research-uk-launches-its-new-equality-diversity-and-inclusion-strategy, 29 January 2021.
11 Val Cipriani, 'Three in four female fundraisers experience gender stereotyping, report finds' [web article], Civil Society Media, www.civilsociety.co.uk/news/three-in-four-female-fundraisers-experience-gender-stereotyping-report-finds.html, 5 March 2020.
12 Mike Zywina, 'Edward Colston: The beginning not the end of the spotlight on hypocritical philanthropy' [blog post], Lime Green Consulting, www.limegreenconsulting.co.uk/blog/edward-colston-the-beginning-not-the-end-of-the-spotlight-on-hypocritical-philanthropy, 18 June 2020.
13 Melissa De Witte, 'Stanford scholar addresses the problems with philanthropy' [web article], https://news.stanford.edu/2018/12/03/the-problems-with-philanthropy, 3 December 2018.
14 Beth Breeze, 'It's time to talk differently – and more carefully – about philanthropy' [blog post], Beacon Collaborative, www.beaconcollaborative.org.uk/blogs/talk-differently-about-philanthropy, 27 September 2020.
15 Vu Le, 'How donor-centrism perpetuates inequity, and why we must move toward Community-Centric Fundraising' [blog post], Nonprofit AF, https://nonprofitaf.com/2017/05/how-donor-centrism-perpetuates-inequity-and-why-we-must-move-toward-community-centric-fundraising, 15 May 2017.
16 Vu Le, 'It's time to expand our perspectives and conversations in fundraising' [blog post], Nonprofit AF, https://nonprofitaf.com/2020/09/its-time-to-expand-our-perspectives-and-conversations-in-fundraising, 28 September 2020.
17 'CCF's 10 principles' [web page], Community-Centric Fundraising, 2021, https://communitycentricfundraising.org/ccf-principles, accessed 19 May 2021.
18 See, for example, Michael Hyman, Alena Kostyk and Haseeb Shabbir, 'Disruptive Events and Associated Discontinuities: A macromarketing prescription', *Journal of Macromarketing*, 2020, doi: 10.1177/0276146720979134; Haseeb Shabbir, Michael Hyman and Alena Kostyk, 'A Macromarketing Prescription for Covid-19', *Journal of Macromarketing*, 2021, doi:10.1177/02761467211001544; Haseeb Shabbir, Michael Hyman, Jon Reast and Dayananda Palihawadana, 'Deconstructing Subtle Racist Imagery in Television Ads', *Journal of Business Ethics*, vol. 123, no. 3, 2014, pp. 421–36.

19 Presentation by Haseeb Shabbir, 'Reflection and action: Diversity, equity and inclusion in philanthropy', Pyrotalks, https://us02web.zoom.us/rec/share/pVfuG3V9CwJRmZLlrGVNwFoE9R2eq_mavX3dUmnItR54ARzudQWSTRK_kcIGEeFl.Z0-ikEu6XErwjV99, 29 October 2020.
20 Haseeb Shabbir, Michael Hyman, Jon Reast and Dayananda Palihawadana, 'Deconstructing Subtle Racist Imagery in Television Ads', *Journal of Business Ethics*, vol. 123, no. 3, 2014, pp. 421–36.
21 Presentation by Haseeb Shabbir, 'Reflection and action: Diversity, equity and inclusion in philanthropy', Pyrotalks, https://us02web.zoom.us/rec/share/pVfuG3V9CwJRmZLlrGVNwFoE9R2eq_mavX3dUmnItR54ARzudQWSTRK_kcIGEeFl.Z0-ikEu6XErwjV99, 29 October 2020.
22 Paul Bain, Jeroen Vaes and Jacques-Philippe Leyens, *Advances in Understanding Humanness and Dehumanization*, New York, Psychology Press, 2014.
23 Presentation by Haseeb Shabbir, 'Reflection and action: Diversity, equity and inclusion in philanthropy', Pyrotalks, https://us02web.zoom.us/rec/share/pVfuG3V9CwJRmZLlrGVNwFoE9R2eq_mavX3dUmnItR54ARzudQWSTRK_kcIGEeFl.Z0-ikEu6XErwjV99, 29 October 2020.
24 See, for example, Ken Burnett, *Storytelling Can Change the World*, London, White Lion Press, 2014.
25 Presentation by Haseeb Shabbir, 'Reflection and action: Diversity, equity and inclusion in philanthropy', Pyrotalks, https://us02web.zoom.us/rec/share/pVfuG3V9CwJRmZLlrGVNwFoE9R2eq_mavX3dUmnItR54ARzudQWSTRK_kcIGEeFl.Z0-ikEu6XErwjV99, 29 October 2020.
26 Jim Waterson, 'Comic Relief stops sending celebrities to African countries' [web article], *The Guardian*, www.theguardian.com/tv-and-radio/2020/oct/27/comic-relief-stops-sending-celebrities-to-african-countries, 27 October 2020.
27 Rob Preston, 'Comic Relief caught up in another "White saviour" controversy' [web article], Civil Society Media, www.civilsociety.co.uk/news/comic-relief-defends-itself-over-latest-white-saviour-controversy.html, 1 March 2019.
28 Emily Burt, 'Comic Relief to stop producing "White saviour" appeal films' [web article], Third Sector, www.thirdsector.co.uk/comic-relief-stop-producing-white-saviour-appeal-films/fundraising/article/1698527, 28 October 2020.
29 Ruby Bayley-Pratt, 'It's time to face up to sexual harassment in fundraising' [web article], www.civilsociety.co.uk/fundraising/ruby-bayley-pratt-agent-provocateur.html, 11 March 2019.
30 Madison Marriage, 'Men only: Inside the charity fundraiser where hostesses are put on show' [web article], *Financial Times*, www.ft.com/content/075d679e-0033-11e8-9650-9c0ad2d7c5b5, 23 January 2018.
31 Alice Sharman, 'Significant failures at Presidents Club, find charity regulators' [web article], Civil Society Media, www.civilsociety.co.uk/news/significant-failures-at-presidents-club-investigations-say.html, 13 July 2018.
32 Peter Kellner, 'The Presidents Club: Lessons for the future' [blog post], NCVO, https://blogs.ncvo.org.uk/2018/01/29/the-presidents-club-lessons-for-the-future, 29 January 2018.
33 *Ibid.*
34 Joe Saxton, 'There is no digital revolution in charities. And probably never will be' [blog post], nfpSynergy, https://nfpsynergy.net/blog/no-charity-digital-revolution, 14 February 2019.

35. *UK Giving 2019: An overview of charitable giving in the UK* [PDF], Charities Aid Foundation, 2019, www.cafonline.org/docs/default-source/about-us-publications/caf-uk-giving-2019-report-an-overview-of-charitable-giving-in-the-uk.pdf, accessed 19 May 2021.
36. *UK Giving and Covid-19: A special report* [PDF], Charities Aid Foundation, 2020, www.cafonline.org/docs/default-source/about-us-publications/caf-uk-giving-2020-covid-19.pdf, accessed 19 May 2021.
37. *The Status of UK Fundraising: 2020 benchmark report*, London, IOF/Blackbaud, 2020.
38. 'Good questions, real answers: How does Facebook use machine learning to deliver ads?' [web article], Facebook, www.facebook.com/business/news/good-questions-real-answers-how-does-facebook-use-machine-learning-to-deliver-ads, 11 June 2020.
39. Allison Fine and Beth Kanter, 'Unlocking generosity with artificial intelligence: The future of giving' [web page], AI4Giving, https://ai4giving.org, accessed 30 May 2021.
40. Allison Fine and Beth Kanter, 'Rehumanising fundraising with artificial intelligence' [web article], *Stanford Social Innovation Review*, https://ssir.org/articles/entry/re_humanizing_fundraising_with_artificial_intelligence, 26 October 2020.
41. *Ibid*.
42. James Manyika, Jake Silberg and Brittany Presten, 'What do we do about the biases in AI?' [web article], *Harvard Business Review*, https://hbr.org/2019/10/what-do-we-do-about-the-biases-in-ai, 25 October 2019.
43. Archana Khatri Das, 'Digitization brings order to philanthropy' [web article], Indvstrvs, https://indvstrvs.com/digitization-brings-order-to-philanthropy, 14 February 2019.
44. *Charity Digital Skills Report* [PDF], Skills Platform/Zoe Amar Digital, 2019, www.skillsplatform.org/charity_digital_skills_report_2019.pdf, accessed 19 May 2021.
45. Sam Taylor, 'WaterAid's Untapped wins major global fundraising award' [web article], www.wateraid.org/uk/media/wateraids-untapped-wins-major-global-fundraising-award, 11 September 2018; 'WaterAid' [web page], The Bot Platform, 2021, https://thebotplatform.com/wateraid-case-study, accessed 14 May 2021.
46. 'How WaterAid made the plight of a village in Sierra Leone feel close to home' [web article], The Drum, www.thedrum.com/news/2020/01/21/how-wateraid-made-the-plight-village-sierra-leone-feel-close-home, 21 January 2020.
47. Melanie May, 'WaterAid chatbot links supporters with benefitting communities' [web article], UK Fundraising, https://fundraising.co.uk/2018/02/09/wateraid-chatbot-links-supporters-benefitting-communities, 9 February 2018.
48. Mark Huffman, 'New study finds most consumers prefer experiences over things' [web article], Consumer Affairs, www.consumeraffairs.com/news/new-study-finds-most-consumers-prefer-experiences-over-things-101519.html, 15 October 2019.
49. 'Nielsen: Consumer disloyalty is the new normal' [press release], Nielsen, www.nielsen.com/eu/en/press-releases/2019/consumer-disloyalty-is-the-new-normal, 19 June 2019.
50. Marian Salzman, 'Marketing to the new consumer' [web article], Forbes, www.forbes.com/sites/mariansalzman/2020/07/10/marketing-to-the-new-consumer, 10 July 2020.

51 *Ibid.*
52 *Ibid.*
53 Katie Hickey, 'What makes a great digital experience?' [blog post], CX Insights, https://usabilla.com/blog/digital-maturity-digital-experience, 30 May 2019.
54 Chloe Green, 'The biggest digital marketing trends we've seen so far in 2020' [web article], Charity Digital, https://charitydigital.org.uk/topics/the-biggest-digital-marketing-trends-weve-seen-so-far-in-2020-7852, 28 August 2020.
55 Aidan Paterson, 'The four trends impacting charity marketing' [web article], Charity Digital, https://charitydigital.org.uk/topics/topics/the-four-trends-impacting-charity-marketing-7839, 24 August 2020.
56 Tom De Fraine, 'Are your donors' expectations changing?' [blog post], JustGiving, https://blog.justgiving.com/are-your-donors-expectations-changing, 27 February 2018.
57 Kirsty Weakley, '"Donor behaviour has changed and it won't change back," says JustGiving boss' [web article], Civil Society Media, www.civilsociety.co.uk/news/charities-should-embrace-ai-and-crowdfunding-to-attract-new-donors-says-justgiving-boss.html, 12 May 2017.
58 Teretza Litsa, 'How the digital donor landscape is changing' [blog post], Lightful, www.lightful.com/blog/fundraising/how-the-digital-donor-landscape-is-changing, 8 July 2019.
59 *UK Giving 2019: An overview of charitable giving in the UK* [PDF], Charities Aid Foundation, 2019, www.cafonline.org/docs/default-source/about-us-publications/caf-uk-giving-2019-report-an-overview-of-charitable-giving-in-the-uk.pdf, accessed 19 May 2021.
60 *Mind the Gap: The growing generational divide in charitable giving* [PDF], Charities Aid Foundation, 2012, www.cafonline.org/docs/default-source/about-us-publications/1190h_partyconf_mindthegap.pdf, accessed 19 May 2021.
61 Aaron D. Warwick, 'Overcoming donor fatigue' [master's dissertation], University of Northern Iowa, 2019, https://stewardshipcalling.com/wp-content/uploads/2015/03/Masters-Degree-Research-Paper-Donor-Fatigue-Fr.-Aaron-Warwick.pdf, accessed 19 May 2021.
62 *Ibid.*
63 Philipp Süssenbach, 'When They Come in Crowds: Charity appeals and moral fatigue', *Basic and Applied Social Psychology*, vol. 40, no. 4, 2018, pp. 171–9.
64 Roger Bennett, 'Factors Influencing Donation Switching Behaviour', *Journal of Customer Behaviour*, vol. 8, no. 4, 2009, pp. 329–45.
65 Marc A. Pitman, 'Donor fatigue is a myth' [web article], Fundraising Coach, https://fundraisingcoach.com/2015/05/20/donor-fatigue-myth, 20 May 2015.
66 Daniel Fluskey, 'Why fewer people are giving to charity and what we can do about it' [web article], Civil Society Media, www.civilsociety.co.uk/voices/daniel-fluskey-why-fewer-people-are-giving-to-charity-and-what-we-can-do-about-it.html, 8 May 2019.
67 Karl Wilding, 'Are fewer people supporting charities?' [blog post], NCVO, https://blogs.ncvo.org.uk/2019/05/07/are-fewer-people-supporting-charities, 7 May 2019.
68 Summer Allen, 'Ten ways to encourage people to give more' [web article], *Greater Good Magazine*, https:// greatergood.berkeley.edu/article/item/ten_ways_to_encourage_people_to_give_more, 27 November 2017. See the source for details of the studies mentioned in the list.

CHAPTER TWELVE
Avoiding strategic wear-out

Introduction

Developing and implementing your fundraising strategy is not the end of your work. You will need to regularly review your strategy to ensure that it remains effective and avoids strategic wear-out.

Strategic wear-out (often referred to more widely as strategic drift) in fundraising can be defined as a gradual deterioration of fundraising effectiveness created by a failure to react to changes in the wider environment.[1] Indeed, organisations tend to change their strategies in a series of small incremental steps based on what has been done before. It's easy for these small steps to lose pace with the changing environment in which your organisation is operating, particularly when major shifts occur in the external environment.[2]

It is therefore essential to view strategy development not as a one-off exercise but as an ongoing cycle of environmental scanning, strategy development and review.

Triggers and methods to avoid strategic wear-out

How then can your organisation avoid strategic wear-out? As fundraising strategies tend to be grounded in an assessment of particular environmental conditions and are commonly based on assumptions about the future state of that environment (see chapter 1), it might be possible to set up a system to avoid strategic wear-out based on flagging environmental change.[3] External issues – such as new competitors entering the market, existing competitors changing their approach, changes in customer or donor requirements, or changes in the macro-environment – can lead to strategic wear-out.[4] It may be helpful here to regularly scan the environment and put in place a process that would trigger an action when environmental signals pass certain thresholds. The action might be a high-level response if the signal is strong (such as pulling the plug on an event altogether) or a lower-level response if the signal is weaker (such as increasing an event's advertising budget).

More broadly, such actions could be classified into five different types:

- **Sitting out the change or waiting for it to cease:** this is an option if the data suggests that the change is temporary.

- **An active intervention:** for example, increasing spending on fundraising advertising to recruit event participants.

- **Moving out of the market:** for instance, if the data suggested a sustained decrease in the number of people interested in cycling, a charity could reduce or even eliminate its cycling events.

- **Changing the overarching strategy:** rather than reacting with more specific interventions, a charity could completely re-evaluate its approach to fundraising.

- **Crisis mode:** although not a proactive choice, if an organisation fails to react in the previous stages or those interventions fail, then it might enter a crisis mode where its very viability might be at stake.

> ### Case study: Parkinson's UK[5]
> The COVID-19 pandemic is an example of an external crisis which forced many commercial and non-profit organisations alike to change how they operated. Parkinson's UK has shared how the pandemic led to an acceleration in how it worked cross-organisationally to share data and break down organisational silos.
>
> In the early stages of the pandemic, although the organisation adapted very quickly, there was an issue with how data was being shared across departments – an issue that was amplified by everyone working from home. In order to combat this challenge, the organisation set up cross-organisational fortnightly synthesis meetings where it could collate disparate pieces of data from different teams, identify key themes, and use that information to write short insight statements that captured the needs of the Parkinson's community. These statements were prioritised, and the team considered how it might take action around each. The statements were then shared across the organisation. The new process has been incredibly successful and is likely to be continued beyond the pandemic.

Difficulties in identifying strategic wear-out

However, it is possible to regularly scan the external environment and still suffer strategic wear-out. Indeed, some have argued that, eventually, strategic wear-out is almost inevitable.[6] There are a number of reasons why scanning the environment alone may not be sufficient to avoid the problem.

Firstly, signals from the external environment may be missed. It's often not easy to understand change as it's happening – for example, you might believe a major change in social attitudes is just a temporary fad.

It's often only with the benefit of hindsight that we actually recognise major changes.[7]

Secondly, signals from the external environment may be misinterpreted. Emeritus Professor of Strategic Management Gerry Johnson describes how signals from the external environment are often interpreted through an organisation's existing perspective or a set of taken-for-granted assumptions: it's that perspective that will decide which factors are seen as relevant and which aren't, and, indeed, those that don't fit with the existing perspective may well be ignored or suggestions for change may become mired in internal political disputes.[8] Johnson also argues that where organisations react to signals, they are likely to do so from inside the perspective in which they currently see the world, rather than changing their views – which might mean that their responses are suboptimal. Ultimately, it may not be until there's a moment of crisis that an organisation is forced to change.[9]

Thirdly, even if signals are recognised and interpreted correctly, there might be other reasons that an organisation can't or won't change. For example, if an organisation has a capability that it's very good at delivering, it might find it difficult to change course. For example, a charity that's very good at delivering its fundraising in the offline world might find it difficult to switch to digital. Johnson and colleagues discuss the concept of path dependency.[10] They use the analogy of a cart regularly travelling along the same road, pointing to how, over time, ruts will form, becoming deeper and deeper – eventually so deep that it's almost impossible to change course. In our example, the charity might have staff who are very skilled in delivering offline direct marketing (such as buying print or advertising space), a database that's ideally configured to manage offline responses, and a supporter care team that is used to managing responses by post and telephone. There might also be cultural reasons an organisation refuses to change, or powerful people who might resist change. In our charity example, there might be trustees who are risk averse and not prepared to invest in new ideas, or a director who is mistrustful of social media.

Case study: Listening to donors

In 2015, very sadly, 92-year-old poppy-seller Olive Cooke took her own life. Several media outlets reported that the volume of charity appeals she received was a factor in her death (although this was denied by her family).[11] The initial media story was followed up by exposés of the use of data by charities, as well as telephone and face-to-face fundraising practices. At the time, renowned fundraiser Giles Pegram stated, 'We fundraisers and fundraising directors got it wrong. We created a fundraising machine that was not attuned to the desires and hopes of our donors. We did it slowly, over decades.

> We did it together. We gave ourselves permission. We knew best. We were wrong.'[12] By not being attuned to the desires and hopes of our donors, the model of how fundraising was typically done was suffering from strategic wear-out.
>
> Fundraising consultant Richard Turner argues that fundraising was built on the paradigm of interrupting the many, through a variety of direct marketing techniques, in order to get a response from the few. Turner suggests that this approach ignored changes in communication that have been going on around us, where, in the wider world, people increasingly react poorly to being interrupted and rely on those whom they know and trust as key sources of information. He argues for an approach which views everyone (for example, the charity, its supporters and volunteers) as channels, enabling supporters to tell charities' stories for themselves.[13]

Cultural signs of strategic wear-out

Given that several of the reasons above are related to organisational culture, there are a number of cultural warning signs which you can watch out for. Professor of Strategic Management Tanya Sammut-Bonnici says that strategic drift can sometimes be avoided before it starts to affect performance, with the early warning signs including:

- people at senior levels having similar mindsets – while similar mindsets can create harmonious organisations, they can also make it easier to miss changes in the broader environment (see page 167 in chapter 11);

- desire to maintain the status quo, which can result in resistance to innovation;

- lack of focus on the external environment, with the organisation often being internally oriented.[14]

In a similar vein, Sammut-Bonnici points to two core underlying cultural issues which can lead to strategic wear-out:

- When mental maps (or fixed ideas and approaches) are shared among the senior management team or organisation leaders, they may make decisions based on ideas and principles that they have constructed over time and through past experience rather than on objective information on the environment around them.

- Culture can have a powerful influence on decision-making, so a culture that doesn't encourage change may mean that people do not recognise the drivers of change or are discouraged from acting if they do.[15]

The two issues are interrelated, with management's mental maps often contributing to an organisation's underlying culture. Sammut-Bonnici goes on to suggest specific actions that organisations can take to try to avoid strategic wear-out:

- encouraging diversity in culture, skills and perspectives;

- encouraging innovation and disincentivising behaviours that suppress innovation;

- generating a flow of information on the external environment and sharing it with key people internally;

- benchmarking against the wider industry;

- investing in market research to spot developing trends;

- ensuring that monitoring and control of strategies are robust, so that signs of strategic drift can be spotted early;

- viewing strategy development as an evolving process.[16]

Proactive reinvention

Rather than just trying to avoid strategic wear-out, organisations can take steps to proactively reinvent themselves when needed. A study in the commercial sector which analysed company performance over a 20-year period found that companies which had successfully strategically transformed themselves had several key factors in common.[17]

Firstly, they built what the authors describe as 'alternative coalitions' internally.[18] In practice, this meant developing two groups of senior executives: one that focused on maintaining the positive aspects of the organisation's existing approach and another that actively sought to develop new approaches. This dual approach became a normal part of how these organisations worked.

Secondly, they encouraged conflict – or, more accurately, constructive challenging – as part of their culture. This often grew out of a history of senior-level conflict, which in its early days may not have been particularly constructive. Over time, however, the companies embedded processes and systems to encourage this challenge-oriented approach.

Thirdly, the companies were able to use what the authors describe as 'happy accidents' to gain support and facilitate change.[19] In practice, this could mean taking problems or challenges and transforming them into opportunities to change things, which could be used by those tasked with developing new approaches. In a fundraising context, one example of a happy accident might be if an organisation which doesn't proactively practise corporate fundraising is approached by a company offering a promising partnership – this might help to show key people internally why corporate fundraising could be a viable approach moving forwards. These processes are repeated continuously as illustrated in figure 12.1.

FIGURE 12.1 THE PROCESS OF PROACTIVE REINVENTION

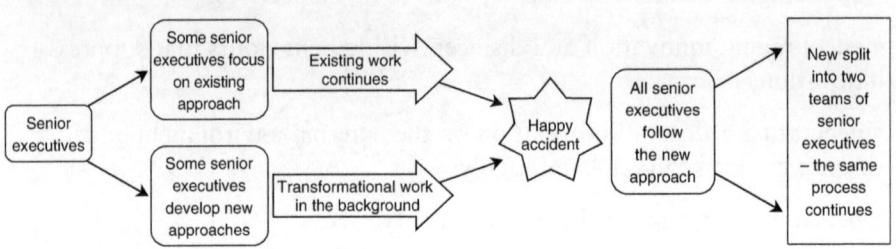

Emergent strategy

There are also other ways in which organisations can take steps to avoid strategic wear-out – for example, by enabling new ideas to flourish alongside the strategy as originally planned. Academic and author Henry Mintzberg discusses strategy as both a planned and an emergent process, leading to what he describes as intended and emergent strategies. Mintzberg and his colleague James Waters say that for an intended strategy to be delivered exactly as originally planned, three conditions need to be in place:[20]

- There must be no ambiguity in the strategy as written.

- Every person involved must be in agreement.

- The wider environment must be either completely predictable or under the full control of the organisation.

Unsurprisingly, this is almost never the case – and therefore strategies are unlikely to be delivered exactly as originally planned. Instead, what is delivered on the ground is likely to be a combination of intended and emergent strategy.

Emergent strategy could be defined as a process of using trial, experimentation and evaluation to understand what works. However, it's not a state of complete randomness, or it wouldn't be a strategy: there is a sense of order and consistency in the choices made.[21] Intended and emergent strategies can co-exist within an organisation, with emergent strategy enabling organisations to respond to unforeseen issues. Indeed, it's been argued that both forms of strategy are important to an organisation's success[22] and even that it's impossible for organisations to sustain their competitive advantage without enabling the development of emergent strategies.[23]

CHAPTER TWELVE **AVOIDING STRATEGIC WEAR-OUT**

The first case study below provides an example of enabling new ideas and the second showcases how organisations can be responsive to a changing environment when considering their fundraising strategy.

Case study: Macmillan's World's Biggest Coffee Morning

A great example of an emergent strategy is Macmillan's World's Biggest Coffee Morning. The initiative was started in 1990 by one of the charity's local fundraising groups.[24] The idea was then picked up by the wider charity. The first nationwide coffee morning took place just a year later, in 1991, with 2,600 supporters taking part.[25]

The coffee morning is a great example of an organisation enabling people on the ground to pilot an idea and then, vitally, listening to that idea and being prepared to develop it. Since 1990, the coffee morning has developed every year, raising more than £290 million in total and earning an award from Guinness World Records.[26]

Case study: Cancer Research UK's #nomakeupselfie campaign

In 2014, Cancer Research UK raised more than £8 million through the #nomakeupselfie campaign. Rather than being instigated by the charity, the campaign was started by 18-year-old Facebook user, Fiona Cunningham, following criticism of a woman attending the Oscars without make-up.[27] Early posts mentioned linking the selfies to raising awareness of cancer, and it evolved into a way of supporting Cancer Research UK after the charity shared a picture of one of its staff members taking part in the campaign alongside a 'text to donate' number.[28] The charity continued to amplify the campaign's messages as it grew and developed.[29] This is a good example of a charity listening carefully in the digital space and staff being able to adapt extremely quickly to a developing trend.

Supporting emergent strategy

While the majority of this book has focused on intentional (or deliberate) strategy development, here we focus on supporting the development of emergent strategy as one way of avoiding strategic wear-out. One key consideration for organisations seeking to enable the development of emergent strategy alongside their deliberate strategy is empowering those people who are closest to the customer – or, in the case of fundraising, the donor.

Associate Professor of Management Karl Moore describes how people who are working in front-line roles are what he calls 'boundary spanners' – they play an important role in an organisation but also have excellent insights into what customers need and what other organisations are doing.[30] They therefore can be very well positioned to come up with new ideas and innovations. For example, in the world of fundraising, someone who works in a supporter care team and regularly speaks to donors is likely to have some good insights into how to address common areas of dissatisfaction for donors. Being open to emergent strategy can therefore be about shifting power from the top of the organisation towards people working on the front lines.[31] The role of senior management then becomes more about creating a culture where people are encouraged to experiment and feel safe to do so; putting in place processes and systems to make the most of the lessons that are gathered; and crafting strategy as it emerges. Indeed, Mintzberg uses the analogy of a potter crafting a pot to describe how a manager can craft a strategy – that is, focus on and bring together the key elements of strategy as it emerges.[32]

If you're the sole fundraiser in a small charity, this might be about giving yourself the freedom to test and learn outside the strategy you've developed. However, if you're the director of fundraising in a larger organisation, it's likely to be more about enabling the members of your team who are regularly meeting and working with donors to pitch and develop new ideas. This approach is practised in the commercial world in a number of innovative firms: Google, for example, has famously encouraged employees to spend 20% of their time developing new ideas.[33]

On the surface, it might seem relatively easy to enable emergent strategy to develop – for example, by ensuring that there is a budget available to test new ideas. However, for emergent strategy to develop optimally, it may require a range of new processes to be put in place. For example, organisations have to ensure that they set up and maintain strong internal information and communication flows, and that they can learn from employees' experiences.[34]

Moore suggests putting in place processes (such as pilot programmes to test new ideas) to allow people to explore their ideas, quickly and cheaply, with the knowledge that many of these experiments will fail.[35] He also suggests taking an in-depth look at what is working well and reflecting on how those insights can be built upon, which could be seen as similar in part to the internal audit we have described previously.

It may also help to have a defined system in place for emergent strategy development. A process for emergent strategy development could include:

1. Creating an initial hypothesis about the market.

2. Testing it quickly and assessing the feedback.

3. Changing either the strategy or the way it is executed.

4. Revising plans and budget, then communicating changes to the organisation and monitoring the execution of the revised strategy.[36]

If you follow a process like this, as your organisation learns, both your strategy and your organisation will evolve.

> **Case study: Design sprint**
>
> There are several parallels between the process of emergent strategy development (see above) and the principles of a design sprint – a short, focused process of understanding an audience, prototyping a product and testing it with customers (or donors). Vicky Reeves, Deputy Group CEO and Digital Managing Director at the agency WPNC, explains how Princess Alice Hospice and WPNC worked together on an intensive three-day sprint to develop the hospice's new website.
>
>> Websites are, of course, a key tool for communicating with donors, but the hospice also needed its website to work for people in need of end-of-life care, their relatives, and health workers looking for qualifications or jobs.
>>
>> Given the importance of the site working for the hospice's users, the sprint started with **understanding** the key audiences and what they needed from the site. This process drew on experts who could shed light on the problems those audiences face, their needs and how those needs would ideally be addressed. The process then moved on to **sketching** new solutions. The solutions were voted on by the participants, then two different site layouts were **prototyped** including a homepage, key landing pages and content pages.
>>
>> Representatives from the core audiences were invited to **test** the clickable prototypes and talk through their honest opinions on what they were seeing and why they were completing certain actions. Due to the speed of the prototyping, the team was able to make iterations based on user feedback in between tests to make some elements clearer. By the end of the three-day process, the team had been able to create a full range of design templates for the new site.
>
> This example demonstrates that, with the right support and processes in place, it's possible to quickly and efficiently test new ideas and iterate elements of your strategy.

Being agile

In recent years there has been increasing interest in agile methodology, which could be argued to be a natural step onwards from embracing the idea of emergent strategy. The agile methodology originated in the world of software design but is increasingly embraced in other sectors, with a number of organisations beginning to adapt its ideas into fundraising. It can be described in various ways: as an organisational mindset or culture, as a way of organising, and as a set of project management techniques or methods (such as the Scrum framework or the design sprint) designed to enable organisations to respond quickly to changes in their environment.

This relatively short chapter cannot do full justice to the varied approaches to the agile methodology. However, agile organisations have been described as ones that are fast-moving, adaptable and robust. This mindset is underpinned by processes and structures that help to deliver speed, adaptation and robustness – for example, by moving from traditional team structures to working within self-contained, cross-functional groups.[37] It has been argued that without the right mindset in place, the agile methodology can become a rigidly applied set of processes in an organisation that is not truly nimble, flexible or quick.[38]

At an operational level, consultant and author Steve Denning has described agility as being underpinned by three laws:

- **The law of the customer:** this defines the core purpose of an organisation as being to add value to its customers (as opposed to other stakeholders).

- **The law of the small team:** this focuses on breaking down problems into small batches of work, delivered by small, cross-functional teams. These teams work quickly and iteratively, drawing on customer feedback.

- **The law of the network:** an organisation operates as a network rather than a set of vertical hierarchies.[39]

Denning argues that it's the three laws in combination that can dramatically increase value for organisations.

Some might argue that strategic planning and an agile approach are incompatible. However, Alessandro Di Fiore, founder of the European Centre for Strategic Innovation, argues that both are necessary.[40] Without planning there wouldn't be an office in which to work or colleagues to work with – planning, Di Fiore says, is essential to ensuring an organisation uses its resources effectively. He suggests that organisations should therefore develop an agile planning process that blends top-down and bottom-up approaches: the bigger-picture (strategic) priorities of the organisation set at the top, balanced with the autonomy of the small teams (as described in the second law above). An agile planning process has a number of elements:

- It has to involve frameworks and tools that can cope with a future which will be different. For example, Di Fiore describes how, in the commercial world, ING Bank reorganised into agile teams. However, they hold quarterly updates to co-ordinate priorities and ensure that their work aligns with the overall strategic goals.
- It has to be able to cope with changes that are likely to be frequent and dynamic.
- It has to ensure that time is invested for strategic conversations.
- It has to ensure that resources and funds will be available as opportunities emerge.

Di Fiore suggests, therefore, developing processes to ensure that teams are able to meet regularly to discuss priorities and share ideas, ensuring that projects will contribute towards larger strategic goals. He also suggests that teams make decisions based on both hard data and softer insights – for example, from talking to customers.

Case study: Save the Children

Having discussed some of the principles of agile and how they might relate to fundraising, it may be interesting to understand how one organisation – Save the Children – has remodelled its fundraising around agile principles.

The fundraising team at Save the Children found that its vision to be more integrated across its communication functions was continually being bogged down in internal silos. Additionally, despite the team's best efforts, the organisation wasn't being responsive enough to external changes.

The team therefore decided to overhaul its fundraising model, drawing on agile principles. Rather than having product teams (such as events, legacies and individual giving), it created four multi-disciplinary squads. Although there were challenges along the way, Gemma Sherrington, Executive Director of Fundraising and Marketing, describes how benefits were felt almost immediately, including a prioritisation of the supporter experience, a much quicker process to move from new ideas to launching fundraising activities in the market, a process of continuous improvement and increased autonomy for staff.

Save the Children's top tips for anyone looking to move to an agile model include:

- It will cost you time and money up front – don't skimp on training.
- Embrace co-design and delivery with your whole leadership team.
- It will be an 18-month to two-year change programme.
- Go for a full operating model change rather than just some tweaks to structures.
- Invest much more time than you think you need to support people through the change.
- Focus on building a brilliant two-way feedback-giving system across the whole organisation which ensures that data is both captured and analysed across your organisation so you can learn and correct fast.
- Agile is not for everyone – you will lose some great people.
- Know what parts of your business don't suit Agile and don't force it. The principles of Agile lend themselves better to areas where there is cross-team collaboration or where the outcomes are less predictable.
- Lead by example.[41]

What does being agile mean in practice?

You might like to consider a range of questions when developing and operationalising your fundraising strategy, including:

- At what point would you consider adjusting your strategy – as the situation changes or as results emerge?
- How can you ensure that your organisation and your fundraising team embrace change and welcome ideas from all levels and that you don't suffer from groupthink, blind spots or a lack of diversity at a senior level?
- Do you have ways of looking outside your organisation at the external environment?
- Do you have strong information and communication flows within your organisation?
- Is your organisation ready to change quickly if needed?

Conclusion

As this chapter shows, your strategies can become ineffective over time as the environment in which you are operating changes. In the most extreme examples, your very future could be at stake if you fail to keep pace with a changing world. However, there are a number of ways in which strategic wear-out can be avoided: most obviously by continuing to scan the environment and flagging – and, of course, reacting to – environmental change with appropriate actions, depending on the magnitude of the change.

Unfortunately, though, avoiding strategic wear-out is not always that simple. It is easy to miss or misinterpret important environmental signals, and sometimes the underlying organisational culture or systems can make change difficult to achieve (in which case it may be necessary to think again about stakeholder management, as discussed in chapter 9).

There are, however, specific actions you can take to try to rectify these cultural issues, such as encouraging diversity and innovation. You can also seek to enable strategy to emerge by empowering people on the front line to innovate and ensuring that their findings are communicated clearly throughout your organisation. Some organisations have also attempted to shift their wider mindset and processes to become increasingly agile and have adapted their planning processes accordingly.

Whether you've reached this point in the book having implemented much of your fundraising strategy or whether you're just about to start that journey, we hope we have helped you to be as strategic as possible in your fundraising. We have found fundraising strategy development and implementation to be instrumental in ensuring organisations' sustainability and success, and we hope you will enjoy implementing these processes as much as we do. It's become something of a passion of ours, which we hope we have conveyed.

We wish you luck in your fundraising. May you change the world with your success.

Notes

1 Tanya Sammut-Bonnici, 'Strategic Drift', in *Wiley Encyclopedia of Management*, edited by Cary Cooper, London, Wiley, 2014, doi:10.1002/ 9781118785317.weom120213.
2 Gerry Johnson, Richard Whittington, Kevan Scholes, Duncan Angwin and Patrick Regnér, *Exploring Strategy: Text and cases*, 11th edition, Harlow, Pearson, 2017, p. 180.
3 Colin Gilligan and Richard Wilson, *Strategic Marketing Planning*, 2nd edition, Abingdon, Taylor & Francis, 2009.
4 Richard Wilson and Colin Gilligan, *Strategic Marketing Management: Planning, implementation and control*, 3rd edition, Abingdon, Routledge, 2005.

5   Based on 'From frenzy to clarity: How our COVID-19 response has helped us put our community and data at the heart of our decision-making' [web article], Parkinson's UK Service Transformation, https://parkinsonsukst.medium.com/from-frenzy-to-clarity-how-our-covid-19-response-has-helped-us-put-our-community-and-data-at-the-a587f5e18693, 6 July 2020.
6   Colin Gilligan and Richard Wilson, *Strategic Marketing Planning*, 2nd edition, Abingdon, Taylor & Francis, 2009.
7   Gerry Johnson, Richard Whittington, Kevan Scholes, Duncan Angwin and Patrick Regnér, *Exploring Strategy: Text and cases*, 11th edition, Harlow, Pearson, 2017.
8   Gerry Johnson, 'Rethinking Incrementalism', *Strategic Management Journal*, vol. 9, no. 1, 1988, pp. 75–91.
9   Gerry Johnson, George Yip and Manuel Hensmans, 'Achieving Successful Strategic Transformation', *MIT Sloan Management Review*, vol. 53, no. 3, 2012, pp. 25–32.
10 *Ibid.*
11 Howard Lake, 'FRSB publishes results of Olive Cooke investigation and related complaints' [web article], UK Fundraising, https://fundraising.co.uk/2016/01/20/frsb-publishes-results-of-olive-cooke-investigation-and-related-complaints, 20 January 2016; Steven Morris, 'Poppy seller who killed herself got 3,000 charity requests for donations a year' [web article], *The Guardian*, www.theguardian.com/society/2016/jan/20/poppy-seller-who-killed-herself-got-up-to-3000-charity-mailings-a-year, 20 January 2016.
12 Giles Pegram, 'Are we managing a fundraising decline? Only if we let ourselves' [web article], 101 Fundraising, https://101fundraising.org/2016/11/are-we-managing-a-fundraising-decline-only-if-we-let-ourselves, 10 November 2016.
13 Richard Turner, 'Why the fundraising model is broken (and why this couldn't be a better time to fundraise)' [blog post], Ifundraiser, https://ifundraiser.wordpress.com/2018/07/01/why-the-fundraising-model-is-broken-and-why-this-couldnt-be-a-better-time-to-fundraise, 1 July 2018.
14 Tanya Sammut-Bonnici, 'Strategic Drift', in *Wiley Encyclopedia of Management*, edited by Cary Cooper, London, Wiley, 2014, doi:10.1002/9781118785317.weom120213.
15 *Ibid.*
16 *Ibid.*
17 Gerry Johnson, George Yip and Manuel Hensmans, 'Achieving Successful Strategic Transformation', *MIT Sloan Management Review*, vol. 53, no. 3, 2012, pp. 25–32.
18 *Ibid.*, p. 26.
19 *Ibid.*, p. 26.
20 Henry Mintzberg and James A. Waters, 'Of Strategies, Deliberate and Emergent', *Strategic Management Journal*, vol. 6, no. 3, 1985, pp. 257–72.
21 Richard Whittington, 'Emergent Strategy', in *The Palgrave Encyclopedia of Strategic Management*, edited by Mie Augier and David Teece, London, Palgrave Macmillan, 2018, pp. 490–3.
22 *Ibid.*
23 Wendy Bodwell and Thomas Chermack, 'Organizational Ambidexterity: Integrating deliberate and emergent strategy with scenario planning', *Technological Forecasting and Social Change*, vol. 77, no. 2, 2010, pp. 193–202.

24 Rachel Beer, 'Macmillan Cancer Support: The World's Biggest Coffee Morning' [web article], The Showcase of Fundraising Innovation and Inspiration (SOFII), https://sofii.org/case-study/the-worlds-biggest-coffee-morning-by-macmillan-cancer-support, 18 June 2012.
25 'Macmillan's World's Biggest Coffee Morning' [web article], Carewatch, www.carewatch.co.uk/macmillan-world-biggest-coffee-morning, 2 October 2016.
26 'What is World's Biggest Coffee Morning?' [web page], Macmillan, 2021, https://coffee.macmillan.org.uk/about/what, accessed 19 May 2021.
27 Amy Duncan, 'Still wondering who kick-started the #nomakeupselfie craze? Creator revealed to be a teenage mum from Stoke-on-Trent' [web article], Metro, https://metro.co.uk/2014/03/25/still-wondering-who-kick-started-the-nomakeupselfie-craze-creator-revealed-to-be-a-teenage-mum-from-stoke-on-trent-4678163, 25 March 2014.
28 Catherine Cottrell, 'Cancer Research UK's "no-make-up selfie" campaign' [web article], The Showcase of Fundraising Innovation and Inspiration (SOFII), https://sofii.org/case-study/cancer-research-uks-no-make-up-selfie-campaign, 30 April 2015.
29 Carlos Miranda and Alissa Steiner, 'No-makeup selfie: Cancer Research's lesson on benefits of quick thinking' [web article], The Guardian, www.theguardian.com/voluntary-sector-network/2014/dec/03/no-makeup-selfie-cancer-research-fundraising-benefit-quick-thinking, 3 December 2014.
30 Karl Moore, 'The emergent way: How to achieve meaningful growth in an era of flat growth' [web article], Ivey Business Journal, https://iveybusinessjournal.com/publication/the-emergent-way-how-to-achieve-meaningful-growth-in-an-era-of-flat-growth, November–December 2011.
31 Richard Whittington, 'Emergent Strategy', in The Palgrave Encyclopedia of Strategic Management, edited by Mie Augier and David Teece, London, Palgrave Macmillan, 2018, pp. 490–3.
32 Henry Mintzberg, 'Crafting strategy' [web article], Harvard Business Review, https://hbr.org/1987/07/crafting-strategy, July 1987.
33 Bill Murphy, 'Google says it still uses the "20-percent rule," and you should totally copy it' [web article], Inc., www.inc.com/bill-murphy-jr/google-says-it-still-uses-20-percent-rule-you-should-totally-copy-it.html, 1 November 2020.
34 Alexis Downs, Rita Durant and Adrian Carr, 'Emergent Strategy Development for Organizations', Emergence, vol. 5, no. 2, 2010, pp. 5–28; Richard Whittington, 'Emergent Strategy', in The Palgrave Encyclopedia of Strategic Management, edited by Mie Augier and David Teece, London, Palgrave Macmillan, 2018, pp. 490–3.
35 Karl Moore, 'The emergent way: How to achieve meaningful growth in an era of flat growth' [web article], Ivey Business Journal, https://iveybusinessjournal.com/publication/the-emergent-way-how-to-achieve-meaningful-growth-in-an-era-of-flat-growth, November–December 2011.
36 Phil Jones, 'Deliberate or emergent strategy: When to choose either or both' [web article], Excitant, www.excitant.co.uk/deliberate-vs-emergent-strategy, 30 May 2020.
37 Yogesh Kumar, 'Agile strategy manifesto' [web article], InfoQ, www.infoq.com/articles/agile-strategy-manifesto, 4 August 2011.
38 Allen Holub, 'Getting started with agility: Essential reading' [web article], https://holub.com/reading, 12 January 2021.
39 Steve Denning, 'What is strategic agility?' [web article], Forbes, www.forbes.com/sites/stevedenning/2018/01/28/what-is-strategic-agility, 28 January 2018.

40 Alessandro Di Fiore, 'Planning doesn't have to be the enemy of agile' [web article], *Harvard Business Review*, https://hbr.org/2018/09/planning-doesnt-have-to-be-the-enemy-of-agile, 13 September 2018.
41 See 'Agile transformation: Save the Children's fundraising lead on its new operating model' [web article], Civil Society Media, www.civilsociety.co.uk/fundraising/agile-transformation-save-the-children-new-operating-model.html, 11 May 2020. The article first appeared in May 2020 issue of *Fundraising Magazine*, published by Civil Society Media.

Index

Page numbers in *italics* refer to figures and illustrations and in **bold** refer to tables.

accountability 180
acquisition, donors 92, 126
advertising 67–8, 76–7, 123, 176
Age UK 71, 98
agencies 52–3
agile methodology 196–8
AI (artificial intelligence) 176
Amazon Alexa 101, 102–3
Ansoff's Growth Matrix 61–4
Arams, Lorraine 111
Arkansas Children's Foundation 124–5
Arkansas University, Little Rock 146–7
artificial intelligence (AI) 176
Ashford, Ruth 63
Ashford, Susan 141–2
asks 97–9
aspirations 16
attrition, loss of donors **12–13**
audience 17–18, 60–73, 76, 96–7 *see also* donors
audits 115
    external 10–20
    internal 22–36
    SWOT analysis 36–9, **38**, **39**, 57–8

Baines, Paul 31
batching 111
Bath University 161
Battersea, charity 117
behaviour, consumer 179–80
Behavioural Insights Team 143
behavioural segmentation 68–70
benchmarking 23–5
beneficiaries 157, 160, 173–4
Bennett, Roger 14, 180
best practice 14
biases 36, 55, 77, 169, 176
Big Idea 84–5
Black Lives Matter 171
Blackbaud 175
Blind Veterans UK 82
Boston Matrix 32–3
Bowcock, Matthew 91
branding 79–82
Breeze, Beth 171

Brickel, Catriona 19
briefs, research 53
British Library 161
Brooks, Jeff 82
budgeting 29, 114–20
Burnett, Ken 100
buy-in 137–42

CAF (Charities Aid Foundation) 14, 91, 175
Cancer Research UK 79, 85, 103, 170, 193
Carpenter, Kathryn 4, 8
case for support 82–7
case studies
    Arkansas Children's Foundation 124–5
    Cancer Research UK's equality, equity, diversity and inclusion strategy 170
    Cancer Research UK's #nomakeupselfie campaign 193
    Church Mission Society audit 19
    Comic Relief 174
    design sprint 195
    developing a new donor journey 106
    getting buy-in from digital teams at St Mungo's 144
    growing internal participation and a culture of giving at the University of Arkansas at Little Rock 146–7
    heart of the Oregon Zoo 83
    how Unicef uses complaints to alter behaviour 131–2
    listening to donors 189–90
    listening to donors at SolarAid 42–3
    Macmillan's World's Biggest Coffee Morning 193
    Mind's Pause box 99
    Operation Smile 122–3
    Parkinson's UK 188
    The Presidents Club 174–5

case studies—*continued*
  rebranding 82
  Save the Children 197–8
  Sue Ryder 100–1
  taking a blended research approach to understanding supporters 51–2
  using Amazon Alexa to encourage giving 101–2
  using qualitative insight to develop a legacy proposition at St Peter's Hospice 50–1
  using quantitative research to develop a training proposition at the Chartered Institute of Fundraising 47–8
  using segmentation in planned (legacy) giving 65
  using sophisticated response modelling in practice 71
  WaterAid's Untapped campaign 178
cash cows, Boston matrix 32, 33
cashflow figures *119–20*
CCEW (Charity Commission for England and Wales) 13, 134, 174–5
change management 139, 142–7, *143*
Channel 4 79
channels (communication routes) 101–3, **102**
Charities (Protection and Social Investment) Act 2016 149–50
Charities Aid Foundation (CAF) 14, 91, 175
Charities and Risk Management (CC26) 134
Charity Commission for England and Wales (CCEW) 13, 134, 174–5
Charity Digital Skills Report, 2019 177
Charity: Water 80
Chartered Institute of Fundraising (CIoF) 25, 47–8, 91, 92, 101, 152, 168, 175
chatbots 176, 178
Church Mission Society 19
class inequality 171 *see also* equality, equity, diversity and inclusion (EEDI)
Clayton, Alan 84
Code of Fundraising Practice 104, 152, 153, 163, 170
cognitive diversity 167–8
collections, street 152
Comic Relief 174

communication 4, 28, 101–3, **102**, 110, 115, 140–1, 173
Community-Centric Fundraising 156, 172
community fundraising 26, 92–3
companies 26, 93–4
competitor analysis 10, *11*, 13–17, 77
complaints 131–2, 163
consequentialist theories 155, 156
consultants 52–3
consumer behaviour 179–80
contingency funds 119
contingency planning 133, 134–5
Cook, Jonathan 47–8
Cooke, Olive 189–90
corporate fundraising 26, 93–4
costs 117–19, **118–19**
Coutts, bank 91
COVID-19 14, 26, 101, 115, 175, 188
Cowley, Edd 13–14
critical path 113–14, *114*
culture, organisational 28, 190–1 *see also* internal environment
Cunningham, Fiona 193
customer behaviour 179–80

data 12, **12–13**, 15–16, 54–5
data protection regulation 92, 153, 181
databases 29, 65, 176
Davison, Ruth 174
de-humanisation 173
decaying dogs, Boston matrix 32, 33
decision-making model 161–2, *162*
demographics 11, 17–18, 66–7, 70
Denning, Steve 196
deontological theories 155, 156, 157
design sprint 195
Detert, James 141–2
Developing your case for support 82
Di Fiore, Alessandro 196–7
Diabetes Canada 106
diagnosis of performance 130–2
digital methods 45, 67–8, 144, 175–8, 179–80
dilemmas, ethical 152–5, 157–8, 161–2, *162*
DiMaggio, Paul 16–17
direct response, giving 91
discrimination *see* equality, equity, diversity and inclusion (EEDI)
diversification 62
diversity 167–8, 191 *see also* equality, equity, diversity and inclusion (EEDI)
donors **12–13**, 14, 96–7 *see also* audience

donors—*continued*
    donor-centrism 156, 158, 159–60, 171
    experience 97, 97–101
    fatigue 180–2
    journey 105–6
    listening to 42–3, 189–90
    messaging for 76–87
    recruitment 92, 126
    retention 4, 24, 124, 179
downsides, of planning process 5
Dowsett, Donna 106
Drucker, Peter 57
Drummond, Graeme 63

EAST framework 143
economy 11, 12
EEDI *see* equality, equity, diversity and inclusion
efficiency 64
emergent strategy 192–8
emotional stimulation 80, 81
Ensor, John 63
environmental aspects 12, 187–90
equality, equity, diversity and inclusion (EEDI) 55, 69–70, 179
    in fundraising practice 170–5
    in fundraising recruitment 167–70
Etherington, Sir Stuart 151
ethics 12, 132, 149–63, 170, 176
event factor review 29–30
events fundraising 18, 26, 33, 92–3, 98
expenditure 117–19, **118–19**
external environment 1–2, 187–90, 191
    analysis 10, *11*, 11–18
    external attractiveness 34–5, **35**

Facebook 123, 178
Farleigh Hospice 161
FastMap, agency 101
fatigue, donor 180–2
feedback 100–1
Fill, Chris 31
financial return 32
Financial Times 174
Fine, Allison 176
Fitzgerald, Julie 83
five Fs, feedback 100
five Ps, strategy 1
focus 9–10, 17, 22
focus groups 49–50, 50–1
following up 100–1
Ford, John 79–82
foundations 25, 100–1
Four Pillars analysis 86

Fundraising Preference Service 151
Fundraising Regulator 151, 163, 174
fundraising strategy cycle 2, *3*
Fundratios project, Chartered Institute of Fundraising 25

gambling 152–3
Gantt charts *112*, 112–14, *114*
General Data Protection Regulation (GDPR) 92, 153, 181
generalisability 54
geographics 66–7, 70
Gift Aid 92, 119
Girl Scouts of Western Washington 159, 160
giving **12–13**, 14
    individual giving 91–2
    staff participation in 146–7
    type of gift 97, 99
goals 4, 9, 10, 28, 44–5, 57–60, 131
GoFundMe 181
good practice 4
Google 67–8, 194
Grain, John 99
grants 25–6, 93
Gray, Dan 178
Grey, Johnty 92
Grow, Pamela 111
growth potential 32
Guide Dogs 117

Hall, Tiffany 103
Help the Aged 71, 98
Henry, Sir Lenny 174
HJC, agency 106
homogenising 16–17
horizontal audits 9–10
humanisation 173

Ice Bucket Challenge 31, 33
ideas, Big Idea 84–5
inclusion *see* equality, equity, diversity and inclusion (EEDI)
income 32, 36, 119–20
individual giving 91–2
informal research 42–3
information gathering 7–8
ING Bank 197
innovation 16–17, 24, 191
institutional isomorphism 16–17
internal environment *see also* organisational culture
    analysing previous fundraising results 22–3
    benchmarking 23–5

internal environment—*continued*
  big picture 27–8
  focused picture 29–30
  internal appropriateness 34–6
  internal processes **103–4**, 103–5, 106
  life cycles of products 30–1
  product portfolios 32–6
  return on investment 25–6, 32
interviews 49–50
investing in fundraising 116–17
involvement 139–40

Jay, Elaine 49
Jenkins, Joe 16
Johnson, Gerry 189
Johnson, Stephanie 91
Johnson, Vicky 131–2
journeys, donor 105–6

Kail, Angela 91
Kanter, Beth 176
Keller, Kevin 76
Kellner, Peter 175
key performance indicators (KPIs) 22, 123–30
  lifetime value 68, 125–8, **127–8**
  return on investment 25–6, 32, 125–6
Koshy, Cherian 54
Kotler, Philip 76
Kotter, John 145, 147

Lammy, David 174
LarkOwl, consultancy 25
Le, Vu 171–2
leadership 27–8, **27–8**, 141–2
learning culture 28
Legacy Foresight 91
legacy fundraising 26, 65, 71, 91, 92, 94, 144
legal aspects 12, 132, 149–50, 151, 152–3
Lepp, John 83
licensing 153
life cycles, product 30–1
lifetime value (LTV) 68, 125–8, **127–8**
listening to donors 42–3, 189–90
Lister, John 70
logos 79
Los Angeles LGBT Center 117
Love, Jen 83
loyalty 179

LTV (lifetime value) 68, 125–8, **127–8**
Lycett, Joe 103

machine learning 176
Macmillan's World's Biggest Coffee Morning 193
MacQuillin, Ian 105, 149, 150, 153, 155–7, 161–2
macro-environmental analysis 10, 11–13, 131
major gifts 91, 92
management buy-in 29, 141–2
The Management Centre, consultancy 32
management information systems 129
Manifesto, digital agency 122–3
mapping
  change 142–3, *143*
  perceptual 77–8
  stakeholder 138–9, *139*
marketing decision and research problems 44
markets 7, 10, *11*, 17–18, 61, 191
  market penetration and development 62
  segmentation 64–73, **67**
matrixes 32–6, 61–4, 138, *139*, 142, *143*
measurement, of performance 122–30
mental models 28
messaging 76–87
methodology, research 46
#MeToo 171
metrics 22–3, 24, 55 *see also* key performance indicators
  lifetime value 68, 125–8, **127–8**
  return on investment 25–6, 32, 125–6
Meyrick, Jane 54
milestones 60, 101, 114
Mind 99
Mintzberg, Henry 1, 192
mission statement 9
mix, fundraising 90–5
Moore, Karl 194
morality 12, 132, 149–63, 170, 176
MQ Mental Health Research 81
Murray, Wayne 2

National Cancer Institute 85
National Lottery grants 93
NCVO (National Council for Voluntary Organisations) 15, 91, 92, 93, 94, 111, 115
NFP Synergy 92

#nomakeupselfie campaign 193
NSPCC 85, 102

objectives 4, 9, 10, 28, 44–5, 57–60, 131
online methods 45, 67–8, 144, 175–8, 179–80
Operation Smile 122–3
opportunities 36–9
Oregon Zoo Foundation 83
organisational culture 28, 190–1 *see also* internal environment
outsourcing 29

Ps, five, strategy 1
Page, Kelly 31
Pallotta, Dan 117
pandemic, COVID-19 14, 26, 101, 115, 175, 188
Pareto Principle 111
Parkinson's UK 188
Pause box 99
Pegram, Giles 189–90
perceptual maps 77–8
performance 3–4, 122–32
personas 76, 77
PEST 11–12
philanthropy 157
Phillips, Mark 85
Pinder, Lesley 51–2
planning 3–4, **5**, 110–20 *see also* contingency planning
policies, ethical fundraising 160–1
political aspects 12
portfolios 32–6, 94–5, **95**
portrayal, of service users 173–4
positioning 76–9
Powell, Walter 16–17
The Presidents Club 174–5
Princess Alice Hospice 195
problem solving 130–2, 167–8
processes, internal 29, **103–4**, 103–5, 106
products 61, 62, 79, 98, 99
 life cycles 30–1
 portfolios 32–6
projects 98, 112
proposition, fundraising 86–7, 97–8, 98
psychology 105–6
public trust 155–6, 159

qualitative research 45, 49–52, 54
quantitative research 45–9, 51–2, 54

question marks, Boston matrix 32, 33
questions, closed 46–7

Race for Life 33
racism 170–1, 173–4 *see also* equality, equity, diversity and inclusion (EEDI)
rebranding 82
recency, frequency and value (RFV) analysis 68–70, **69**
recruitment
 staff, and EEDI 167–70
 supporters 92, 126
Reeves, Vicky 195
regulation 149–50, 151, 152–3
reinvention 191–2, *192*
relationships with donors 65, 92, 94, 101, 105–6, 130
reliability 54
research 42–56, *44*
retention
 donors 4, 24, 124, 179
 staff 129–30
return on investment (ROI) 25–6, 32, 125–6
reward 105
RFV (recency, frequency and value) 68–70, **69**
Ries, Al 76–8
rights-balancing 157, 158, 160
rising stars, Boston matrix 32, 33
risk management 93, 111, 132–5, **133**
Rogare's decision-making model 161–2, *162*
ROI (return on investment) 25–6, 32, 125–6
The Royal British Legion 80

St Dunstan's 82
St Michael's Hospital Foundation, Toronto 65
St Mungo's 144
St Peter's Hospice 50–1
Sammut-Bonnici, Tanya 190–1
sampling 46
Sargeant, Adrian 4, 7–8, 27–8, 34, 49, 65, 67, 79–82, 84, 105
Savani, Sharmila 14
Save the Children 85, 197–8
scheduling 110–14
Scottish Fundraising Standards Panel 151, 163
secondary research 45
segmentation, of markets 64–73, **67**
Seiler, Timothy 82, 84
Sellu 178

207

service 80, 81
service users 157, 160, 173–4
sexism 170, 174–5 *see also* equality, equity, diversity and inclusion (EEDI)
Shabbir, Dr Haseeb 173
Shang, Jen 7–8, 27–8, 84, 100, 105
Sherrington, Gemma 197
Shuchman, Abe 7
Siciliano, Julie 3
SLEPT 11–12
slogans 79
SMART objectives 58–60
Smith, Sarah 13–14
Smith, Wendell 64
SolarAid 42–3
sophisticated response models 70–1
sources of funding 90–5
specificity 64
staff
    participation in giving 146–7
    recruitment, and EEDI 167–70
    retention 129–30
stakeholder mapping 138–9, *139*
Stand Up To Cancer 79, 103
standards 152
statistical analysis 46, 49
STEEPLE 11–12
story-telling 140, 173
strategic wear-out
    avoiding 187–91
    emergent strategy 192–8
    proactive reinvention 191–2
strategy *see also* tactics
    fundraising strategy cycle 2, *3*
    relationship between organisational and fundraising 9
street collections 152
strengths 36–9
stress 111
success factors 16
Sue Ryder 100–1
Sun Tzu 57
support, case for 82–7
support, senior-level 29
supporters *see* donors
surveys 45–9, 50
Süssenbach, Philipp 180
SWOT analysis 36–9, **38**, **39**, 57–8
Syed, Matthew 167–8
systematic research 54
systems thinking 28

tactics 15 *see also* strategy
    delivering tactics 95–106, *96*
    developing fundraising mix 90–5

targeting 64–73, **67**
task method of budgeting 116, 117–20
teams 28, 167–8
testing 49
thanking 99–100
theories, ethical 155–8
threats 14, 16, 36–9
time management 110–11
tradition 80, 81
training 47–8
transparent research 54
trends 15, 18, 22–3
Trout, Jack 76–8
trustism 155–6, 158, 159
trusts 25, 100–1
Turner, Richard 42–3, 189–90
turnover, of staff 129–30

UK Giving, 2019 report 175, 180
Unicef UK 131–2
University of Arkansas, Little Rock 146–7
University of Bath 161
Untapped campaign, WaterAid 178

validity 54
value-exchange 19
values 179 *see also* equality, equity, diversity and inclusion (EEDI)
vertical audits 9–10
virtual methods 45, 67–8, 144, 175–8, 179–80
vision 9, 86
voice 81
voice assistants 101, 102–3
volunteers 92–3

Warner, Claire 129–30
Warwick, Aaron 180
WaterAid 92, 178
Waters, James 192
weaknesses 36–9
websites 195
well-being 111
White Helmets in Syria 80
Wild Welfare 161
WPNC, agency 195
WWF (World Wide Fund for Nature) 68

young people 58, 59, 99, 180